THE SPHERE ILLUSTRATED

HISTORY OF BRITAIN

1485 – 1789

Derived from The Oxford Illustrated History of Britain

Edited by Kenneth O. Morgan

Sphere Reference

Sphere Books Ltd
30–32 Gray's Inn Road
London WC1X 8JL

© Oxford University Press

First published as part of
The Oxford Illustrated History of Britain in 1984

First published in this paperback edition
in 1985

Printed and bound in Great Britain by
Collins, Glasgow

CONTENTS

EDITOR'S FOREWORD
TO THE OXFORD EDITION

THE distinctiveness, even uniqueness, of the British as a people has long been taken for granted by foreign observers and native commentators alike. Visitors from overseas, from those omnipresent Venetian ambassadors in the late fifteenth century, through intellectuals like Voltaire or Tocqueville, to American journalists in the twentieth century, have all been convinced of the special quality of British society. This has equally been assumed by modern native chroniclers of the British scene, as opposed in their ideological outlooks as Sir Winston Churchill and George Orwell, patriots both. But the nature or essence of the Britishness of the British is far easier to proclaim than to define, let alone to explain. Very few attempts to encapsulate its quality have been more than marginally successful. One of the most celebrated, addressing itself to the English people alone and first published in 1926, came in G. M. Trevelyan's remarkable synoptic *History of England*. Trevelyan here focused on a number of themes which he believed to have marked out the separate experience of the English through the centuries—geographical severance from the European continent, with the consequent centrality of sea-power; a broad social fluidity in which the early demise of feudalism helped generate a new industrial and commercial enterprise; a flowing cultural continuity from the time of Chaucer and Wycliffe onwards; and above all—a theme especially dear to the heart of an old late-Victorian Liberal like Trevelyan—a long political and legal evolution expressed in the durability of parliamentary institutions and the rule of law. Secure in itself, a vibrant, outward-looking island had proceeded to colonize and civilize the world. None of Trevelyan's themes can be dismissed. Equally, none can be accepted uncritically in the more tormented, doubt-ridden age of the late twentieth century, with its well-founded suspicion of national and racial stereotypes. The problem of trying to come to grips with the essential reality of the British experience remains as pressing and as fascinating as ever.

The purpose of this book is to isolate and uncover the main elements in that experience throughout British history, from the earliest Roman period down to the later twentieth century. It is not concerned with the protean concept of 'national character', a difficult and perhaps unrewarding enterprise even when considering the English alone—and almost impossible when the distinct traditions of the Welsh, Scots, and Irish are included. It is rather intended to disentangle the main political, social, economic, religious, intellectual, and cultural features of these islands as they have revealed themselves to successive generations, and as trained scholars have tried to examine them. The illustrations provided in this book are offered not merely as physical embellishments, important though that may be, but as vital explanatory tools in demonstrating key points in the narrative. The question of a British 'national character', or the lack of it, will, therefore, be implicit rather than explicit. Readers will be left to draw their own conclusions, and to form their own personal visions. This is, inevitably, a multi-author volume, written by ten professional historians in close collaboration with one another. Such a collective approach is inescapable, since the days when one compendious mind such as Trevelyan's could have the capacity and the confidence to treat all aspects of British history with equal ease probably died with the Liberal intelligentsia some time after 1914. It is certainly neither practicable nor desirable, now that Renaissance men have vanished from the earth. Rather, each major phase in the history of Britain is examined here in depth by a specialist working in that field, but always directing his findings to the general reader. A basic premiss of this book is that it deals with the history of Great Britain, two partitioned, poly-cultural islands, and not merely with England alone. Indeed, the fact that the ten authors include three Welshmen and two Scots may help towards that end! Again, while the geographic and other distinctiveness of Britain from the European continent and the world beyond may constantly emerge, so too will the economic, intellectual, cultural, and religious links by which Britain and overseas nations helped shape each other's experience. The dynamic urge for exploration, colonization, and conquest from the Tudor period onwards, which led in time to the creation of the greatest empire the world had ever seen, also lent an outward-looking aspect to British historical development. Britain in this book remains the geographical island familiar to schoolchildren. But it is an island whose physical insularity was always qualified by a wider process of transmission from continental Europe, and later from

North America, Africa, Asia, and Australasia, from the first arrival of the Roman legions onwards.

These chapters help to show how old clichés have dissolved in the searching light of modern research and scholarship. The 'anarchy' of the mid-twelfth century, the chaos of the Wars of the Roses, the inevitability of the Civil Wars, the serenity of Victorian England, familiar to readers of *1066 and All That*, tend to disappear like the autumn leaves at Vallombrosa. Again, the notion that British history, unlike that of less fortunate nations elsewhere, is uniquely marked by a kind of seamless, peaceful continuity emerges here as needing the most severe qualification. The history of the British people is a complex, sometimes violent or revolutionary one, full of disjunctions and abrupt changes of pace or of course. The idea of a tranquil, undisturbed evolutionary progress even for England, let alone the turbulent, fractured, schizophrenic history of the Celtic nations, comes out here as little more than a myth, fit for the refuse-heap of history, like romances of 'golden ages' over the centuries from Arthurian times onwards.

Roman Britain, as Peter Salway shows, was marked by constant, alternating phases of social upheaval and readjustment, long before the final retreat of the Romans in the early fifth century. John Blair describes the dynastic turbulence and the dramatic growth of urban life in the Anglo-Saxon period, until the final, violent end at Hastings. In the early Middle Ages, John Gillingham depicts a saga of conquest punctuated by frequent defeats on French and British soil, with an exploding society under such strain by the late thirteenth century that it is described here as being possibly on the verge of class war. Although that was avoided, in the later Middle Ages, as Ralph Griffiths writes, long wars in France were followed by aristocratic turmoil in Britain in the fifteenth century, accompanied by domestic recovery from plague and social revolt. The Tudor Age, as John Guy demonstrates, suffused in a golden glow in the patriotic effusions of later generations, was marked in fact by extreme pressure of population upon economic resources, by religious conflict, and the threat of foreign invasion. The resultant political and religious tensions inherited by the house of Stuart are analysed by John Morrill for a century in which—despite a marked decline in internal lawlessness—two civil wars, regicide, a republic, a restoration, and a revolution, followed each other in bewildering, breathless profusion. The apparent surface stability, prosperity, and cultural expansiveness of the Georgian age, as Paul Langford shows, gave way to an explosive tumult of industry, trade, and technology unprecedented in the history of the world, and also to the new revolutionary impulses surging in from the American colonies and from republican France. Somehow, the picture of Edward Gibbon, the urbane chronicler of the Rome of the Antonines and their successors, fleeing across Europe in the face of the Jacobin hordes in his beloved France, is symbolic. The early nineteenth century, as Christopher Harvie explains, did indeed manage to avoid the revolutionary malaria raging through other European states. But instead it brought massive dislocations in the social fabric and the notion of the legal community, and a seemingly unbridgeable class division that led Marx, fancifully, to see Britain as being in the forefront of the revolutionary apocalypse. The later nineteenth and early twentieth centuries, as outlined by H. C. G. Matthew, moved on rapidly from the bland self-assurance of the Great Exhibition, to the anxieties of the *fin de siècle* period, with its social tensions, imperialist neuroses, and sense of national vulnerability. The years since 1914, described by the present writer, saw two world wars, pulverizing economic pressures in the thirties and the seventies, and a forcible wrenching of Britain out of its place in the sun. The history of Britain, then, is not one of harmonious continuity, broadening from precedent to precedent, or from status to contract, as Victorian intellectuals would have it. It is a dramatic, colourful, often violent story of an ancient society and culture torn apart by the political, economic, and intellectual turmoil of human experience. Britain in many ways has been the cockpit of mankind.

And yet, a reading of these chapters may also leave the clear impression that, however elusive in definition, the sense of Britishness always survived in the post-Roman and post-Norman periods. Some elements of that consciousness, not necessarily closely related, can be clearly traced through the centuries. There were, variously, that Celtic Christian identity that survived the invasion of the Romans; the artistic flowering seen in the miniatures and sculpture of the late Anglo-Saxon era; the centralized governmental and ecclesiastical system created by the Normans and Angevins; the vivid sense of an English nationality emerging in the poetry, and perhaps even the architecture, of the fourteenth century. Even in the Tudor twilight, Shakespeare's plays testify to a growing sense of national cohesion—while the presence of that ubiquitous Elizabethan Welshman, John Dee, who invented the ambiguous term 'British Empire', indicates some wider horizons, too. Equally, the intellectual values embodied in the revolution of

1688, Macaulay's famous 'preserving revolution', suggests a social and cultural continuity beneath the surface turbulence of high politics in the seventeenth century. The communal stability of much of the eighteenth and nineteenth centuries, together with their integrative developments in industry, transport, and communication, and perhaps even the democratic advances, political and social, of the present century, have reinforced this perceptible current of national awareness. At key moments in British history, society coalesced rather than divided. Class war, however defined, did not in fact take place in the later Middle Ages; while Marx's prophecies of violent revolutionary upheaval in the modern industrial period were, fortunately, not fulfilled. That Britain was able to assimilate the strains of its political revolution as early as the seventeenth century and of its industrial revolution as early as the eighteenth, in each case long before other European nations did so, testified to the rooted strength of its institutions and its culture. Consensus, no less than conflict, is a central part of our story.

In its many forms, this rooted patriotism, embracing the Welsh, Scots, and Ulstermen over the centuries—though, significantly, never the southern Irish—endured and remained unquenchable. The visible, recognized symbols of that patriotic sense still survive—Crown, Parliament, the processes of law, the legacy of empire, the urge for individuality and domestic privacy, the collective enthusiasm for recreation and mass sport. But what is equally striking, perhaps, is the patriotism of the dissenting critics also, with their alternative scenarios. The Levellers, Daniel Defoe, William Cobbett, William Morris, R. H. Tawney, George Orwell, all in their time emerged as passionate, libertarian opponents of the social inequalities and political imbalance of their day. Yet each of them emerged, also, as deeply committed to an almost religious sense of the civilized essence of their country and its people, their history and destiny. By setting this sense of national continuity against the recurrence of disruption and crisis through the centuries, the historian derives perhaps his ultimate justification in thrusting the British people face to face with their past and with the image of themselves. We hope that general readers will understand themselves, their society, neighbours, and an encompassing world with more clarity, subtlety, enthusiasm, and even affection, after reading this book.

KENNETH O. MORGAN

INTRODUCTION TO VOLUME 2

TUDOR England has always been suffused with a golden glow in the eyes of posterity. In many ways this later reputation was amply justified. Under Henry VII and Henry VIII, a new political stability and a more masterful royal authority were established. Economic advance meant that a growing population was able to feed itself despite price inflation and occasional crises of starvation. Most striking of all, the Henrician reformation saw the fabric of religious life and institutions utterly transformed, partly the result of intellectual humanism or popular anti-clericalism, more the outcome of the royal thrust for supremacy. The union with Wales and a renewed control over Ireland were further testimony to Tudor power. The long reign of Elizabeth I, with its glorious achievements in architecture and music and the immortal legacy of Shakespeare in literature, appeared to mark the climax of national progress and creativity. And yet the later Tudor period witnessed a series of strains and challenges, barely concealed by the splendour of court life or the cult of 'Gloriana'. Mounting religious antagonisms meant a rising challenge from Puritan critics within the realm and from exiled Catholics overseas. Elizabethan foreign policy was in many respects damaging and unsuccessful, despite such spectacular triumphs as the repulse of the Spanish armada. Inexorable problems of finance testified to a steady loss of royal control, and perhaps a growing cultural introspection and loss of self-confidence. In its twilight period, Tudor England was a land lurching into instability and decay, a nation becoming steadily ungovernable.

This dangerous legacy was inherited by James I and the Scottish house of Stuart. Yet for some decades the Stuarts seemed to bring a more stable order, and a moderation of the extremes of religious conflict. More immediately alarming were the huge rise in the birth-rate, and renewed pressure upon economic resources as a result. Against the resilience of the new gentry and the commercial expansion of London must be measured the increase of the landless poor and a growing crisis in the finances of government. Quite unexpectedly, between 1637 and 1642 Charles I blundered into a crisis with his parliaments. Constitutional and fiscal disputes were reinforced by renewed religious conflict with the Puritan minority, exacerbated by troubles with the Presbyterian Scots and an uprising of the Catholic southern Irish. There resulted two decades of extraordinary upheaval, a prolonged civil war between the King and a financially and militarily superior Parliament; the execution of Charles I in Whitehall; the ascendancy of Cromwell's protectorate during Britain's only experiment with republicanism; and the eventual restoration of the monarchy under Charles II. But the restoration did not mean greater tranquillity either in political or religious life. The renewal of sectarian conflict, followed by the bigoted Romish obstinacy of James II, led to the expulsion of the king and the bloodless revolution of 1688 to legitimize the succession of the Dutchman, William of Orange, and his wife. Only after this did the passionate tensions within British society seem to moderate. In line with the increased secularization, urbanity and rationalism of the arts and science, and in the realm of ideas, Britain's peaceful, permanent revolution meant the succession of a more pragmatic, less fevered and tormented age.

Yet the reigns of William III and of Anne were anything but tranquil. There were lengthy wars with France, militarily triumphant but politically largely unproductive. A new British empire overseas began to emerge in north America and shortly in India. At home, there was vicious religious and party friction, and a threat of Jacobite restoration. However, the era of Walpole brought with it a degree of social stability and political calm. The economy now prospered markedly, and displayed the early signs of an industrial and manufacturing take-off without precedent in human history, with the centre of activity clearly shifting to the midlands and north of England. If the country houses of the Georgian age, with their Palladian splendours, testified to the authority of the landowners, the sophistication of cities like London and Edinburgh and Bristol showed the growing social and cultural influence of a commercial, urban middle class, steadily encroaching upon the hegemony of land. At work and at play, in religious and intellectual toleration, and philanthropic reform, the influence of 'middle England' was clearly visible. But the serenity and order of the Augustan age marked profound new tensions abroad and at home. Overseas, the revolt of the American colonies brought a crisis of empire, born of unique military disaster across the Atlantic. In Britain, political radicalism, spurred on by industrial change and a transformed social balance, led to a mood of popular protest. The apparently unchanged world of the Younger Pitt and the evangelical conservatives of the 1780s provided the backdrop for a new explosive surge of dynamic, almost revolutionary activity.

KENNETH O. MORGAN

JOHN GUY

5. *The Tudor Age*

(1485–1603)

Population Changes

THE age of the Tudors has left its impact on Anglo-American minds as a watershed in British history. Hallowed tradition, native patriotism, and post-imperial gloom have united to swell our appreciation of the period as a true golden age. Names alone evoke a phoenix-glow—Henry VIII, Elizabeth I, and Mary Stuart among the sovereigns of England and Scotland; Wolsey, William Cecil, and Leicester among the politicians; Marlowe, Shakespeare, Hilliard, and Byrd among the creative artists. The splendours of the Court of Henry VIII, the fortitude of Sir Thomas More, the making of the English Bible, Prayer Book, and Anglican Church, the development of Parliament, the defeat of the Armada, the Shakespearian moment, and the legacy of Tudor domestic architecture—these are the undoubted climaxes of a simplified orthodoxy in which genius, romance, and tragedy are superabundant.

Reality is inevitably more complex, less glamorous, and more interesting than myth. The most potent forces within Tudor England were often social, economic, and demographic ones. Thus if the period became a golden age, it was primarily because of the considerable growth in population that occurred between 1500 and the death of Elizabeth I did not so dangerously exceed the capacity of available resources, particularly food supplies, as to precipitate a Malthusian crisis. Famine and disease unquestionably disrupted and disturbed the Tudor economy, but they did not raze it to its foundations, as in the fourteenth century. More positively, the increased manpower and demand that sprang from rising population stimulated economic growth and the commercialization of agriculture, encouraged trade and urban renewal, inspired a housing revolution, enhanced the sophistication of English manners, especially in London, and (more arguably) bolstered new and exciting attitudes among

Tudor Englishmen, notably individualistic ones derived from Reformation ideals and Calvinist theology.

The matter is debatable, but there is much to be said for the view that England was economically healthier, more expansive, and more optimistic under the Tudors than at any time since the Roman occupation of Britain. Certainly, the contrast with the fifteenth century was dramatic. In the hundred or so years before Henry VII became king of England in 1485, England had been underpopulated, underdeveloped, and inward-looking compared with other Western countries, notably France. Her recovery after the ravages of the Black Death had been slow—slower than in France, Germany, Switzerland, and some Italian cities. The process of economic recovery in pre-industrial societies was basically one of recovery of population, and figures will be useful. On the eve of the Black Death (1348), the population of England and Wales was between 4 and 5 millions; by 1377, successive plagues had reduced it to 2.5 millions. Yet the figure for England (without Wales) was still no higher than 2.26 millions in 1525, and it is transparently clear that the striking feature of English demographic history between the Black Death and the reign of Henry VIII is the stagnancy of population which persisted until the 1520s. However, the growth of population rapidly accelerated after 1525:

English population totals 1525–1601

Year	Population total in millions
1525	2.26
1541	2.77
1551	3.01
1561	2.98
1581	3.60
1601	4.10

(Source: E. A. Wrigley and R. S. Schofield, *The Population History of England, 1541–1871*, London, 1981)

Between 1525 and 1541 the population of England grew extremely fast, an impressive burst of expansion after long inertia. This rate of growth slackened off somewhat after 1541, but the Tudor population continued to increase steadily and inexorably, with a temporary reversal only in the late 1550s, to reach 4.10 millions in 1601. In addition, the population of Wales grew from about 210,000 in 1500 to 380,000 by 1603.

While England reaped the fruits of the recovery of population in the sixteenth century, however, serious problems of adjustment were encountered. The impact of a sudden crescendo in demand, and pressure on available resources of food and clothing, within a society that was still overwhelmingly agrarian, was to be as painful as it was, ultimately, beneficial. The morale of countless ordinary Englishmen was to be wrecked irrevocably, and ruthlessly, by problems that were too massive to be ameliorated either by governments or by traditional, ecclesiastical philanthropy. Inflation, speculation in land, enclosures, unemployment, vagrancy, poverty, and urban squalor were the most pernicious evils of Tudor England, and these were the wider symptoms of population growth and agricultural commercialization. In the fifteenth century farm rents had been discounted, because tenants were so elusive; lords had abandoned direct exploitation of their demesnes, which were leased to tenants on favourable terms. Rents had been low, too, on peasants' customary holdings; labour services had been commuted, and servile villeinage had virtually disappeared from the face of the English landscape by 1485. At the same time, money wages had risen to reflect the contraction of the wage-labour force after 1348, and food prices had fallen in reply to reduced market demand. But rising demand after 1500 burst the bubble of artificial prosperity born of stagnant population. Land hunger led to soaring rents. Tenants of farms and copyholders were evicted by business-minded landlords. Several adjacent farms would be conjoined, and amalgamated for profit, by outside investors at the expense of sitting tenants. Marginal land would be converted to pasture for more profitable sheep-rearing. Commons were enclosed, and waste land reclaimed, by landlords or squatters, with consequent extinction of common grazing rights. The literary opinion that the active Tudor land market nurtured a new entrepreneurial class of greedy capitalists grinding the faces of the poor is an exaggeration. Yet it is fair to say that not all landowners, claimants, and squatters were entirely scrupulous in their attitudes; certainly a vigorous market arose among dealers in defective titles to land, with resulting harassment of many legitimate occupiers.

The greatest distress sprang, nevertheless, from inflation and unemployment. High agricultural prices gave farmers strong incentives to produce crops for sale in the dearest markets in nearby towns, rather than for the satisfaction of rural subsistence. Rising population, especially urban population, put intense strain on the markets themselves: demand for food often outstripped supply, notably in years of poor harvests due to epidemics or bad weather. In cash terms, agricultural prices began to rise faster than industrial prices from the beginning of

The double-wheeled plough. The ploughs used by Tudor cultivators varied according to the soil they were designed to turn. The double-wheeled plough was used on flinty or gravelly soil, and was drawn by horses or oxen double abreast. (John Fitzherbert, *Newe Tracte for husbandeman, c.*1525)

the reign of Henry VIII, a rise which accelerated as the sixteenth century progressed. Yet in real terms, the price rise was even more volatile than it appeared to be, since population growth ensured that labour was plentiful and cheap, and wages low. The size of the work-force in Tudor England increasingly exceeded available employment opportunities; average wages and living standards declined accordingly. Men (and women) were prepared to do a day's work for little more than board wages; able-bodied persons, many of whom were peasants displaced by rising rents or the enclosure of commons, drifted in waves to the towns in quest of work.

The best price index hitherto constructed covers the period

Churning butter. Of the various types of husbandry, dairy farming was best suited to domestic producers. Although much milk had to be converted into butter or cheese before it could be sold, the necessary butter churns, cheese tubs, etc. were inexpensive. (*Grete herball*, 1527)

1264–1954, and its base period is most usefully 1451–75—the end of the fifteenth-century era of stable prices. From this index, we may read the fortunes of the wage-earning consumers of Tudor England, because the calculations are based on the fluctuating costs of composite units of the essential foodstuffs and manufactured goods, such as textiles, that made up an average family shopping basket in southern England at different times. Two indexes are, in fact, available: first the annual price index of the composite basket of consumables; secondly the index of the basket expressed as the equivalent of the annual wage rates of building craftsmen in southern England. No one supposes that building workers were typical of the English labour force in the sixteenth century, or at any other time. But the indexes serve as a rough guide to the appalling reality of the rising household expenses of the majority of Englishmen in the Tudor period.

Indexes (1451–75 = 100) of
(1) price of composite unit of consumables;
(2) equivalent of wage rate of building craftsman

Year	(1)	(2)
1450	102	98
1490	106	94
1510	103	97
1530	169	59
1550	262	48
1570	300	56
1590	396	51
1610	503	40

(Source: E. H. Phelps Brown and S. V. Hopkins, *Economica*, no. 92, Nov. 1956, n.s. vol. xxiii)

It is clear that in the century after Henry VIII's accession, the average prices of essential consumables rose by some 488 per cent. The price index stood at the 100 or so level until 1513, when it rose to 120. A gradual rise to 169 had occurred by 1530, and a further crescendo to 231 was attained by 1547, the year of Henry VIII's death. In 1555 the index reached 270; two years later, it hit a staggering peak of 409, though this was partly due to the delayed effects of the currency debasements practised by Henry VIII and Edward VI. On the accession of Elizabeth I, in 1558, the index had recovered to a median of 230. It climbed again thereafter, though more steadily: 300 in 1570, 342 in 1580, and 396 in 1590. But the later 1590s witnessed exceptionally meagre harvests, together with regional epidemics and famine: the index read 515 in 1595, 685 in 1598, and only settled back to 459 in 1600.

The index expressed as the equivalent of the building craftsman's wages gives an equally sober impression of the vicissitudes of Tudor domestic life. An abrupt decline in purchasing power of wages occurred between 1510 and 1530, the commodity equivalent falling by some 40 per cent in twenty years. The index fell again in the 1550s, but recovered in the next decade to a position equivalent to two-thirds of its value in 1510. It then remained more or less stable until the 1590s, when it collapsed to 39 in 1595, and to a catastrophic nadir of 29 in 1597. On the queen's death in 1603 it had recovered to a figure of 45—which meant that real wages had dropped by 57 per cent since 1500.

These various data establish the most fundamental truth about the age of the Tudors. When the percentage change of English population in the sixteenth century is plotted against that of the index of purchasing power of a building craftsman's wages over the same period, it is immediately plain that the two lines of development are opposite and commensurate (see graph). Liv-

———— Percentage change of population since last total
(Source: E. A. Wrigley and R. S. Schofield, *The Population History of England, 1541-1871*, London, 1981)
– – – – Percentage change since last total (averaged over three years) in index of purchasing power of building craftsman's wages as compared to index of his purchasing power in 1510
(Source: E. H. Phelps Brown and S. V. Hopkins, *Economica*, no. 92, Nov. 1956, n.s. vol. xxiii)

ing standards declined as the population rose; recovery began as population growth abated and collapsed between 1556 and 1560. Standards then steadily dropped again, until previous proportions were overthrown by the localized famines of 1585–8 and 1595–8—though the cumulative increase in the size of the wage-labour force since 1570 must also have had distorting effects.

In other words, population trends, rather than government policies, capitalist entrepreneurs, European imports of American silver, the more rapid circulation of money, or even currency debasements, were the key factor in determining the fortunes of the British Isles in the sixteenth century. English government expenditure on warfare, heavy borrowing, and debasements unquestionably exacerbated inflation and unemployment. But the basic facts of Tudor life were linked to population growth.

In view of this fundamental truth, the greatest triumph of Tudor England was its ability to feed itself. A major national subsistence crisis was avoided. Malthus, who wrote his historic *Essay on the Principle of Population* in 1798, listed positive and preventive checks as the traditional means by which population was kept in balance with available resources of food. Preventive checks included declining fertility, contraception, and fewer, or later, marriages; positive ones involved heavy mortality and abrupt reversal of population growth. Fertility in England indeed declined in the later 1550s, and again between 1566 and 1571. A higher proportion of the population than hitherto did not marry in the reign of Elizabeth I. Poor harvests resulted in localized starvation, and higher mortality, in 1481–3, 1519–21, 1527–8, 1544–5, 1549–51, 1555–8, 1585–8, and 1595–8. Yet devastating as these years of dearth were for the affected localities, especially for the towns of the 1590s, the positive check of mass mortality on a national scale was absent from Tudor England, with the possible exception of the crisis of 1555–8. On top of its other difficulties, Mary's government after 1555 faced the most serious mortality crisis since the fourteenth century: the population of England quickly dropped by about 200,000. Even so, it is not proved that this was a 'national' crisis in terms of its geographical range, and population growth was only temporarily interrupted. In fact, the chronology, intensity, and geographical extent of famine in the sixteenth century were such as to suggest that starvation crises in England were abating, rather than worsening, over time. Bubonic plagues were likewise confined to the insanitary towns after the middle of the century, and took fewer victims in proportion to the expansion of population.

The inescapable conclusion is that, despite the vicissitudes of the price index, the harsh consequences for individuals of changed patterns of agriculture, and the proliferation of vaga-bondage, an optimistic view of the age of the Tudors has sufficiently firm foundations. The sixteenth century witnessed the birth of Britain's pre-industrial political economy—an evolv-ing accommodation between population and resources, econ-omics and politics, ambition and rationality. England aban-doned the disaster-oriented framework of the Middle Ages for the new dawn of low-pressure equilibrium. Progress had its price, unalterably paid by the weak, invariably banked by the strong. Yet the tyranny of the price index was not ubiquitous. Wage rates for agricultural workers fell by less than for building workers, and some privileged groups of wage-earners such as the Mendip miners may have enjoyed a small rise in real income. Landowners, commercialized farmers, and property investors were the most obvious beneficiaries of a system that guaranteed fixed expenses and enhanced selling prices—it was in the Tudor period that the nobility, gentry, and mercantile classes alike came to appreciate fully the enduring qualities of land. But many wage-labouring families were not wholly dependent upon their wages for subsistence. Multiple occupations, domestic self-employment, and cottage industries flourished, especially in the countryside; town-dwellers grew vegetables, kept animals, and brewed beer, except in the confines of London. Wage-labourers employed by great households received meat and drink in addition to cash income, although this customary practice was on the wane by the 1590s.

Finally, it is not clear that vagabondage or urban population outside London expanded at a rate faster than was commensu-rate with the prevailing rise of national population. It used to be argued that the English urban population climbed from 6.2 per cent of the national total in 1520 to 8.4 per cent by the end of the century. However, London's spectacular growth alone explains this apparent over-population: the leading provincial towns, Norwich, Bristol, Coventry, and York, grew slightly or remained stable in absolute terms—and must thus have been inhabited by a reduced share of population in proportional terms.

Henry VII

Yet if the new dawn was marked by England's espousal of a system of low-pressure equilibrium, the quest for political stability at the end of the fifteenth century remained of paramount importance to future progress. No one now thinks that the thirty years' internal commotion known as the Wars of the Roses amounted to more than an intermittent interruption of national life, or that Henry VII's victory at Bosworth Field (22 August 1485) rates credit beyond that due to an improbably fortunate accident. Bosworth Field was, indeed, conclusive only because Richard III, together with so many of his household men and supporters, was slain in the battle; because Richard had eliminated in advance the most plausible alternatives to Henry VII; and because Henry was ingenious enough to proclaim himself king with effect from the day before the battle, thus enabling the Ricardian rump to be deemed traitors. By marrying Elizabeth of York, daughter of Edward IV, Henry VII then proffered the essential palliative to those Yorkist defectors who had joined him against Richard in the first place—the ensuing births of Arthur in 1486, Margaret in 1489, Henry in 1491, and Mary in 1496 achieved the 'Union of the Two Noble and Illustrious Families of Lancaster and York' upon which the pro-Tudor chronicler Edward Hall lavished his laudatory eloquence.

But the need for stability went far beyond Henry VII's accession and marriage. The victor of Bosworth Field could found a new dynasty; it remained to be seen whether he could create a new monarchy. The essential demand was that someone should restore the English Crown to its former position above mere aristocratic faction. The king should not simply reign; he should also rule. For too long, the king of England had been *primus inter pares*, rather than *rex imperator*. The Wars of the Roses had done negligible permanent damage to agriculture, trade, and industry, but they had unquestionably undermined confidence in monarchy as an institution: the king was repeatedly seen to be unable, or unwilling, to protect the rights of all his subjects. In particular, royal government had ceased to be politically neutral, having been excessively manipulated by individuals as an instrument of faction. All aspects of the system, especially the legal system, had been deeply permeated by family loyalties, aristocratic rivalries, favouritism, and a web of personal connections.

In fairness to Edward IV, whom Sir Thomas More thought had left his realm 'in quiet and prosperous estate', the work of reconstruction had already been started. Edward IV's failure to make sufficient progress was primarily due to his excessive generosity, his divisive marriage to Elizabeth Woodville, and his

Henry VII. Portrait by Michiel Sittow, 1505. The king holds a red rose of Lancaster, and wears the collar of the Golden Fleece over a cloth of gold surcoat lined with white fur.

barely-controlled debauchery. His premature death had become the cue for the usurpation of Richard III, who was leader of a large and unusually powerful northern faction. Henry VII was, by contrast, dedicated and hard-working, astute and ascetic, and financially prudent to the point of positive avarice, or even culpable rapacity, as some have maintained. Yet Henry's strategic advantage in the campaign for stability was that his extraordinary good luck in sweeping the board at Bosworth, as in the case of William the Conqueror in 1066, had freed him, temporarily at least, from dependence on any one group or faction. Henry's continued independence and security naturally had to be earned, consolidated, and defended—a formidable task that absorbed many years. In fact, the first of the Tudor kings had specifically to combine the task of restoring the monarchy with that of protecting its flank from hyperactive Yorkist conspiracy.

Of the two Yorkist impostures, that of Lambert Simnel as earl of Warwick in 1487, although the more exotic, was, thanks to Irish support, the more menacing; that of Perkin Warbeck, as Richard of York during the 1490s, was more easily contained despite Scottish involvement. Simnel was routed at Stoke (16 June 1487); his promoters were killed or pardoned, and the young impostor was taken into the royal household as a servant. Warbeck fell into Henry's hands in August 1497; before long he had abused the king's leniency and was hanged in 1499. His demise was then made an occasion for executing the real earl of Warwick. But it was another seven years before the incarceration in the Tower of the last premier representative of the White Rose, Edmund de la Pole, earl of Suffolk, completed the defensive process.

By that time, it was clear that Henry VII, if not to be distinguished as the inventor of new methods of government, had, nevertheless, mastered the art of streamlining the old. The touchstone of his policy was enforcement—the enforcement of political and financial obligation to the Crown, as much as of law and order. In achieving the restoration of the monarchy, the Tudors practised their belief that ability, good service, and loyalty to the regime, irrespective of a man's social origins and background, were to be the primary grounds of appointments, promotions, favours, and rewards. This belief was most evident in Henry VII's use of royal patronage and in his appointments of ministers and councillors. Patronage was the process by which the Crown awarded grants of offices, lands, pensions, annuities, or other valuable perquisites to its executives and dependants, and was thus its principal weapon of political control, its most powerful motor of political ascendancy. Subjects, from great peers of the realm to humble knights and gentry, vied with each

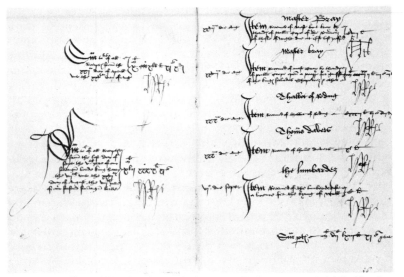

Extract from Henry VII's chamber book of receipts. Each entry was initialled by the king, who changed the style of his signature in 1492. Both versions are illustrated here.

other for a share of the spoils—no nobleman was too high to join in the undignified scramble. Henry VII gradually restructured the patronage system to reflect more realistically the Crown's limited resources, and next ensured that the values of grants made under the great seal were fully justified in terms of return on expenditure. The resources of Tudor monarchy were relatively meagre in the years before the Dissolution of the Monasteries, and again in the later part of Elizabeth I's reign. Henry VII set the pace and the standards for distributing royal bounty for much of the sixteenth century; indeed, the only danger inherent in the Tudor model of cash efficiency was that it might veer towards meanness or excessive stringency. The level and flow of grants might become so far diminished in relation to expectations as to ferment impatience, low morale, and even active disloyalty among the Crown's servants and suitors.

Henry VII's ministers were all personally selected by the king for their ability, assiduity, shrewdness, and loyalty—again a pattern for the most part emulated by his Tudor successors. Yet at first sight, Reynold Bray, Richard Empson, and Edmund Dudley seemed to hold quite minor offices. Bray was Chancellor of the duchy of Lancaster; soon after he died, in 1503, Empson succeeded him; Dudley was 'president of the Council', which effectively meant minister without portfolio. But Bray and the rest exercised control, under the king, far in excess of their apparent status. For Henry VII managed in an absurdly short space of time to erect a network of financial and administrative checks and blueprints, the records of which never left the hands of himself and the selected few, and the methods of which were equally of their own devising. Financial accounting, the exploitation of the undervalued resources of the Crown lands along the most modern lines known to the land-holding aristocracy, the collection of fines and obligations, and the enforcement of Henry VII's morally-dubious but probably necessary system of compelling political opponents, or even apparent friends, to enter into coercive bonds for good behaviour—these vital matters were dealt with only by the king and his inner ring. It was a system that owed nothing to Parliament; it owed something to the Council in so far as Bray and the others sat there as Henry's most trusted councillors; but it owed everything to the king himself, whose vigilance and attention to detail were invincible. Nothing slipped past Henry's keen eye, least of all money through his twitching fingers. The extant Chamber books, the master-documents of the early Henrician nexus of administrative co-ordination, are signed, and thus checked, on every page, and even beside every entry, by the king who was the best businessman ever to sit on the English throne.

Tudor government, however, was as much a question of partnership as of dictatorship. England lacked a police force and a standing army. The revenues of the Tudors were increasingly inadequate in proportion to the expanding functions of central bureaucracy, the escalating costs of Renaissance warfare, and the need, never tackled by anyone until the Protectorate of Oliver Cromwell, to provide a system of local government better than that furnished by unsalaried, overworked, and often barely qualified Justices of the Peace. James Harrington wrote in *Oceana*, first published in 1656, that government could be based either upon a nobility or upon an army. He was right; in the absence of the permanent militia, the Tudors were significantly vulnerable to their own partial dependence upon the local authority of their territorial magnates. It was for Henry VII and his successors at best to subdue, at worst to preside over, aristocratic faction, while positively deploying the existing private resources of the peerage along channels commensurate with wider royal interests. In other words, 'overmighty subjects', whose existence and persistence Sir John Fortescue in the fifteenth century, and Francis Bacon in the seventeenth, imperceptively lamented, were essential to the running of the country. Both Henry VII and Cardinal Wolsey appreciated this conventional wisdom: between them, they tamed the aristocracy in order to ride upon its back.

Henry VII's methods here were a judicious combination of carrot and stick. In his large and active King's Council, the first of the Tudors practised consultation in a way calculated to inspire, alternately, supportive enthusiasm and vapid boredom. A nobleman was *ipso facto* a royal councillor prior to the historic reform of the Council by Thomas Cromwell in 1536, and political identity involved attending Council meetings from time to time. Before 1536, the Council's chief work was done in Star Chamber, which was both a meeting place for the working Council (literally *Camera Stellata*, the room's azure ceiling being decorated with stars of gold leaf) and a court of law. Star Chamber thus formed the premier point of contact between the Crown, its ministers, and the nobility until Wolsey's fall in 1529, and under Henry VII it discussed those issues, such as internal security, the armed defences, and foreign affairs, which, of necessity, had to secure the support of the magnates, who were also the muster-men and captains of armies. The Council never debated fiscal or enforcement policies under Henry VII, matters which remained firmly vested in the hands of ministers and those of two tribunals known as the Council Learned in the Law and the Conciliar Court of Audit. But by making conciliar involvement a new and subtle dimension of magnate status, Henry VII went far towards filtering out the threat of an alienated nobility that sprang from lack of communications and isolation in the political wilderness.

Next, Henry VII made an overtly determined bid to concentrate the command of castles and garrisons, and, as far as possible, the supervision of military functions, in the members of the royal Household, and he launched direct attacks on the local, territorial powers of the magnates, if he felt that those powers had been exercised in defiance of perceived royal interests. Such attacks normally took one of two forms, either that of prosecutions and fines at law for misfeasance, or the most drastic resort of attainder and forfeiture.

George Neville, Lord Burgavenny, for instance, was tried in King's Bench in 1507 on a charge of illegally retaining what amounted to a private army. He pleaded guilty (people did under Henry VII, for it was cheaper), and was fined £70,650, being the price, at the rate of £5 per man per month, for which he was liable for having hired 471 men for 30 months from 10 June 1504 to 9 December 1506. It seems that the 'army' comprised 25 gentlemen,

4 clerics, 440 yeomen, one cobbler, and one tinker—the Tudors got details right. But Henry VII was not opposing retaining purely on principle on the occasion of this prosecution; he *valued* Burgavenny's force, down to that last Kentish tinker, just as much as did its true territorial proprietor—it was even better that Burgavenny was footing the bill. Despite Henry VII's peaceful foreign policy, England was within the mainstream of European affairs, quite apart from her fluctuating relations with Scotland and Ireland. The all-too-brief marriage of Prince Arthur to Catherine of Aragon in 1501 had sharpened England's perspective in Continental eyes, and even the preliminary negotiations and marriage treaty had sucked Henry VII into the French war of 1489–92. England, or rather the king of England, had virtually no army beyond that recruited on demand from the royal demesne, and that provided on request by the nobility. Thus, in Burgavenny's case, it was an essential aspect of his prosecution, which may in any case have been partly *in terrorem tantum*, that the peer was by birth a Yorkist, and that he had been implicated *inter alia* in an unsuccessful rising of Cornishmen in 1497.

The modern cash equivalent of Burgavenny's fine is around £1 million, and it was never supposed that he should pay quite all of it. In a broader perspective, his case became the first of a long series of exemplary and admonitory prosecutions brought by the Tudors in order to transform the fifteenth-century imbalance between royal and magnate power back irrevocably in favour of the former. Yet far more drastic, and effective, was the weapon of attainder and forfeiture. Acts of attainder were parliamentary statutes proclaiming convictions for treason, and declaring the victim's property forfeit to the king and his blood 'corrupted'. The method almost always involved execution of the victim, but did not necessarily lead to the total forfeiture of his lands. Most attainders were by tradition repealed later in favour of the heirs, though not always with full restoration of property. Henry VII's reign saw 138 persons attained, and 86 of these attainders were never reversed. Only 46 were reversed by Henry VII, and six by Henry VIII. These figures compare unfavourably with those of the reigns of Henry VI, Edward IV, and even Richard III—reflecting the toughness of Tudor policy. Henry VII realized that attainders were not simply a tool of faction and dynastic intrigue: they could be used constructively in favour of the monarchy to wipe out at a stroke the territorial powers of 'overmighty' or hostile magnates, while at the same time significantly augmenting the Crown's own power and income. In similar fashion, Henry VIII, after the Pilgrimage of Grace (1536), and Elizabeth I, after the Northern Rebellion (1569), used attainders to bolster the Crown's territorial strength and to eradicate pockets of baronial resistance to royal authority. However, finesse was required if the method was not to backfire. Its excessive use, and repeated failure to reverse attainders in favour of heirs, could provoke burning resentment among the peerage, whose partnership with the monarchy was thus impaired. Attainders could also do serious damage if they left a territorial power vacuum in a particular local area, as occurred in East Anglia when the third duke of Norfolk was attainted by Henry VIII in 1547. His attainder, reversed by Mary in 1553, created instability which the Crown could not easily correct, and resulted in the proliferation of the disturbances known as Ket's Rebellion in 1549.

Historians suspect that Henry VII overdid his policy of enforcement in the latter part of his reign. In 1506, Henry himself commissioned one Polydore Vergil, who was a visiting collector of papal taxes, to write a history of England, and it was Polydore who opined that the first of the Tudors had practised financial rapacity after 1502.

For he began to treat his people with more harshness and severity than had been his custom, in order (as he himself asserted) to ensure that they remained more thoroughly and entirely in obedience to him. The people themselves had another explanation for his action, for they considered they were suffering not on account of their own sins but on account of the greed of their monarch. It is not indeed clear whether at the start it was greed; but afterwards greed did become apparent.

The debate concerning Henry's alleged rapacity still rages. Whatever the eventual outcome, three points are proven. First, Henry VII used penal bonds in sums ranging from £100 to £10,000 to enforce what *he* considered to be acceptable behaviour on his subjects. These bonds had a dual purpose, namely to hold the political nation, especially the nobility, at the king's mercy, and to short-circuit due process of common law in case of offence by the victims. If a man was deemed to have misbehaved, he would simply be sued for debt on his bond—it was not possible to litigate over the nature or extent of the allegedly substantive offence. In other words, Henry VII used bonds to defeat due legal process in the way that King John and Richard II had used blank charters as instruments of tyranny. Secondly, Empson and Dudley perverted juries at inquisitions *post mortem*, and inquests of office, to find verdicts in favour of Henry VII's feudal rights. The best example is the case of the inquests held into the estates of the earl of Westmorland. A full-scale conciliar inquiry had to be launched to rectify this matter in Henry VIII's reign. Thirdly, Henry VII sold offices, including important legal ones.

He twice sold the chief justiceship of the Court of Common Pleas, and at exorbitant prices. Not even Elizabeth I, during whose reign large-scale corruption permeated English administration, stooped to so blatant a sale after the French model.

Henry VIII

Henry VII's death in 1509 was greeted with feasting, dancing, and universal rejoicing—for no one who survived until 1547 could have thought, with hindsight, that it was the accession of Henry VIII that inspired the nation's confidence. Henry VIII succeeded, at barely eighteen years of age, because his elder brother, Arthur, had died in 1502. Under pressure from his grandmother, the iron maiden Margaret Beaufort, Henry began his 'triumphant' reign by marrying his late brother's widow, Catherine of Aragon—a union that was to have momentous, not to say revolutionary, consequences. He continued by executing Empson and Dudley, who were now thrown to the wolves in ritual expiation of their former employer's financial prudence. Needless to say, these executions were a calculated ploy to enable the new regime to profit from the stability won by Henry VII without incurring any of its attendant stigma—no one complained that Henry VIII's government omitted to cancel the last batch of outstanding bonds until well into the 1520s. Yet Henry VIII had started as he meant to go on; something of the king's natural cruelty, and inherent assumption that clean breaks with the past could solve deep-rooted problems, was already evident.

Henry VIII's character was certainly fascinating, threatening, and intensely morbid, as Holbein's great portrait illustrates to perfection. The king's egoism, self-righteousness, and unlimited capacity to brood over suspected wrongs, or petty slights, sprang from the fatal combination of a relatively able but distinctly second-rate mind and a pronounced inferiority complex that derived from Henry VII's treatment of his second son. For the first of the Tudors had found his younger son unsatisfactory; on Arthur's death, Henry had been given no functions beyond the title of Prince of Wales—a signal of unmistakable mistrust. As a result, Henry VIII had resolved to rule, even where, as in the case of the Church, it would have been enough merely to reign. He would put monarchic theory into practice; would give the words *rex imperator* a meaning never dreamt of even by the emperors of Rome, if he possibly could. Henry was eager, too, to conquer—to

Henry VIII. Portrait by Hans Holbein the Younger, 1536.

emulate the glorious victories of the Black Prince and Henry V, to quest after the golden fleece that was the French Crown. Repeatedly the efforts of Henry's more constructive councillors were bedevilled, and overthrown, by the king's militaristic dreams, and by costly Continental ventures that wasted men, money, and equipment. Evaluation is always a matter of emphasis, but on the twin issues of monarchic theory and lust for conquest, there is everything to be said for the view that Henry VIII's policy was consistent throughout his reign; that Henry was himself directing that policy; and that his ministers and officials were allowed freedom of action only within accepted limits, and when the king was too busy to take a personal interest in state affairs.

Cardinal Wolsey was Henry VIII's first minister, and the fourteen years of that proud but efficient prelate's ascendancy (1515–29) saw the king in a comparatively restrained mood. Henry, unlike his father, found writing 'both tedious and painful'; he preferred hunting, dancing, dallying, and playing the lute. In his more civilized moments, Henry studied theology and astronomy; he would wake up Sir Thomas More in the middle of the night in order that they might gaze at the stars from the roof of a royal palace. He wrote songs, and the words of one form an epitome of Henry's youthful sentiments.

> Pastime with good company
> I love and shall until I die.
> Grudge who lust, but none deny;
> So God be pleased, thus live will I;
>> For my pastance,
>> Hunt, sing and dance;
>> My heart is set
>> All goodly sport
>> For my comfort:
>> Who shall me let?

Yet Henry himself set the tempo; his pastimes were only pursued while he was satisfied with Wolsey. Appointed Lord Chancellor and Chief Councillor on Christmas eve 1515, Wolsey used the Council and Star Chamber as instruments of ministerial power in much the way that Henry VII had used them as vehicles of royal power—though Wolsey happily pursued uniform and equitable ideals of justice in Star Chamber in place of Henry VII's selective justice linked to fiscal advantage. But Wolsey's greatest asset was the unique position he obtained with regard to the English Church. Between them, Henry and Wolsey bludgeoned the pope into granting Wolsey the rank of legate *a latere* for life, which meant that he became the superior ecclesiastical authority in England, and could convoke legatine synods. Using these powers, Wolsey contrived to subject the entire English Church and clergy to a massive dose of Tudor government and taxation, and it looks as if an uneasy *modus vivendi* prevailed behind the scenes in which Henry agreed that the English Church was, for the moment, best controlled by a churchman who was a royal servant, and the clergy accepted that it was better to be obedient to an ecclesiastical rather than a secular tyrant—for it is unquestionably true that Wolsey protected the Church from the worst excesses of lay opinion while in office.

The trouble was that, with stability restored, and the Tudor dynasty apparently secure, England had started to become vulnerable to a mounting release of forces, many of which were old ones suppressed beneath the surface for years, and others which sprang from the new European mood of reform and self-criticism. Anticlericalism was the most volcanic of the smouldering emotions that pervaded the English laity; an ancient 'disease', it had been endemic in British society since Constantine's conversion to Christianity. By the sixteenth century, English anticlericalism centred on three major areas of lay resentment: first, opposition to such ecclesiastical abuses as clerical fiscalism, absenteeism, pluralism, maladministration, and concubinage; secondly, the excessive numbers of clergy, as it appeared to the laity—monks, friars, and secular priests seemed to outnumber the laity, and form a caste of unproductive consumers, which was untrue but reflected lay xenophobia; and thirdly, opposition to the jurisdiction of the bishops and Church courts, especially in cases of heresy. It was pointed out by prominent writers, notably the grave and learned Christopher St. German (1460–1541), that the Church's procedure in cases of suspected heresy permitted secret accusations, hearsay evidence, and denied accused persons the benefit of purgation by oath-helpers or trial by jury, which was a Roman procedure contrary to the principles of native English common law—a clerical plot to deprive Englishmen of their natural, legal rights. Such ideas were manifestly explosive; for they incited intellectual affray between clergy and common lawyers.

Popular religious idealism was another major problem faced by the English ecclesiastical authorities. Late medieval religion was sacramental, institutional, and ritualistic; for ordinary people it seemed excessively dominated by 'objective' Church ritual and obligation, as opposed to 'subjective' religious experience based on Bible reading at home. The educated classes, who were the nobility, clergy, and rich merchants, knew that traditional Catholic piety and meditation did not lack for subjectivity and individual introspection, but few non-literate persons had the mental discipline needed to meditate with any degree of fulfilment. For ordinary people, personal religion had to be founded on texts of Scripture and Bible stories (preferably illustrated ones), but vernacular Bibles were illegal in England—the Church authorities believed that the availability of an English Bible, even an authorized version, would ferment heresy by permitting Englishmen to form their own opinions. Sir Thomas More, who was Wolsey's successor as Lord Chancellor, was the premier lay opponent of the commissioning of an English Bible, and ally of the bishops. He declared, in his notorious proclamation of 22 June 1530, that 'it is not necessary the said Scripture to be in the English tongue and in the hands of the common people, but that the distribution of the said Scripture, and the permitting or denying thereof, dependeth only upon the discretion of the superiors, as they shall think it convenient'. More pursued a policy of strict censorship: no books in English printed outside the realm on *any* subject whatsoever were to be imported; he forbade the printing of Scriptural or religious books in England, too, unless approved in advance by a bishop. It was a case of one law for the rich and educated, who could read the Scriptures in Latin texts and commentaries, and another for the poor, who depended on oral instruction from semi-literate artisans and travelling preachers. But More and the bishops were swimming against the tide. The invention of printing had revolutionized the transmission of new ideas across Western Europe, including Protestant ideas. Heretical books and Bibles poured from the presses of English exiles abroad, notably that of William Tyndale at Antwerp. The demand for vernacular Scriptures was persistent, insistent, and widespread; even Henry VIII was enlightened enough to wish to assent to it, and publication of an English Bible in Miles Coverdale's translation was first achieved in 1536, a year after More's death.

Of the forces springing from the new European mood of reform and self-criticism, Christian Humanism and the influence of Greek learning came first. The humanists, of whom the greatest was Erasmus of Rotterdam (1467–1536), rejected scholasticism and elaborate ritualism in favour of wit and simple biblical piety, or *philosophia Christi*, which was founded on primary textual scholarship, and in particular study of the Greek New Testament. Erasmus read voraciously, wrote prodigiously, and travelled extensively; he made three visits to England, and it

was in Cambridge in 1511–14 that he worked upon the Greek text
of his own edition of the New Testament, and revised his Latin

Children in school. The sixteenth century saw the expansion of English
education, inspired by the humanists and new demand fed by the output of the
printing presses. John Colet founded St. Paul's school in 1509. Yet most lower
schools still met in church porches or chantry chapels. (*Parvulorum Institutio,*
1512–13)

version that improved significantly on the standard Vulgate text.

But the renaissance of Greek learning owed as much to a native Englishman, John Colet, the gloomy dean of St. Paul's and founder of its school. Colet, who was also young Thomas More's spiritual director, had been to Italy, where he had encountered the neoplatonist philosophy of Marsilio Ficino and Pico della Mirandola. He had mastered Greek grammar and literature, which he then helped to foster at Oxford and at his school, and the fruits of his philosophical and literary knowledge were applied to Bible study—especially to the works of St. Paul. The result was a method of Scriptural exegesis that broke new ground. Colet emphasized the unity of divine truth, a literal approach to texts, concern for historical context, and belief in a personal and redemptive Christ. These were exciting ideas, and they inspired both Erasmus and the younger generation of English humanists.

The clarion call of humanist reform was sounded in 1503, when Erasmus published *A Handbook of a Christian Knight*, a compendium, or guide, for spiritual life. This book encapsulated the humanism, evangelism, and laicism that its author had imbibed from Colet, and made Europe uncomfortably aware that the existing priorities of the Church would not do. Erasmus added reforming impetus to traditional lay piety, and his pungent criticisms of the scholastic theologians, of empty ritual, ecclesiastical abuses, and even the mores of the Papacy, were as stimulating as they were embarrassing. For Erasmus, whose classic satire was *Praise of Folly* (1514), highlighted his reforming posture by means of his immortal wit, combining the serious, the humorous, and the artistic in peerless texture, and delighting everyone except the senior Church authorities. Wit is an essential literary commodity, and Erasmus drew on his as from a bottomless purse—which was just as well, for it was his sole pecuniary endowment. His effervescent humour flowed quite naturally. Works of piety, that might otherwise have been mere pebbles thrown into the European pond, thus generated ripples that increasingly had the force of tidal waves.

The best English exponent of humanist satire in the wake of *Praise of Folly* was Thomas More, whose *Utopia*, first published at Louvain in 1516, described an imaginary and idealized society of pagans living on a remote island in accordance with principles of natural virtue. By implicitly comparing the benign social customs and enlightened religious attitudes of the ignorant Utopians with the inferior standards, in practice, of (allegedly) Christian Europeans, More produced a strident indictment of

The imaginary island of Utopia. Woodcut by Ambrosius Holbein, 1518, from the third edition of More's *Utopia.*

the latter, based purely on deafening silence—a splendid, if perplexing, achievement of the sort More perennially favoured.

But to the distress of Erasmus, More abandoned reform for repression and extermination of heresy during his thousand days as Lord Chancellor, and has gone down to history, save in the writings of his apologists, as a persecutor rather than a prophet. However, his terrible end in 1535 as a victim of Henry VIII's vengeance, and his willingness to suffer torment for the truth he had discovered in the (then controversial) dogma of papal primacy, perpetually guarantee that his steadfastness was not a delusion; when the axe fell, *Utopia*'s author earned his place among the few who have enlarged the horizons of the human spirit.

In fairness to More, the Brave New World of *Utopia* had been crudely shattered by Luther's début upon the European stage in 1517. For the Christian Humanists, to their sorrow, had unintentionally, but irreversibly, prepared the way for the spread of Protestantism. In England, the impact of Lutheranism far exceeded the relatively small number of converts, and the rise of the 'new learning', as it was called, became the most potent of the forces released in the 1520s and 1530s. Luther's ideas and numerous books rapidly penetrated the universities, especially Cambridge, the City of London, the inns of court, and even reached Henry VIII's Household through the intervention of Anne Boleyn and her circle. At Cambridge, the young scholars influenced included Thomas Cranmer and Matthew Parker, both of whom later became Archbishops of Canterbury. Wolsey naturally made resolute efforts as legate to stamp out the spread of Protestantism, but without obvious success. His critics blamed his reluctance to burn men for heresy as the cause of his failure—for Wolsey would burn books and imprison men, but shared the humane horror of Erasmus at the thought of himself committing bodies to the flames. However, the true reason for Luther's appeal was that he had given coherent doctrinal expression to the religious subjectivity of individuals, and to their distrust of Rome and papal monarchy. In addition his view of the ministry mirrored the instincts of the anticlerical laity, and his answer to concubinage was the global solution of clerical marriage.

Into this religious maelstrom dropped Henry VIII's first divorce. Although Catherine of Aragon had borne five children, only the Princess Mary (b. 1516) had survived, and the king demanded the security of a male heir to protect the fortunes of the Tudor dynasty. It was clear by 1527 that Catherine was past the age of childbearing; meanwhile Henry coveted Anne Boleyn, who would not comply without the assurance of marriage. Yet royal annulments were not infrequent, and all might have been resolved without drama, or even unremarked, had not Henry VIII himself been a proficient, if mendacious, theologian.

The chief obstacle was that Henry, who feared international humiliation, insisted that his divorce should be granted by a competent authority in England—this way he could deprive his wife of her legal rights, and bully his episcopal judges. But his marriage had been founded on Pope Julius II's dispensation, necessarily obtained by Henry VII to enable the young Henry VIII to marry his brother's widow in the first place, and hence the matter pertained to Rome. In order to have his case decided without reference to Rome, in face of the Papacy's unwillingness to concede the matter, Henry had to prove against the reigning pope, Clement VII, that his predecessor's dispensation was invalid—then the marriage would automatically terminate, on the grounds that it had never legally existed. Henry would be a bachelor again. However, this strategy took the king away from matrimonial law into the quite remote and hypersensitive realm of papal power. If Julius II's dispensation was invalid, it must be because the successors of St. Peter had no power to devise such instruments, and the popes were thus no better than other human legislators who had exceeded their authority.

Henry was a good enough theologian and canon lawyer to know that there *was* a minority opinion in Western Christendom to precisely this effect. He was enough of an egotist, too, to fall captive to his own powers of persuasion—soon he believed that papal primacy was unquestionably a shám, a ploy of human invention to deprive kings and emperors of their legitimate inheritances. Henry looked back to the golden days of the British imperial past, to the time of the Emperor Constantine and of King Lucius I. In fact, Lucius I had never existed—he was a myth, a figment of pre-Conquest imagination. But Henry's British 'sources' showed that this Lucius was a great ruler, the first Christian king of Britain, who had endowed the British Church with all its liberties and possessions, and then written to Pope Eleutherius asking him to transmit the Roman laws. However, the pope's reply explained that Lucius did not need any Roman law, because he already had the *lex Britanniae* (whatever that was) under which he ruled both *regnum* and *sacerdotium*:

For you be God's vicar in your kingdom, as the psalmist says, 'Give the king thy judgments, O God, and they righteousness to the king's son' (Ps. lxxii: 1) . . . A king hath his name of ruling, and not of having a realm. You shall be a king, while you rule well; but if you do otherwise, the name of a king shall not remain with you . . . God grant you so to rule the realm of Britain, that you may reign with him for ever, whose vicar you be in the realm.

Vicarius Dei—vicar of Christ. Henry's divorce had led him, incredibly, to believe in his royal supremacy over the English Church.

With the advent of the divorce crisis, Henry took personal charge of his policy and government. He ousted Wolsey, who was hopelessly compromised in the new scheme of things, since his legatine power came directly from Rome. He named Sir Thomas More to the chancellorship, but this move backfired owing to More's scrupulous reluctance to involve himself in Henry's proceedings. He summoned Parliament, which for the first time in English history worked with the king as an omnicompetent legislative assembly, if hesitatingly so. Henry and Parliament finally threw off England's allegiance to Rome in an unsurpassed burst of revolutionary statute-making: the Act of

The hanging and disembowelling of the London Carthusians, convicted of high treason in 1535 for denying Henry VIII's royal supremacy. This print was engraved at Rome in 1555.

Annates (1532), the Act of Appeals (1533), the Act of Supremacy (1534), the First Act of Succession (1534), the Treasons Act (1534), and the Act against the Pope's Authority (1536). The Act of Appeals proclaimed Henry VIII's new imperial status—all English jurisdiction, both secular and religious, now sprang from the king—and abolished the pope's right to decide English ecclesiastical cases. The Act of Supremacy declared that the king of England was supreme head of the *Ecclesia Anglicana*, or Church of England—not the pope. The Act of Succession was the first of a series of Tudor instruments used to settle the order of succession to the throne, a measure which even Thomas More agreed was in itself unremarkable, save that this statute was prefaced by a preamble denouncing papal jurisdiction as a 'usurpation' of Henry's imperial power. More, together with Bishop Fisher of Rochester, and the London Carthusians, the most rigorous and honourable custodians of papal primacy and the legitimacy of the Aragonese marriage, were tried for 'denying' Henry's supremacy under the terms of the Treasons Act. These terms *inter alia* made it high treason maliciously to deprive either king or queen of 'the dignity, title, or name of their royal estates'—that is to deny Henry's royal supremacy. The victims of the act, who were in reality martyrs to Henry's vindictive egoism, were cruelly executed in the summer of 1535. A year later the Reformation legislation was completed by the Act against the Pope's Authority, which removed the last vestiges of papal power in England, including the pope's 'pastoral' right as a teacher to decide disputed points of Scripture.

Henry VIII now controlled the English Church as its supreme head in both temporal and doctrinal matters; his ecclesiastical status was that of a lay metropolitan archbishop who denied the validity of external, papal authority within his territories. He was not a priest, and had no sacerdotal or sacramental functions—the king had tried briefly to claim these but had been rebuffed by an outraged episcopate. Yet Henry was not a Protestant, either. Until his death in 1547, Henry VIII believed in Catholicism without the pope—a curious but typically Henrician application of logic to the facts of so-called British 'history' as exemplified by King Lucius I. As a lay archbishop, Henry could make ecclesiastical laws and define doctrines almost as he pleased—provided he did not overthrow the articles of faith. In fact, this gave him a wider latitude than might be thought, because the bishops could not agree what the articles of faith were, beyond the fundamentals of God's existence, Christ's divinity, the Trinity, and some of the sacraments. The Greek scholarship of the Christian

Humanists had weakened the structure of traditional, medieval Christian doctrine by questioning texts and rejecting scholasticism: a mood of uncertainty prevailed.

Before 1529, then, Henry had ruled his clergy through Wolsey; after 1534 he did so personally, and through his new chief minister, Thomas Cromwell, whom Henry soon appointed his (lay) vicegerent in spirituals. A former aide of Wolsey, Cromwell had risen to executive power as a client of the Boleyn interest, and had taken command of the machinery of government, especially the management of Parliament, in January 1532. By combining the offices of Lord Privy Seal and vicegerent, Cromwell succeeded Wolsey as the architect of Tudor policy under Henry, until his own fall in July 1540—but with one striking difference. As vicegerent he was entirely subordinate to Henry; Wolsey, as legate, had been subordinate only as an Englishman.

Yet the accomplishment of Henry's dream to give the words *rex imperator* literal meaning raises a key historical question. Exactly why did the English bishops and abbots, the aristocracy of the spirit who held a weight of votes in the House of Lords, permit the Henrician Reformation to occur? The answer is partly that Henry coerced his clerical opponents into submission by threats and punitive taxation; but some bishops actually *supported* the king, albeit sadly, and a vital truth lies behind this capitulation. Those clerics who were politically alert saw that it was preferable to be controlled by the Tudor monarchs personally, with whom they could bargain and haggle, than to be offered as a sacrifice instead to the anticlerical laity in the House of Commons, which was the true alternative to compliance. For as early as 1532 it was on the cards that the Tudor supremacy would be a parliamentary supremacy, not a purely royal one, and only the despotic king's dislike of representative assemblies ensured that Parliament's contribution was cut back to the mechanical, though still revolutionary, task of enacting the requisite legislation. It was plain to all but the most ultramontane papalists on the episcopal bench that a parliamentary supremacy would have exposed the clergy directly to the pent-up emotional fury and hatred of the anticlerical laity and common lawyers. The laity, furthermore, were fortified for the attack by the humanists' debunking of ritualism and superstition. In short, royal supremacy was the better of two evils: the clergy would not have to counter the approaching anticlerical backlash without the necessary filter of royal mediation.

Henry VIII's supremacy did save the bishops from the worst excesses of lay anticlericalism, and the king's doctrinal conservatism prevented an explosion of Protestantism during his reign. However, nothing could save the monasteries. Apart from anticlericalism, three quite invincible forces merged after 1535 to dictate the dissolution of the religious houses. First, the monastic communities almost invariably owed allegiance to parent institutions outside England and Wales—this was juridically unacceptable after the Acts of Appeals and Supremacy. Secondly, Henry VIII was bankrupt. He needed to annex the monastic estates in order to restore the Crown's finances. Thirdly, Henry had to buy the allegiance of the political nation away from Rome and in support of his Reformation by massive injections of new patronage—he must appease the lay nobility and gentry with a share of the spoils. Thus Thomas Cromwell's first task as vicegerent was to conduct an ecclesiastical census under Henry's commission, the first major tax record since Domesday Book, to evaluate the condition and wealth of the English Church. Cromwell's questionnaire was a model of precision. Was divine service observed? Who were the benefactors? What lands did the houses possess? What rents?—and so on. The survey was completed in six months, and Cromwell's genius for administration was shown by the fact that *Valor Ecclesiasticus,* as it is known, served both as a record of the value of the monastic assets, and as a report on individual clerical incomes for taxation purposes.

The lesser monasteries were dissolved in 1536; the greater houses followed two years later. The process was interrupted by a formidable northern rebellion, the Pilgrimage of Grace, which was brutally crushed by use of martial law, exemplary public hangings, and a wholesale breaking of Henry's promises to the 'pilgrims'. But the work of plunder was quickly completed. A total of 560 monastic institutions had been suppressed by November 1539, and lands valued at £132,000 per annum immediately accrued to the Court of Augmentations of the King's Revenue, the new department of state set up by Cromwell to cope with the transfer of resources. Henry's coffers next received £15,000 or so from the sale of gold and silver plate, lead, and other precious items; finally, the monasteries had possessed the right of presentation to about two-fifths of the parochial benefices in England and Wales, and these rights were also added to the Crown's patronage.

The long-term effects of the dissolution have often been debated by historians, and may conveniently be divided into those which were planned, and those not. Within the former category, Henry VIII eliminated the last fortresses of potential

The Entombment (detail). East Anglian School, early fifteenth century. Despite restoration, mutilation of the faces by iconoclasts during the Protestant Reformation is still plainly visible.

resistance to his royal supremacy. He founded six new dioceses upon the remains of former monastic buildings and endowments—Peterborough, Gloucester, Oxford, Chester, Bristol, and Westminster, the last-named being abandoned in 1550. The king then reorganized the ex-monastic cathedrals as Cathedrals of the New Foundation, with revised staffs and statutes. Above all, though, the Crown's regular income was seemingly doubled— but for how long? The bitter irony of the dissolution was that Henry VIII's colossal military expenditure in the 1540s, together with the laity's demand for a share of the booty, politically irresistible as that was, would so drastically erode the financial gains as to cancel out the benefits of the entire process. Sales of the confiscated lands began even before the suppression of the greater houses was completed, and by 1547 almost two-thirds of the former monastic property had been alienated. Further grants by Edward VI and Queen Mary brought this figure to over three-quarters by 1558. The remaining lands were sold by Elizabeth I and the early Stuarts. It is true that the lands were not given away: out of 1,593 grants in Henry VIII's reign, only 69 were gifts or partly so; the bulk of grants (95.6 per cent) represented lands sold at prices based on fresh valuations. But the proceeds of sales were not invested—quite the opposite under Henry VIII.

In any case, land *was* the best investment. The impact of sales upon the non-parliamentary income of the Crown was thus obvious, and there is everything to be said for the view that it was Henry VIII's constant dissipation of the monarchy's resources that made it difficult for his successors to govern England.

Of the unplanned effects of the dissolution, the wholesale destruction of fine Gothic buildings, melting down of medieval metalwork and jewellery, and sacking of libraries were the most extensive acts of licensed vandalism perpetrated in the whole of British history. The clergy naturally suffered an immediate decline in morale. The number of candidates for ordination dropped sharply; there was little real conviction that Henry VIII's Reformation had anything to do with spiritual life, or with God. The disappearance of the abbots from the House of Lords meant that the ecclesiastical vote had withered away to a minority, leaving the laity ascendant in both Houses. With the sale of ex-monastic lands usually went the rights of parochial presentation attached to them, so that local laity obtained a considerable monopoly of ecclesiastical patronage, setting the pattern for the next three centuries. The nobility and gentry, especially moderate-sized gentry families, were the ultimate beneficiaries of the Crown's land sales. The distribution of national wealth shifted between 1535 and 1558 overwhelmingly in favour of Crown and laity, as against the Church, and appreciably in favour of the nobility and gentry, as against the Crown. Very few new or substantially enlarged private estates were built up solely out of ex-monastic lands by 1558. But if Norfolk is a typical county, the changing pattern of wealth distribution at Elizabeth's accession was that 4.8 per cent of the county's manors were possessed by the Crown, 6.5 per cent were episcopal or other ecclesiastical manors, 11.4 per cent were owned by East Anglian territorial magnates, and 75.4 per cent had been acquired by the gentry. In 1535, 2.7 per cent of manors had been held by the Crown, 17.2 per cent had been owned by the monasteries, 9.4 per cent were in the hands of magnates, and 64 per cent belonged to gentry families.

Without Henry VIII's preparatory break with Rome, there could not have been Protestant reform in Edward VI's reign— thus evaluation can become a question of religious opinion, rather than historical judgement. However, it is hard not to regard Henry as a despoiler; he was scarcely a creator. Thomas Cromwell did his utmost, often behind the king's back, to endow his contemporaries with Erasmian, and enlightened, idealism: the Elizabethan *via media* owed much to the eirenic side of

Cromwell's complex character. But Cromwell's reward was the block—*ira principis mors est*. He was cast aside by his suspicious employer, and fell victim to the hatred of his enemies. And without Wolsey or Cromwell to restrain him, Henry could do still more harm. He resolved to embark on French and Scottish wars, triggering a slow-burning fuse that was extinguished only by the execution of Mary Stuart in February 1587.

Yet if Henry turned to war and foreign policy in the final years of his reign, it was because he felt secure at last. Cromwell had provided the enforcement machinery necessary to protect the supreme head from spontaneous internal opposition; Jane Seymour had brought forth the male heir to the Tudor throne; Henry was excited about his marriage to Catherine Howard, and was happily cured of theology.

The matrimonial adventures of Henry VIII are too familiar to recount again in detail, but an outline may conveniently be given. Anne Boleyn was already pregnant when the king married her, and the future Elizabeth I was born on 7 September 1533. Henry was bitterly disappointed that she was not the expected son, blaming Anne and God—in that order. Anne had turned out to be a precocious flirt, who meddled fatally in politics: she was ousted and executed in a coup of May 1536. Henry immediately chose the homely Jane Seymour, whose triumph in producing the baby Prince Edward was Pyrrhic, for she died of Tudor surgery twelve days later. Her successor was Anne of Cleves, whom Henry married in January 1540 to win European allies. But this gentle creature, whom Henry rudely called 'the Flemish mare', did not suit; divorce was thus easy, as the union was never consummated. Catherine Howard came next. A high-spirited minx, she had been a maid of honour to Anne of Cleves—entirely inappropriately—and became Henry's fifth queen in July 1540 as the key to the coup that destroyed Cromwell. She was executed in February 1542 for adultery. Finally, Henry took the amiable Catherine Parr to wife in July 1543. Twice widowed, Catherine was a cultivated Erasmian, under whose benign influence the royal children lived under one roof, and were spared the more malign components of Henry's paternal indulgence.

Henry VIII's plans for war, which were conceived after his marriage to Catherine Howard, and which hardened when he learned of her infidelity, resurrected youthful dreams of French conquests. Wolsey had monitored the king's futile early campaigns of 1511–16, and brilliantly transformed Henry's military failures into the diplomatic prize of the treaty of London (1518).

At the Field of Cloth of Gold in 1520, Henry had fêted Francis I of France in a Renaissance extravaganza that was hailed as the eighth wonder of the world, for Francis was the king whom Henry loved to hate. More wasteful campaigns in 1522 and 1523 were curtailed by England's financial exhaustion—then Henry's policy fell into labyrinthine confusion. England was at war with France; then in alliance with France. In the end, Henry was perhaps grateful for the European peace which prevailed from 1529 to 1536, and even more relieved by the resumed rivalry that kept Habsburg and Valois mutually engaged until the reverberations of the Pilgrimage of Grace had died away.

By 1541 Henry was moving towards a renewed amity with Spain against France, but he was prudent enough to hesitate. Tudor security required that, before England went to war with France, no doors should be open to the enemy within Britain itself. This meant an extension of English hegemony within the British Isles—Wales, Ireland, and Scotland. Accordingly Henry undertook, or continued, the wider task of English colonization that was ultimately completed by the Act of Union with Scotland (1707).

The Union of England and Wales had been presaged by Cromwell's reforming ambition, and was legally accomplished by Parliament in 1536 and 1543. The marcher lordships were shired, English laws and county administration were extended to Wales, and the shires and county boroughs were required to send twenty-four MPs to Parliament at Westminster. In addition, a refurbished Council of Wales, and new Courts of Great Sessions, were set up to administer the region's defences and judicial system. Wales was made subject to the full operation of royal writs, and to English principles of land tenure. The Act of 1543 dictated that Welsh customs of tenure and inheritance were to be phased out, and that English rules were to succeed them. Welsh customs persisted in remoter areas until the seventeenth century and beyond, but English customs soon predominated. English language became the fashionable tongue, and Welsh native arts went into decline.

Englishmen have regarded the Union as the dawn of a civilizing process that ended with the abolition of the Council of Wales in 1689 and of the Great Sessions in 1830. Welshmen, by contrast, view Henry VIII's Acts as a crude annexation, which technically they were—for they were not in the nature of a treaty between negotiating parties as was the case with Scotland in 1707. In fact, Welsh civilization was already advanced in the sixteenth century, and flourished despite the Acts. Sir John Prise,

The Principality of Wales 1284–1536
Boundary of Wales as subject to the jurisdiction of the Court of Great Sessions, 1542-1830
Boundary of Wales and the Border Counties subject to the Council of Wales

0   10   20 miles
0 10 20 30 km

The union of England and Wales

a relation of Thomas Cromwell, defended Welsh history against the scepticism of Polydore Vergil; Humphrey Llwyd of Denbigh supported him with geographical learning—and there were others. John Owen of Plas Du, Llanarmon, and New College, Oxford, enjoyed a higher literary reputation abroad during his lifetime than did William Shakespeare, his contemporary. He wrote 1,500 Latin epigrams in the style of Martial. Welsh grammars were compiled to perpetuate the native tongue—by Sion Dafydd Rhys (1592), who wrote in Latin in order to reach the widest European audience, and by John Davies of Mallwyd (1621), who publicly justified the utility of Welsh studies.

Tudor Irish policy had begun with Henry VII's decision that all laws made in England were automatically to apply to Ireland, and that the Irish Parliament could only legislate with the king of England's prior consent. English territorial influence, in reality, did not extend much beyond the Pale—the area around

Dublin—and the Irish chiefs held the balance of power. Henry VIII ruled mainly through the chiefs before the Reformation, but was obliged to protect England in the 1530s from a possible papal counter-attack launched from Ireland. Lord Leonard Grey was named deputy of Ireland by Cromwell, but his coercive actions proved counter-productive. He was replaced by Sir Anthony St. Leger, who made a fresh start.

St. Leger reshaped the Irish policy of the Tudors, and his basic philosophy persisted until 1783. Instead of consolidation and coercion, he proposed friendship and conciliation, but the essence of the plan was to create a subordinate national superstructure for Ireland by translating Henry VIII's lordship into kingship. The kings of England were *dominus Hiberniae*, not *rex*. But St. Leger persuaded Henry to assume the Crown—that would overthrow papal claims to feudal overlordship, and subordinate the chiefs to royal authority. Henry assented, and was proclaimed king in June 1541. His understanding was probably that kingship would enhance his security within the British Isles, Moreover, if the idea was to form a framework for peaceful, constitutional relations between the Crown and the Irish nation, that was laudable and altruistic. Yet it was also visionary and impractical. The Irish revenues were insufficient to maintain royal status—a separate Council, Star Chamber, Chancery, and Parliament in Dublin, operating independently of, but subject to controls from, the English Parliament and Privy Council. Above all, kingship committed England to a possible full-scale conquest of Ireland in the future, should the chiefs rebel, or should the Irish Reformation, begun by Cromwell, fail. As it turned out, 'conciliation' by benevolent kingship was probably worse than external 'consolidation' and 'coercion', since Tudor attitudes to conquest in Ireland were based on experiences in the New World, something the disillusioned Edmund Spenser, who lived in Ireland, pointed out in Elizabeth's reign.

The harsh vicissitudes of Irish history, especially in the seventeenth century, were hardly attributable to Henry VIII and St. Leger. However, the new policy of the Tudors perpetuated the disadvantages both of subordination and of autonomy. In the wake of Irish pressure and the revolt of the American Colonies, the British Parliament abandoned its controls over Ireland in 1783. The Act of Union of 1801 reversed this change in favour of direct rule from Westminster, after which Irish history owed nothing to the Tudors.

Yet the linchpin of Tudor security was the need to control

Scotland. James IV (1488–1513) had renewed the Auld Alliance with France in 1492 and further provoked Henry VII by offering support for Perkin Warbeck. But the first of the Tudors declined to be distracted by Scottish sabre-rattling, and forged a treaty of Perpetual Peace with Scotland in 1502, followed a year later by the marriage of his daughter, Margaret, to King James. However, James tried to break the treaty shortly after Henry VIII's accession; Henry was on campaign in France, but sent the earl of Surrey northwards, and Surrey decimated the Scots at Flodden on 7 September 1513. The élite of Scotland—the king, three bishops, eleven earls, fifteen lords, and some 10,000 men—were slain in an attack that was the delayed acme of medieval aggression begun by Edwards I and III. The new Scottish king, James V, was an infant, and the English interest remained safe for the next twenty years or so in the hands of his mother, Henry VIII's own sister. But Scottish panic after Flodden had, if anything, confirmed the nation's ties with France, epitomized by the regency of John duke of Albany, who represented the French cause but nevertheless kept Scotland at peace with England for the moment.

The French threat became overt when the mature James V visited France in 1536, and married in quick succession Madeleine, daughter of Francis I, and on her death Mary of Guise. In 1541 James agreed to meet Henry VIII at York, but committed the supreme offence of failing to turn up. By this time, Scotland was indeed a danger to Henry VIII, as its government was dominated by the French faction led by Cardinal Beaton, who symbolized both the Auld Alliance and the threat of papal counter-attack. In October 1542 the duke of Norfolk invaded Scotland, at first achieving little. It was the Scottish counterstroke that proved to be a worse disaster even than Flodden. On 25 November 1542, 3,000 English triumphed over 10,000 Scots at Solway Moss—and the news of the disgrace killed James V within a month. Scotland was left hostage to the fortune of Mary Stuart, a baby born only six days before James's death. For England, it seemed to be the answer to a prayer.

Henry VIII and Protector Somerset, who governed England during the early years of Edward VI's minority, none the less turned advantage into danger. Twin policies were espoused by which war with France was balanced by intervention in Scotland designed to secure England's back door. In 1543 Henry used the prisoners taken at Solway Moss as the nucleus of an English party in Scotland; he engineered Beaton's overthrow, and forced on the Scots the treaty of Greenwich, which projected union of the

Crowns in the form of marriage between Prince Edward and Mary Stuart. At the end of the same year, Henry allied with Spain against France, planning a combined invasion for the following spring. But the invasion, predictably, was not concerted. Henry was deluded by his capture of Boulogne; the emperor made a separate peace with France at Crépi, leaving England's flank exposed. At astronomical cost the war continued until June 1546. Francis I then finally agreed that England could keep Boulogne for eight years, when it was to be restored to France complete with expensive new fortifications. He also abandoned the Scots, endorsing by implication the terms of the treaty of Greenwich. But it was too late: Henry's 'rough wooing' of Scotland had already backfired. Beaton had trumped Henry's English party and repudiated the treaty; the earl of Hertford, the future Protector Somerset, was sent north with 12,000 men. Hertford's devastation of the border country, and Lothian, was successful, but was culpably counter-productive. In particular, the sack of Edinburgh united Scottish resistance to English terrorism. Henry VIII had thus engineered exactly what he wished to avoid—simultaneous conflict with France and Scotland. Hertford returned to Scotland in 1545, but the French faction remained ascendant, even after Beaton was murdered in May 1546 by a group of Fife lairds.

Edward VI

The death of Henry VIII in 1547, and the Protectorate until 1549 of the obsessional, vacillating Hertford as duke of Somerset left a power vacuum at the centre. This was paralleled locally by the temporary inability of county governments to contain outbreaks of violence and rebellion springing mainly from the decline in living standards in the 1540s. Riot and commotion were virtually ubiquitous from 1548 to 1550, save in the north where memories of the ill-fated Pilgrimage of Grace were perhaps still fresh. Coinage debasements designed to help pay for the French war had caused rampant inflation, and the most abrupt decline in the purchasing power of money coincided with Somerset's enclosure commissions and sheep tax, a platform that fermented rumours that the Protector supported the poor against the rich. The most serious uprisings took place in Devon and Cornwall, and in East Anglia, culminating in formal sieges of Exeter and Norwich by rebels. Somerset's equivocation, and inability to end this domestic crisis, prompted the earl of Warwick's coup against him in October 1549.

Edward VI as Prince of Wales. Although this portrait claims to depict Edward 'Anno Aetis suae 10', it must have been painted before his accession on 28 January 1547, since he wears the Prince of Wales's feathers as a jewel. By William Scrots or his circle.

Yet Somerset's most spectacular failure was his continued adherence to the defunct treaty of Greenwich. His desire to realize Henry VIII's plan to subdue French influence in Scotland and achieve the union of the Crowns became an obsession. His victory at the battle of Pinkie (10 September 1547) was justified as an attempt to free Scotland from the Roman clergy, but the Scottish Reformation was hardly helped by a policy that pushed Scotland ever closer into the embrace of France. In June 1548, 6,000 French troops landed at Leith, and Mary Stuart was removed to France. When Somerset continued to threaten Scotland, Henry II of France declared war on England. Boulogne was blockaded; French forces in Scotland were strengthened. The Scots then agreed that Mary should eventually marry the Dauphin, heir to the French throne. That provision hammered the last nail into Somerset's coffin.

The earl of Warwick's coup, and the realignment of the Privy Council, was completed by February 1550. Warwick shunned the title of Protector; instead he assumed that of Lord President of the Council, an interesting choice, since it revived an office effectively obsolete since the fall of Edmund Dudley, Warwick's father. Posthumous tradition has vilified Warwick as an evil schemer—a true 'Machiavel'. But it is hard to see why, for expediency in the interests of stability was the most familiar touchstone of Tudor policy. Three episodes allegedly prove Warwick's criminal cunning: his original coup against Somerset, the subsequent trial which ended in Somerset's execution in January 1552, and the notorious scheme to alter the succession to the throne in favour of Lady Jane Grey, Warwick's daughter-in-law. However, only the last of these charges seems justifiable by Tudor standards, and even this would be regarded differently by historians had the plot to exclude the Catholic Mary actually succeeded.

Warwick, who created himself duke of Northumberland in October 1551, made, in fact, a laudable effort to reverse the destabilization permitted, or left unchecked, by Somerset. Domestic peace was restored by the use of forces which included foreign mercenaries; England's finances were put back on course by means of enlightened reforms and retrenchments. Above all, Somerset's disastrous wars with France and Scotland were quickly terminated. Northumberland sought peace with dishonour—a humiliating but attractive alternative to fighting. Boulogne was returned to France at once; English garrisons in Scotland were withdrawn, and the treaty of Greenwich was quietly forgotten. It thus became inevitable that Mary Stuart would marry the Dauphin, but considerations of age ensured that the union was postponed until April 1558.

The English Reformation had meanwhile reached its crossroads. After Thomas Cromwell's execution, Henry VIII had governed the Church of England himself: his doctrinal conservatism was inflexible to the last. But Somerset rose to the Protectorate as leader of the Protestant faction in the Privy Council, and the young Edward VI—he was nine years old in 1547—mysteriously became a precocious and bigoted Protestant too. In July 1547, Somerset reissued Cromwell's Erasmian injunctions to the clergy, followed by a Book of Homilies, or specimen sermons, which embodied Protestant doctrines. He summoned Parliament four months later, and the Henrician doctrinal legislation was repealed. At the same time, the chantries were dissolved. These minor foundations existed to sing masses for the souls of their benefactors; as such, they encouraged beliefs in purgatory and the merits of requiems, doctrines which Protestants denied. Somerset thus justified their abolition on religious grounds, but it is plain that he coveted their property even more to finance his Scottish ambitions. Next, the Privy Council wrote to Archbishop Cranmer, ordering the wholesale removal of images from places of worship, 'images which be things not necessary, and without which the churches of Christ continued most godly many years'. Shrines, and the jewels and plate inside them, were promptly seized by the Crown; the statues and wall-paintings that decorated English parish churches were mutilated, or covered with whitewash. In 1538 Henry VIII had suppressed shrines which were centres of pilgrimages, notably that of St. Thomas Becket at Canterbury. Protector Somerset finalized the destruction already begun, ensuring that the native art, sculpture, metalwork, and embroidery associated with Catholic ritual were comprehensively wiped out.

The danger was always that Protestant reform would over-reach itself—in the Cornish rebellion of 1549, opposition to the first of Cranmer's Prayer Books provided the chief rallying point. The system for licensing public preachers had broken down by September 1548, and Somerset was obliged, temporarily, to ban all preaching, whether licensed or not, in favour of readings of the official homilies. The Protector, though, promised 'an end of all controversies in religion' and 'uniform order', and Cranmer likewise aspired to this visionary goal. He wrote to Albert Hardenberg, leader of the Bremen Reformed Church:

We are desirous of setting forth in our churches the true doctrine of God, neither have we any wish to be shifting and unstable, or to deal in ambiguities: but, laying aside all carnal considerations, to transmit to posterity a true and explicit form of doctrine agreeable to the rule of the scriptures; so that there may be set forth among all nations a testimony respecting our doctrine, delivered by the grave authority of learned and pious men; and that all posterity may have a pattern which they may imitate. For the purpose of carrying this important design into effect we have thought it necessary to have the assistance of learned men, who, having compared their opinions together with us, may do away with doctrinal controversies, and establish an entire system of true doctrine.

Protestant theologians who responded to Cranmer's call included John Knox from Scotland, Martin Bucer from Strasbourg, John à Lasco from Poland, Peter Martyr Vermigli from Italy, and Bernardino Ochino, the controversial ex-vicar-general of the Capuchins, who had made a sensational conversion to Protestantism in the early 1540s.

Yet Protestants were even less capable of consensus than were Catholics. John Knox, to whom Northumberland inadvertently offered the bishopric of Rochester (fortunately Knox refused), was particularly atavistic; he thrived on crisis. Cranmer soon came to see that unity could only be achieved at the price of uniformity—this was the fundamental lesson of the English Reformation. Accordingly the two editions of his Book of Common Prayer (1549, 1552), which enshrined the pure and Scriptural doctrines for which the primate had craved since 1537, not only had to be approved by Parliament; they had to be enforced by Acts of Uniformity. The advantages from Cranmer's viewpoint were that the Books were in English, and the second was unambiguously Protestant; the drawback was that the Prayer Books were first published as schedules to the Uniformity Acts, so that the doctrines and ceremonies of the English Church now rested on parliamentary authority, rather than on the independent legislative power of the supreme head. This constitutional amendment marked the final triumph of the Tudor laity over the *Ecclesia Anglicana*, for Elizabeth I, in fashioning the religious settlement of 1558–9, was obliged to regard Cranmer's Prayer Books as a precedent.

Queen Mary

Northumberland's patronage of Knox, who in exile during Mary's reign scandalized Europe by theorizing upon the rights of subjects to rebel against idolatrous rulers, illustrates how far the duke had linked his future to the Protestant cause. Edward VI had never enjoyed good health, and by the late spring of 1553 it was plain that he was dying. By right of birth, as well as under

Henry VIII's will, Mary, Catherine of Aragon's Catholic daughter, was the lawful successor. But Northumberland's attempted *putsch* in July 1553 needs more than a casual explanation. The facts are that Northumberland bound his family to the throne on 21 May by marrying his eldest son to Lady Jane Grey. Jane was the eldest daughter of the marquis of Dorset, and residuary legatee of the Crown, after the Princesses Mary and Elizabeth, under Henry VIII's will. Next, a documentary 'device' was drafted, by which Edward VI disinherited his sisters and bequeathed his throne to Jane and her heirs. Edward died on 6 July 1553; Northumberland and the Council proclaimed Jane queen four days later. The duke's treachery seems proved. Yet the plot may have been Edward's. The Protestant boy-bigot hated his sisters, especially Mary; the 'device' was drafted in his own hand, and corrected by him. At the very least, Edward had been Northumberland's willing collaborator.

Jane Grey ruled for nine days. Knox preached on her behalf, and threatened popery and tyranny should Mary enforce her claim. But the *putsch* was doomed. Mary was allowed to escape to Framlingham, the walled fortress of the Catholic Howard family. Proclaimed by the East Anglian gentry, she marched south. London changed sides; Northumberland, Jane, and their principal adherents eventually went to the block.

Yet Mary triumphed because she cheated. The Norfolk gentry was persuaded of her Tudor legitimism; they learned the terrible extent of her Catholicism only after she was safely enthroned at Westminster. Even so, we should beware of the bias of John Foxe and other Protestant polemicists writing in Elizabeth's reign, who would prefer us to believe that Mary did nothing but persecute. It is true that Mary burned a minimum of 274 persons after February 1555, when the law again permitted such horrors. Moreover, the premier Protestant martyrs, Bishops Hooper, Ridley, Latimer, and Archbishop Cranmer, suffered agony at the stake far exceeding the sheer physical torment suffered earlier by their Catholic opponents—for Bishop Fisher and Sir Thomas More had been granted the privilege of simple decapitation. Yet these leaders of Edwardian Protestantism were primarily the victims of straightforward political vengeance. Stephen Gardiner, the failed conservative manipulator of Henry VIII's reign, who had been outwitted by Thomas Cromwell in the 1530s, was abandoned by the king in the 1540s, and had languished in the Tower during Edward's reign, had become Lord Chancellor in 1553; he had bitter scores to settle. Secondly, we should appreciate that many of the Marian 'martyrs' would have been burnt as

Mary I, 1554. One of three certain versions by Antonio Mor, who was sent to England to paint Mary as the prospective wife of Philip of Spain. She holds a Tudor rose, and her pendant jewel may be that given her by Henry VIII in 1542.

anabaptists, or Lollards, under Henry VIII. By sixteenth-century standards there was nothing exceptional about Mary's reign of terror beyond the fact that, as in the case of More when he had persecuted Protestants as Lord Chancellor, she regarded her work as well done, and that it enhanced her appetite for dinner. Even the scale of Mary's persecution may have been exaggerated, for the figures come from the biased Foxe, who reported the same examples twice whenever possible, and who conveniently forgot that the unpersecuted Lollards of Edward's reign had created a backlog.

Mary's true goal was always England's reunion with Rome; persecution was a minor aspect of her programme. It was thus to her advantage that the parliamentary landed laity were, by this date, thoroughly secular-minded, for they repealed the Henrician and Edwardian religious legislation almost without comment, and re-enacted the heresy laws—all the time their sole condition was that the Church lands taken since 1536 should not be restored. Yet Mary needed papal assistance; she could not work alone. In November 1554, Cardinal Pole, an English Catholic exile of Plantagenet lineage, landed in England, absolved the kingdom from sin, and proclaimed papal reunion. Pole, who was appointed Archbishop of Canterbury, then attempted to implement intelligent ecclesiastical reforms in the spirit of the Counter-Reformation: these covered such areas as the liturgy, clerical manners, education, and episcopal supervision. But Pole, too, was a fascinating relic of Christian Humanism as practised by Colet, Erasmus, and Thomas More before 1517—for he was of their generation and had shared their illusions; it was no accident that More's idealized memory was rediscovered in Mary's reign to a fanfare of hagiographical trumpetings. However, Pole was afforded neither the time nor the money needed to accomplish his tasks: three years, and virtually no money, were not enough. The ecclesiastical machine ground slowly; standards of clerical education could not be raised without the augmentation of stipends, especially in the north.

Mary's short reign was, nevertheless, surprisingly successful in other spheres. The financial reforms of Northumberland were completed; the Exchequer was revitalized and reorganized; a blueprint for recoinage was prepared, and was adopted under Elizabeth. In 1557, a committee was named to investigate 'why customs and subsidies be greatly diminished and decayed'. The outcome was a new Book of Rates in May 1558, which increased customs receipts by 75 per cent. Nothing on this scale would be tried again until James I's reign, when the Great Contract of 1610 proved such a disastrous failure.

Yet Mary made two bad mistakes. The first was to allow some 800 English Protestants to emigrate to Frankfurt, Zurich, and Geneva. For not only did these exiles launch a relentless crusade of anti-Catholic propaganda and subversive literature against England, which the government was obliged to suppress or refute as best it could; they also flocked home again upon the accession, in 1558, of Elizabeth, the Protestant Deborah, as they believed her to be, when many were appointed bishops, despite the inherent tension between the Anglican ceremonials they became obliged to enforce, and the Genevan distaste for popish rituals and vestments they had so recently shared. Mary's second mistake was her Spanish marriage. Her union with Philip, son of the Emperor Charles V, was her own idea, celebrated in July 1554 despite the pleas of privy councillors and Parliament. Philip was styled king jointly with Mary as queen during her lifetime; however, his rights in England were to expire if Mary died childless, as proved to be the case. Yet even these terms did not appease opponents of the match: four simultaneous rebellions were planned for 1554, of which Sir Thomas Wyatt's, in Kent, began prematurely in January. Wyatt led 3,000 men to London, proclaiming that 'we seek no harm to the Queen, but better council and counsellors'. But Wyatt declined to pillage London; he removed his force to Kingston—a fatal diversion. His army was defeated, and 100 rebels, including Wyatt, were executed as traitors. The other projected rebellions came to nothing.

Wyatt's fear that England would become a Spanish pawn was, none the less, justified. In 1556, Philip became king of Spain, following Charles V's abdication. Within a year, he had dragged his wife into a war with Henry II of France, which culminated in the recapture of Calais by the duke of Guise (7 January 1558). Calais, apart from its commercial value as the wool Staple, was symbolic of the glorious French campaigns of the Black Prince and Henry V: its loss was more than bad luck. Mary's death in November 1558 was thus unmourned, and the fact that Cardinal Pole died within a few hours of the queen was a positive fillip. Henry II meanwhile exulted with Te Deum and bonfires, and the marriage of Mary Stuart to the Dauphin, the perilous consequence of the aggression of Henry VIII and Somerset, was expedited.

Elizabeth I

Elizabeth I, daughter of Henry VIII and Anne Boleyn, ascended her throne on 17 November 1558. Ruler of England for forty-four years, Elizabeth has attained a posthumous reputation far in excess of her actual achievements. It is plain that her own propaganda, the cult of Gloriana, her sheer longevity, the coincidence of the Shakespearean moment, and the lucky defeat of the Armada have beguiled us into joining a crescendo of adulation that ignores the simple fact that she quietly allowed England to become ungovernable.

> Are you then travelling to the temple of Eliza?
> Even to her temple are my feeble limbs travelling.
> Some call her Pandora: some Gloriana: some
> Cynthia: some Belphoebe: some Astraea; all by
> several names to express several loves: Yet
> all those names make but one celestial body,
> as all those loves meet to create but one soul.
> I am of her own country, and we adore her by the
> name of Eliza.
> Thomas Dekker, *Old Fortunatus* (1600)

Against such patriotic rhetoric historical truth dims into mere dusty pedantry.

At first, though, the emphasis was strictly on stability and religious settlement. Even the positive, if differing, efforts of Northumberland and Mary to reverse the destabilization endemic between 1547 and 1549 had failed to recover enough lost ground. Hence Elizabeth's password was 'concord'; at her first official reception in the City of London in January 1559, she was hailed as the royal peacemaker. The theme of her first coronation pageant was 'Unity': her throne was garnished with red and white roses, beneath which was written:

THE UNITING OF THE TWO HOUSES OF YORK AND LANCASTER.

For the symbolism was that, just as Henry VII had ended civil strife in England when he had married Elizabeth, daughter of Edward IV, so the new Elizabeth, granddaughter of the Tudor dynasty's founder, would also strive for the perpetual preservation of concord. As the child-narrator of the pageant intoned:

> Therefore as civil war and shed of blood did cease;
> When these two Houses were united into one:
> So now, that jar shall stint and quietness increase,
> We trust, O noble Queen! thou wilt be cause alone!

It was hardly great verse, but the sentiment was genuine.

Religious concord was, however, the issue in 1559. Another pageant portrayed Elizabeth as judge and restorer of Israel, enthroned beneath a palm tree:

> Jabin, of Canaan King, had long, by force of arms,
> Oppressed the Israelites; which for God's people went:
> But God minding, at last, for to redress their harms;
> The worthy DEBORAH, as judge among them sent.

Yet concord was easier to desire than to achieve. Elizabeth originally aimed to revive Henry VIII's religious legislation, to re-establish her royal supremacy and the break with Rome, and to permit communion in both kinds (bread and wine) after the Protestant fashion—but nothing else. In 1559, such terms were visionary and unattainable: they ignored Parliament's new role as partner with the supreme head in prescribing uniformity and in enacting and repealing the requisite legislation; they disappointed the aspirations of the Protestant exiles, who had to be appeased because none of Mary's bishops would serve in the new Anglican Church. In the end, William Cecil, who became Elizabeth's premier councillor from the start of her reign, arranged a compromise by which Elizabeth was styled 'supreme governor' of the English Church, thus placating male chauvinism; and by which Cranmer's 1552 Book of Common Prayer, with minor modifications, was to be enforced by an Act of Uniformity. Another act then confirmed to the Crown such monastic and chantry property as Mary had begun to return; and a third measure strengthened further the Crown's estates at the expense of the bishops. The Elizabethan Settlement was completed in 1563, when Convocation approved Thirty-nine Articles defining the Anglican Church's doctrine—these were based on forty-two articles drafted by Cranmer in Edward VI's reign. The Settlement gained teeth sharper than the Act of Uniformity in 1571, when a Subscription Act required the beneficed clergy to assent to the Thirty-nine Articles, or resign their livings.

The Anglican Church now became the most powerful motor of Tudor domestic stability. Despite its faults, the framework that John Jewel defended in his *Apology of the Church of England* (1562), and to which the 'judicious' Richard Hooker gave rational credibility in *The Laws of Ecclesiastical Polity* (1593–1600), the 'Church by law Established' saved England from the religious strife that so sorely afflicted other European countries at the time, notably France. But the Settlement was only the first of several tests faced by the Elizabethan regime. In April 1559, the peace of Cateau-Cambrésis (between Spain, France, and England) ended the débâcle of Mary's French war; it meant, too, that the Catholic powers had temporarily acknowledged Elizabeth's sovereignty, since they had signed a treaty with her. However, the Anglican Church was plainly Protestant, even if it retained altars and vestments. Toleration was not granted to Catholics, unless they were prepared to become 'church papists'. The others had to pay fines for not attending church under the Uniformity Act, although Elizabeth did not persecute her Catholic subjects except at times of international crisis. In short, English Catholics, the Papacy, Spain, and France were the

Robert Dudley, Earl of Leicester. Drawing by Federigo Zuccaro, 1575.

natural enemies of the Settlement; the real danger was the threat of a Catholic league against England. After 1559, the Catholic cause was directly linked to that of dynastic intrigue, which aimed to depose Elizabeth in favour of Mary Stuart.

Mary had married the Dauphin in April 1558, and seven months later the Scottish Parliament agreed to offer him the crown matrimonial in exchange for support for the Scottish Reformation. Mary Tudor's death unleashed new French intervention in Scotland; there was sporadic fighting, enlivened only by Mary of Guise's jest, 'Where is now John Knox's God? My God is stronger than his, yea, even in Fife.' (The Catholic Mary of Guise had ousted the earl of Arran from the regency of Scotland in 1554.) Yet by August 1561 the Queen of Scots was a widow and living in Scotland—*sic transit gloria mundi*. Furthermore, Elizabeth and Cecil were cautiously assisting Knox: the Scottish Reformation had become the effective vehicle for the expulsion of Continental influence from the British Isles, and the assertion of the hegemony sought by Henry VIII.

Elizabeth I, meanwhile, declined to marry, or name her successor. Mary Stuart's supporters hoped that the Virgin Queen would die, and that Mary would succeed her in a Catholic coup. For Mary's grandmother had been Henry VIII's sister, Margaret. The union of the Scottish and English Crowns was a distinct possibility. But Mary made mistakes as ruler of Scotland, she lost the battle of Langside, and fled to England in May 1568. Elizabeth, in effect, imprisoned her. A labyrinthine chain of intrigues then took shape, in which native Catholic, papal, and Spanish ambitions allied, threateningly, with domestic political factions opposed to Cecil's monopoly of influence—strange bedfellows indeed. Fortunately the Northern Rebellion, led by the disillusioned Catholic earls of Northumberland and Westmorland, was incoherently attempted and easily crushed. By the summer of 1572, Elizabeth and Cecil had passed their second major test. Stability had been preserved; Cecil took care to demand a peerage in reward.

Mary Stuart's imprisonment, nevertheless, began a new phase in Tudor politics; international involvement became integral to the formulation of policy. First, Pope Pius V had issued a bull, *Regnans in Excelsis*, in February 1570, declaring Elizabeth excommunicated and deposed, and calling upon loyal Catholics to remove her. Secondly, outright revolt in the Spanish Netherlands after 1572 caused a crisis among Protestant consciences, which felt obliged to offer direct aid to the Prince of Orange. Thirdly, Elizabeth's threat of support for French invasion of the

Low Countries as a counter against Spain, which was twice taken to the point of Anglo-French marriage negotiations, was regarded as hostile by Philip II. On these matters the Privy Council was, in fact, divided. The dominant faction led by Cecil, now Lord Burghley, and the earl of Sussex, favoured renewed amity with Spain. Against this the earl of Leicester, Elizabeth's favourite and Burghley's chief rival, and Sir Francis Walsingham, an avowed left-wing Protestant, pleaded for material assistance for the Dutch. The tension was between *realpolitik* and religion, with the result that Elizabeth opted for the indirect strategy of alliance with France. Less confident in foreign than domestic statecraft, her innate conservatism, secular-mindedness, and abhorrence for rebels silenced her intuitive Protestant leanings; in short, she played safe. Mid-Elizabethan policy was thus defensive and immobile, shunning obvious initiatives. For the queen and Burghley were convinced that England could not survive alone the ultimate test of war with Spain.

Yet when war with Spain came in 1585, England was isolated. From 1580 to 1583, Elizabeth pursued her strategy of support for French intervention in the Netherlands, backing Francis duke of Anjou, brother and heir of Henry III of France, and her most plausible suitor. The Leicester–Walsingham faction carried the Council against the marriage plan, which they held to be political dynamite—for once Burghley and Sussex were outflanked. But Anjou died in 1584, having failed to halt Spanish recovery in the Low Countries. The Protestant Henry of Navarre was now heir to the French throne, and the Guise Court party made an immediate effort to counterbalance this threat, espousing a pro-Spanish policy. Philip II meanwhile prospered. His forces captured the Azores in 1583; the Prince of Orange was assassinated in June 1584. In May 1585, Philip felt confident enough to seize all English ships in Iberian ports, a step that was a covert declaration of war. Elizabeth responded by giving Leicester his head, allying with the Dutch States General in August 1585, and dispatching the earl to Holland with an army. But Leicester's mission was a fiasco; his ignominious return in December 1587 was soon followed by his death. Only Sir Francis Drake, a patriotic pirate, who was permitted to take revenge on Spanish ports and property, enjoyed any degree of success.

Outright war followed the execution of Mary Stuart in February 1587. Further Catholic plots, one of which involved the assassination of Elizabeth, had hardened the Privy Council's attitude. Elizabeth stood indecisive and immobile; Mary had been tried and convicted, but she was of the royal blood.

The 'Ark Royal'. Built in 1581 for Sir Walter Raleigh as the *Ark Raleigh*, she was bought by the Crown, renamed, and used as flagship for Lord Howard of Effingham against the Armada.

However, the Council could wait no longer: the law was put into effect. Scotland fulminated, but the twenty-one-year-old James VI was appeased by subsidies and enhanced prospects of the greatest of glittering prizes—succession to the English Crown. (In any case, James had no illusions about Spanish support for the Scottish Reformation.) Philip II, though, regarded Mary's execution as provocation: he launched the *impresa d'Inglaterra*—the 'invincible' Armada. Protestant England's ultimate test was approaching.

The Armada sailed from Lisbon in May 1588. Philip's plan was to win control of the English Channel, to rendezvous with the duke of Parma off the coast of Holland, and to transport Parma's army of some 30,000 men from the Netherlands across the Channel. The main fleet was to cover Parma's crossing to England, and then unite troops carried by the Armada itself with Parma's army in a combined invasion of England. The Armada was commanded by the duke of Medina Sidonia; the English fleet was led by Lord Howard of Effingham, Lord High Admiral, with Sir Francis Drake as second-in-command. Effingham sailed in the *Ark Royal*, built for Sir Walter Raleigh in 1581; Drake captained the *Revenge*, commissioned in 1575. In England the local militias were mobilized; possible landing places were mapped, and their defences charted. But had Parma landed, his army would have decimated English resistance; the effectiveness of English sea-power was vital.

In the event, the historic defeat of the Armada was not far removed from traditional legend, romantic games of bowls excepted. A two-pronged English assault, organized in squadrons, trapped Medina Sidonia in Calais Roads, where Parma could not join him for fear of the Dutch. The fire-ships sent in by the English at Calais were virtually harmless, but they appeared to be bomb-ships, which were deadly. The Armada cut cables and dispersed in confusion, the loss of anchors causing problems later. The main battle was then fought off Gravelines. The English used long-range guns to advantage; Spanish ships were holed, and men died in considerable numbers. Suddenly a change of wind enabled the battered Armada to flee north, with Howard and Drake in pursuit as far as the Firth of Forth. Many Spanish ships rounded the Orkneys, but Atlantic gales and loss of anchors created havoc. In August 1588, Protestant England celebrated her deliverance with prayers and public thanksgiving, and a victory parade at St. Paul's Cathedral.

It had been a narrow escape, as everyone realized. England had gained considerable prestige, but Elizabeth never again committed her whole fleet in battle at once. During the remainder of the long war, she instead refashioned her former defensive policy against Spain. This was streamlined to comprise modest though active assistance for the Dutch cause; support for the Protestant Henry of Navarre, who succeeded to the French Crown in 1589; and literally thousands of privateering expeditions against Spain in the Caribbean, and off the Azores and Iberian coast. Formal military-style expeditions against specifc Spanish targets in 1589, 1594, 1596, and 1597 were relatively small-scale, though dangerous enough. But nothing strategic was achieved, and the war dragged on amid invasion scares until 1604, when it was ended by James I.

Yet late Elizabethan policy was increasingly damaging from both diplomatic and domestic viewpoints. First, Henry IV of France, who controlled Normandy but not the capital, resolved in 1593 that Paris was distinctly worth a mass; he converted to Catholicism, thus souring hopes of a Protestant alliance against Spain and Rome. Secondly, Elizabeth quarrelled with the Dutch over their mounting debts and cost of English garrisons and forces led by Sir Francis Vere. Thirdly, the cost of the war, over the years, was unprecedented in English history—even with parliamentary subsidies, it could only be met by borrowing and

Battle of Gravelines, 27–29 July 1588. The Spanish fleet disperses in confusion, pursued by the English, past Gravelines on the Flemish coast. This engraving was first published in 1612.

by sales of Crown lands, both of which created major problems for the future. Fourthly, the war, in effect, spread to Ireland. The Irish Reformation had not proved successful, and the threat of Spanish landings there, together with serious internal rebellions, obliged the Privy Council to think in terms of the full-scale conquest of Ireland logically induced by Henry VIII's assumption of the kingship. Elizabeth hesitated—as well she might. At last her second favourite, the dazzling but paranoid earl of Essex, was dispatched in 1599 with a large army. But Essex's failure surpassed even Leicester's in the Netherlands; he deserted his post in a last-ditch attempt to salvage his career by personal magnetism, and was executed in February 1601 for leading his faction in a desperate rebellion through the streets of London. Lord Mountjoy replaced him in Ireland, reducing the chiefs to submission and routing a force of 4,000 Spanish infantry in 1601. The conquest of Ireland was completed in 1603. Yet the results were inherently contradictory: English hegemony seemed irrevocably confirmed, but the very fact of conquest vanquished any further hope of advancing the Irish Reformation, and thus achieving cultural unity with England.

Such contradictions were not, however, confined to Irish history. Internal tension became inexorably pronounced in Elizabethan government and society. If the English Deborah had constructed the Anglican Church, thwarted rebellion, defeated the Armada, and pacified Ireland, the Tudor stability thus restored, and preserved, was none the less vulnerable to structural decay. Problems that were at first relatively minor gained momentum as the reign progressed, but the queen's caution and immobility prevented her from taking remedial action in time. It was as if the sheer effort of making the Settlement of 1559 had sapped away Elizabeth's creative powers, or perhaps the extent to which she had been pushed into Protestantism then had dissuaded her from permitting further changes in any sphere. Perhaps she was simply too much her father's daughter? In any event, her constancy, so admired in her youth, deteriorated with age into indecisiveness, inertia, and benign neglect.

The most obvious area was that of government. First, Elizabeth and Burghley allowed the English system of taxation to go into irretrievable decline. The value of a parliamentary subsidy not only failed to keep up with inflation, because tax assessments remained static at a time when levels of government expenditure were soaring in real terms; its mere money value even depreciated owing to tax evasion, which became endemic after 1558. The yield of one subsidy fell from £140,000 at the beginning of Elizabeth's reign to £85,000 at the end—a steady drop which reached £70,000 by 1624. In Sussex, the average tax assessment of leading families fell from £61 in 1540 to £14 in 1620, and some potential taxpayers managed to escape inclusion on the subsidy rolls altogether. Burghley himself evaded tax, despite being Lord Treasurer from 1572 to his death in 1598. He grumbled hypocritically in Parliament about tax cheating, but kept his own assessment of income static at £133. 6s. 8d. throughout his life—his real income was £4,000 per annum. In Kent, William Lambarde protested that cheating was so extensive that dishonest assessors should be prosecuted. Here Lambarde had spotted the true focus of Elizabethan neglect, because the fault lay in the local system of central government, which simply turned a blind eye. The English landed gentry formed the backbone of local government under the Tudors—as deputy lieutenants, JPs, sheriffs, subsidy commissioners, clerks of the peace, and constables. Yet despite the enhanced sophistication of sixteenth-century life, Elizabeth did little to raise standards among these unpaid local grandees, who served the Crown mainly to gain prestige; if anything, standards were lower by

1603 than they had been under Cardinal Wolsey. Burghley, in particular, was insufficiently original to appreciate that the local governors had urgently to be enthused with a sense of collective responsibility for national, as opposed to local, affairs. But nothing was done, and when widespread reform was attempted under Charles I, it proved to be politically unacceptable in many counties.

Next, Elizabeth and Burghley permitted central government to become permeated by corruption, in face of their inability to supply sufficient patronage from their available resources. The cost of the war with Spain, some £250,000 a year, more than devoured frequent parliamentary subsidies, the profits of the Crown lands, the customs revenues, and the receipts from fiscal feudalism; Elizabeth sold lands worth £126,000 in 1588, and more worth £213,000 in 1599–1601, a process which in turn further reduced the Crown's income. Forced loans, benevolences, ship money, purveyance, borrowing, and the profits of privateering gave temporary relief, though at the price of burgeoning political friction. In 1603, the national debt was £400,000. Yet even this record was achieved only by Elizabeth's studied parsimony; she refrained from granting titles, lands, annuities, and pensions to her subjects save in exceptional cases, and any lands were normally assigned at realistic rents payable to the Exchequer. Inflation had meanwhile eroded the value of the fees and salaries earned by royal servants, thus compounding the problem of insufficient patronage.

Elizabeth fell back in despair on three policies, each of which was injurious in the long term, quite apart from the fact that James I was left with inadequate resources. First, grants in reversion to offices or lands were made on a large scale. Four, five, or more reversioners might stand waiting for a position or a property to fall vacant—this expedient mortgaged the future, and even allowed key posts to become hereditary. In addition, the long queue was a barely satisfactory solution of the lack of patronage. Secondly, sales of offices proliferated, despite being contrary to a statute of 1551–2. Two hundred pounds would be offered for this or that minor post; competitive bids of £1,000 to £4,000 were taken for such lucrative offices as the treasurership of the wars, or the receivership of the Court of Wards. Yet such bids were regarded as investments; if a sale went through, the newly-appointed official would aim to recoup his outlay at handsome interest—hence England became obliged to tolerate premeditated corruption. Two-thirds of Burghley's annual £4,000, for instance, comprised the profits of office—his official salary was about £866. His son, Robert Cecil, received £6,900 per annum from political offices between 1608 and 1612, when the system was at its acme. Other men's profits were smaller, but the damage to Tudor integrity was manifest. Thirdly, Elizabeth capitalized on earlier practices by which trading licences, and monopolies, were granted as perquisites to courtiers or favourites. The earl of Leicester obtained £750 a year from the customs; Sir Walter Raleigh had a monopoly for playing-cards; the earl of Essex bought the right to collect customs on sweet wines—and so on.

Behind these issues lurks a historical conundrum. Henry VIII's dissipation of the monastic assets had made it virtually impossible for his successors to sustain a war economy for more than a few years without major reforms in taxation. Elizabeth's policies of parsimony, and patronage on the cheap, covered up this constitutional flaw until 1603, but in doing so perpetuated it. For corruption created an insuperable obstacle to financial reform under the early Stuarts. Whose offence was worse?

The other key area in which the Elizabethan State was racked by internal tension was religion. The loyal obedience of Englishmen to the Settlement of 1559 was challenged by both Protestant and Catholic activists. The Marian exiles had accepted the Settlement, but yearned to purify the Anglican Church of 'popish' ceremonies and vestments. They also imported into England the radical ideas they had learned abroad concerning forms of worship and church government. The ambitions of these and other Protestant crusaders, who came to be known as Puritans, were fourfold: the elimination of 'popish' rituals (the sacraments were to be administered after the fashion of primitive Christianity, rather than the Prayer Book); the rebirth of preaching, which was to be made a priority, to be undertaken by properly educated ministers, and based exclusively on the Bible; the propagation of a living, regenerative faith among believers destined by God's grace to be among his elect (the radicals emphasized the terrible consequences of the Fall, and denied man's ability to redeem himself, for instance by good works); and lastly 'godly discipline' throughout the congregation, without clerical, and especially episcopal, domination. In addition, a number of Puritan sectarians promoted the idea of independent 'churches', or congregations, outside the framework of the Elizabethan Church, which devised their own forms of worship and church government. But such separatists were quickly disowned and persecuted as seditious revolutionaries by a polity that had already agreed on the need for a national church structure in principle. The real question was whether the Settlement of 1559 was the beginning or the end of Protestant development.

The extent to which Elizabeth refused to adjust the Settlement even in the smallest detail over the ensuing forty years was almost obsessional. Archbishop Parker's *Advertisements* (1566) required rigorous adherence to the rubrics of the Prayer Book; the government argued that ceremonies and vestments were not fundamentals of faith or practice, but merely *adiaphora*—or 'things indifferent'. Naturally the Puritans replied that, if the points raised were not essential, why was conformity required? In turn, this focused attention on enforcement and the wider question of episcopal discipline, even on the validity of a bishop's powers. The Protestants successfully mustered support in Parliament, notably in 1566, 1571, 1572, and 1586–7. Elizabeth outflanked such political moves by wielding familiar weapons: the monarch's right to veto bills and to prorogue or dissolve Parliament. She also declared religious policy to be, in effect, reserved business—a 'matter of state' in which no subject could meddle without royal permission. Yet such an exalted view of royal prerogative was controversial, since the Settlement of 1559 had manifestly been the combined achievement of Crown and Parliament. Thus while Elizabeth managed to sustain her position throughout her reign, she bequeathed to her successors a monarchic theory that depended primarily on political acumen; the abuse of that legacy is the life story of Charles I. However, Elizabeth was driven to take a hard line against the Puritans. Archbishop Whitgift (1583–1604) was expressly appointed by the queen to silence them, and the Court of High Commission, together on occasion with Star Chamber, was used to detect and prosecute nonconforming clergy. In the last resort, separatist activists such as Henry Barrow, John Greenwood, and John Penry were tried and hanged for sedition and treason.

The Catholic question was more intractable than that of Protestantism. The Settlement of 1559 left Catholics isolated, and Elizabeth hoped that their cause would evaporate through sheer inertia. English Catholics had no indigenous leaders after the deprivation of the Marian bishops and death of Cardinal Pole, and no guidance issued from Rome (or Spain) until 1570. The faithful were initially left in the refrigerator. In Louvain, their exiled brethren preached temporal loyalty and non-resistance. But the Northern Rebellion in 1569, followed by Pius V's bull *Regnans in Excelsis* a year later, shattered this mood. Catholics had become potential traitors, under orders to depose Elizabeth in favour of Mary Stuart—or so the government believed. Parliament and the Privy Council united in self-defence: in 1571, an act made it treason to bring into England or publish documents from Rome; an act of 1581 further extended the treason laws, and increased recusancy fines for not attending the Anglican Church to £20 per month. Catholic loyalism gave place in consequence to resistance theory, expressed in Nicholas Sander's *De Visibili Monarchia Ecclesiae* (1571). Sander listed the Catholic clergy and laity who had suffered exile, imprisonment, or loss for recusancy since 1558; he validated the rebellion of 1569; and he justified the papal bull of deposition. However, Catholic political action failed, and in 1580 the Jesuits secured a new ruling from Pope Gregory XIII that *Regnans in Excelsis* was only binding upon Catholic consciences when its implementation was politically feasible. Resistance theory was to be silenced in favour of renewed loyalism.

William Allen, an English exile, had meanwhile founded a seminary at Douai to train English missionary priests. His ardent young men, together with Jesuit missionaries trained in Rome and Spain, started to arrive in England. By December 1580 over 100 priests had landed. The plan was partly to convince Elizabeth that religious recusancy was commensurate with secular obedience, and partly to offer long-awaited spiritual and sacramental relief to English Catholics. This twin policy was epitomized by two gentle Jesuits, Edmund Campion and Robert Persons, who denied that the Catholic faith was automatically treason, and who maintained that their mission was purely spiritual. Yet the Northern Rebellion, the numerous plots linked to Mary Stuart, and the Catholic fanaticism of Philip II militated against such eirenic vision. The Armada unleashed a frenzy of anti-Catholic xenophobia conditioned by fifty years of Reformation propaganda: a myth of Catholic conspiracy was created that generated spontaneous combustion in English society as late as the reign of James II. Galvanized by international crisis, Elizabeth and Burghley gave Protestantism its desire; the government adopted a policy of religious persecution. No Catholic had been martyred between 1558 and 1577, but between 1577 and 1603 some 200 priests and laymen were executed. The crunch came in 1584–5, when Parliament enacted that it was treason simply to *be* a Catholic priest in England. Catholic Englishmen who had become priests since 1558 were to seek exile within forty days, or face arraignment.

Elizabeth's last years were tainted by the cumulative strain of a war economy, the Irish crisis, Essex's rebellion, and a series of localized famines from 1595 to 1598. Except for one calamitous season in 1556, the harvests in 1594–7 were the worst since 1482 and 1527, and their social impact was exacerbated by increased poverty and vagrancy linked to the effects of war. The Poor Laws of 1597–8 and 1601 offered limited parish relief, but did not innovate. Nothing was attempted by a Tudor Parliament on a

Holbein's design for a fireplace for Henry VIII, 1540. This fine example of a design for the interior decoration of a room was perhaps intended for Bridewell Palace.

welfare issue that was not already established practice in such leading cities as London, Hull, and Norwich. Furthermore, the motivation behind the Elizabethan legislation was the fear of vagrancy and urban insurrection shared by property owners in Parliament, rather than genuine human concern for the living conditions of the poor.

Yet the pessimism of the Tudor twilight was outweighed by positive advances, notably in domestic housing. The years from 1570 to 1610 have no formal significance, but they nevertheless mark the first key phase of the English housing revolution. Probate inventories suggest that from 1530 to 1569 the average size of the Tudor house was three rooms. Between 1570 and the end of Elizabeth's reign it was four or five rooms. The period 1610–42, which was the second phase of the revolution, saw the figure rise to six or more rooms. After 1570, prosperous yeomen might have six, seven, or eight rooms; husbandmen might aspire to two or three rooms, as opposed to the one-room cottages ubiquitous in 1500. Richer farmers would build a chamber over the open hall, replacing the open hearth with a chimney stack. Poorer people favoured ground-floor extensions: a kitchen, or second bedchamber, would be added to an existing cottage. Kitchens were often separate buildings, probably to reduce the risk of fire. A typical late-Elizabethan farmstead might be described as 'one dwelling house of three bays, one barn of three bays, one kitchen of one bay'. Meanwhile there were corresponding improvements in domestic comfort. The average investment in hard and soft furniture, tableware, and kitchenware in Tudor England prior to 1570 was around £7. Between 1570 and 1603 it rose to £10. 10s., and in the early Stuart period it climbed to £17. The value of household goods of wealthier families rose by 250 per cent between 1570 and 1610, and that of middling and lesser persons slightly exceeded even that high figure. These percentages were in excess of the inflation rate.

In the upper echelons of society, Elizabethan great houses were characterized by innovations founded on Tudor stability and rising standards of comfort. English architecture after about 1580 was inspired by Gothic ideals of chivalry as much as by Renaissance classicism. The acres of glass and towering symmetry of Hardwick Hall, Derbyshire, built in 1591–7 by Robert Smythson for Elizabeth, countess of Shrewsbury, paid homage to the Perpendicular splendour of King's College Chapel, Cambridge. But if Elizabethan Gothic architecture was neo-medieval in its outward profile, the aim was for enhanced standards of sophistication within. In any case, the neo-medieval courtyards, gatehouses, moats, parapets, towers, and turrets of Tudor England were ornamental, not utilitarian. The parapets at Hardwick incorporated the initials E.S. (Elizabeth Shrewsbury)—the decorative device that proclaimed the parvenue. Brick chimneys became a familiar feature of Tudor mansions, and they signified the arrival of the kitchen and service quarters within the main house, either into a wing or a semi-basement. As time progressed, basement services became fairly common, and were particularly favoured in town houses built on restricted sites. Household servants began to be relegated to the subterranean caverns from which it took three centuries to rescue them.

Yet this was not coincidental. The Elizabethan mansion was the first of its genre to equate privacy with domestic comfort. The great hall of the medieval manor house was not abandoned, but it gave way to the long gallery, hung with historical portraits, where private conversations could be conducted without constant interruption from the traffic of servants. In fact, these Elizabethan long galleries were modelled on those erected in Tudor palaces earlier in the century. An interesting early example was Wolsey's gallery at Hampton Court, where in 1527 Henry VIII and Sir Thomas More had paced uneasily together as they first discussed the terms of the king's proposed divorce. In

The west front, Hardwick Hall, Derbyshire. Built in 1591–7 by Robert Smythson for Bess of Hardwick.

similar fashion, ground-floor parlours replaced the great hall as the customary family sitting and dining-rooms—at least for normal daily purposes. The family lived in the ground-floor parlours and the first-floor chambers; the servants worked on both these floors and in the basement, and slept in the attics or turrets. Staircases were revitalized as a result: the timber-framed structure gradually became an architectural feature in itself. Finally, provision of fresh-water supplies and improved sanitary arrangements reflected the Renaissance concern with private and public health. In the case of town houses, the family would often go to immense lengths to solve drainage problems, sometimes paying a cash composition to the municipal authorities, but frequently performing some service for the town at court or at Westminster in return for unlimited water or drainage.

These improvements in Tudor housing were complemented by technical progress in the fields of art and music. Nicholas Hilliard became the most influential painter at the Elizabethan court on the strength of his ravishing miniatures. Trained as a goldsmith, Hilliard earned renown for his techniques as a 'limner', or illuminator of portrait gems that captured the 'lovely graces, witty smilings, and these stolen glances which suddenly like lightning pass, and another countenance taketh place.' Intimacy was the key to this style, combined with a wealth of emblematic allusion that added intellectual depth to the mirror-like image portrayals. In Hilliard's hands, the miniature was far more than a mere reduced version of an ordinary life-scale painting—but that was thanks to his creative invention. To enhance the techniques learned in the workshops of Ghent and Bruges, where the miniature was painted on fine vellum and pasted on to card, Hilliard used gold as a metal, burnishing it 'with a pretty little tooth of some ferret or stoat or other wild little beast'. Diamond effects were simulated with utter conviction, and Hilliard's jewel-bedecked lockets were often worn as talismans, or exchanged as pledges of love between sovereign and subject or knight and lady. Hilliard's techniques were passed on to his pupil, Isaac Oliver, and finally to Samuel Cooper. The miniature was ultimately confounded by the invention of photography.

Tudor music was invigorated by royal and noble patronage, by the continued liturgical demands of the Church, and by the steady abandonment of the strict modal limitations of the medieval period in favour of more progressive techniques of composition and performance. The Tudor monarchs, together with Cardinal Wolsey, were distinguished patrons of music both

Miniature portrait by Nicholas Hilliard, of Sir Walter Raleigh. Hilliard was the
most important artist of the Elizabethan period. His style was based on
Holbein's but was also influenced by French court portraiture. He believed that
the face was the mirror of the soul.

sacred and secular. An inventory of Henry VIII's musical
instruments suggests that as lavish a selection was available in
England as anywhere in Europe—the king himself favoured the
lute and organ. His and Wolsey's private chapels competed to
recruit the best organists and singers to be found in England and
Wales. In Mary's reign, England was exposed to the potent
artistry of Flemish and Spanish music, while the seminal
influence of Italy was always present in the shape of Palestrina's
motets and the works of the Florentine madrigalists. Elizabeth I
retained a large corps of court musicians drawn from Italy,

Germany, France, and England itself. But her Chapel Royal was the premier conservatoire of Tudor musical talent and invention, for Thomas Tallis, William Byrd, and John Bull made their careers there. The Protestant Reformation happily encouraged, rather than abandoned, composers—the Edwardian and Elizabethan injunctions left liturgical music intact, and many of the gentlemen of the Chapel discreetly remained Catholics, including Byrd and Bull. Yet it was the technical advances that really mattered. Byrd and Bull gradually freed themselves from the old ecclesiastical modes, or ancient scales. Tallis and Byrd gained a licence for music printing that enabled them to pioneer printed musical notation, albeit unsuccessfully. Melody, harmony, and rhythm became as important to music as plainsong and counterpoint, and the arts of ornamentation and extemporization thrived among the virginalists, and among the lute and consort players. Such developments presaged the music of seventeenth-century English and Continental composers, and ultimately that of J. S. Bach.

The age of the Tudors ended on an equivocal note, which is best discerned in its literature. Erasmus's wit and More's satirical fiction expressed (though in Latin) the intellectual exuberance of pre-Reformation Europe. Sir Thomas Elyot, Sir John Cheke, and Roger Ascham translated Renaissance ideals into pedestrian but tolerable English prose. Sir Thomas Wyatt, Henry Howard, earl of Surrey, and Sir Philip Sidney reanimated English lyric poetry and rekindled the sonnet as the vehicle of eloquent and classical creativity. But it was Edmund Spenser who rediscovered to perfection what English prosody had lacked since the time of Chaucer. Once again, music tutored the ear, and the connections between ear and tongue were fully realized. Spenser attained an impeccable mastery of rhythm, time, and tune—his work was no mere 'imitation of the ancients'. In particular, his harmonious blend of northern and midland with southern dialects permitted verbal modulations and changes of diction and mood akin to those of lute players. His pastoral sequence, *The Shepheards Calendar* (1579), was a landmark in the history of English poetry, its melodious strains encapsulating the pains and pleasures of pastoral life.

> Colin, to heare thy rymes and roundelayes,
> Which thou wert wont on wastfull hylls to singe,
> I more delight then larke in Sommer dayes;
> Whose Echo made the neyghbour groves to ring,
> And taught the byrds, which in the lower spring
> Did shroude in shady leaves from sonny rayes,
> Frame to thy songe their cherefull cheriping,
> Or hold theyr peace, for shame of thy swete layes.

Spenser's masterpiece was *The Faerie Queene* (1589 and 1596), an allegorical epic poem, which examined on a dazzling multiplicity of levels the nature and quality of the late-Elizabethan polity. The form of the poem was Gothic as much as Renaissance: the Gothic 'revival' in architecture after 1580 was paralleled by its episodic sequences, within which details took on their own importance, decorating the external symmetry without damaging the total effect. The poem above all, though, was an allegory. As Spenser explained in a dedicatory epistle to Sir Walter Raleigh, 'In that Fairy Queen I mean glory in my general intention, but in my particular I conceive the most excellent and glorious person of our sovereign the Queen, and her kingdom in Fairy land. And yet, in some places else, I do otherwise shadow her.' In other words, Spenser's allegory was part moral, part fictional—there was no easy or straightforward correspondence of meaning. Yet the allegory had a single end; as in *Piers Plowman* before it, and *Pilgrim's Progress* afterward, *The Faerie Queene* led the reader along the path upon which truth was distinguishable from falsehood. To this end, the ambition, corruption, intrigue, and secular-mindedness of Elizabethan power politics were sublimated into the 'delightful land of Faerie', clothed in the idyllic garments of romance, and exalted as the fictional realization of the golden age of Gloriana.

It was inevitable that Spenser should fail to impress the Elizabethan establishment. He informed Raleigh that his 'general end' was 'to fashion a gentleman or noble person in virtuous and gentle discipline'. Yet the ambiguities were pervasive, and Spenser manifestly perceived his goal as already archaic. Chivalry had been soured by Renaissance politics and statecraft; the 'verray parfit, gentil knyght' of Chaucer's age had been displaced by the Tudor courtier. The golden age had passed, if it had ever existed:

> So oft as I with state of present time
> The image of the antique world compare,
> When as mans age was in his freshest prime,
> And the first blossome of faire vertue bare;
> Such oddes I finde twixt those, and these which are,
> As that, through long continuance of his course,
> Me seemes the world is runne quite out of square
> From the first point of his appointed sourse;
> And being once amisse growes daily wourse and wourse.

Spenser's allegory in *The Faerie Queene* was unquestionably over-complex; his attempt to fuse worldly and idealized principles of behaviour into a single dramatic epic was bound to prove unmanageable. Moreover, the reader was obliged to unriddle endless personifications of Elizabeth as the moon-goddess Diana (or Cynthia or Belphoebe), of Sir Walter Raleigh as Timias, of Mary Stuart as Duessa, who also doubled as Theological Falsehood—and so on. However, Spenser's failure to convince, as opposed to his poetic ability to delight, actually *heightens* our impression of his disillusion and despair. We are taught to debunk the myth of Gloriana; art has held 'the mirror up to nature' and shown 'the very age and body of the time his form and pressure'.

Another faithful mirror of the Tudor age was that held by the immortal William Shakespeare. Author of thirty-four plays that included *Hamlet* (1600–1), *King Lear* (1605–6), and *Othello* (1604), and of 154 Sonnets (1593–7), together with *Venus and Adonis* and *The Rape of Lucrece* (1593–4), Shakespeare has exerted greater influence on English literature and European drama than any other single writer. The sheer vitality, power, and virtuosity of his work remain unmatched in any European language; his genius exceeded that of Chaucer or Tennyson—it need not be justified or explained. Even so, it is necessary to remember that Shakespeare was not an 'intellectual' or 'élitist' writer, like Milton or Voltaire. His orbit centred on Stratford and London, not Oxford and Cambridge. His was the mundane world of life, death, money, passion, stage business, and the alehouse—such matters became the stuff of peerless drama and poetry. The rich variety of his experience is perhaps the chief reason for the universality of his appeal; certainly there is no hint of the bigot or intellectual snob in his work.

Shakespeare's experience was, nevertheless, that of a writer at the cultural crossroads of Europe. After about 1580, European literature explored increasingly the modes of individual expression and characterization associated with modern processes of thought. Authors and the fictional characters they created simultaneously displayed awareness both of experience in general, and of themselves as the particular agents of unique experiences. Shakespeare's *Hamlet* and Christopher Marlowe's *Doctor Faustus* (1592) epitomize the dramatic depiction of individual experience in Elizabethan literature; the principal protagonists express their private despair, and submit to the inexorable forces of personal motivation. Of the two plays, *Hamlet* is the more advanced. Shakespeare took a familiar plot and transformed it into a timeless masterpiece. But Marlowe's *Faustus* was not far behind. Both dramatists were eager to pursue psychology, rather than ethics. The difference is that Faustus does not pass beyond the bounds of egotism and self-dramatiza-

tion to realize self-analysis, whereas Hamlet's subjective introspection and self-doubts are the keystones of the action.

> What a piece of work is a man! how noble in reason! how infinite in faculties! in
> form and moving, how express and admirable! in action, how like an angel! in
> apprehension, how like a god! the beauty of the world! the paragon of animals!
> And yet to me, what is this quintessence of dust?
> (*Hamlet*, II. ii. 323–9)

Neoplatonist philosophy as practised at the dawn of the
sixteenth century by John Colet and his circle had dealt with the
objective appreciation of senses, natures, and truth—this
reflected the medieval cast of mind. Eighty or so years later, the
emphasis had shifted towards subjectivity and self-expression,
paradoxically under the influence of Calvinist theology, which so
stressed the inflexibility of God's predestined Word that a
person's quest for grace necessarily came to depend on systematic self-scrutiny. Calvinism was also replacing the medieval ideal
of chivalry with the notion of the permanent spiritual warfare of
God's elect against worldly thraldom.

Marlowe and Shakespeare dominated Elizabethan drama,
although they did not monopolize it. The allegories and morality
plays of the fifteenth century flourished as much as ever,
especially in such provincial towns as Chester, Coventry, and
York. But the Brave New World was symbolized by Shakespeare's Globe Theatre in London, where the impact of the
Protestant Reformation had combined with the enhanced
sophistication of metropolitan life to give distinctive shape to
the preferred drama of modern Britain. Self-expression, individuality, and the soliloquy were the cultural developments that
paralleled the expansion of education and literacy, the birth of
the nonconformist conscience, and the growth of cosmopolitan
attitudes.

Yet Hamlet's melancholy ultimately defeated his self-
knowledge. He remained uncertain of his destiny, and of the
reason for his existence:

> To be, or not to be: that is the question:
> Whether 'tis nobler in the mind to suffer
> The slings and arrows of outrageous fortune,
> Or to take arms against a sea of troubles,
> And by opposing end them? To die: to sleep;
> No more; and, by a sleep to say we end
> The heart-ache and the thousand natural shocks
> That flesh is heir to, 'tis a consummation
> Devoutly to be wish'd.
> (*Hamlet*, III. i. 56–64)

Such sentiments were equally applicable to the dusk of Tudor

England. When the bell tolled for the age of Gloriana, on 24 March 1603, Elizabeth had already lost her will to survive, Burghley was five years dead, and a newly ambitious and less scrupulous generation of courtiers was ascendant. It is easy to romanticize or eulogize such Tudor triumphs as stability, economic expansion, the Reformation, the repulse of Spain, the defeat of Protestant and Catholic extremism, and the unification of Britain—finally attained on Elizabeth's death. But reality is more abrasive. Stability had begun to breed instability through structural decay. The institutions of government were relatively slender, especially at local level. The financial resources of the Crown were woefully inadequate. National defences, too, were weak, for Elizabeth had unwisely permitted her land forces to wither away, while English sea-power depended on privateering and piracy. Religious extremism had admittedly been silenced, but had not been absorbed within the framework of Anglicanism. Finally, the benefits of the Poor Laws were in many areas simply crushed beneath the weight of the rise in population.

By 1603 Elizabeth's inertia and immobility had established a pattern that precluded comprehensive reform. The country had become quietly ungovernable. In particular, England was unable to fight a protracted war without engendering domestic political friction. This is not to say that total collapse under the early Stuarts was inevitable; there was no high road to civil war. Yet the Tudor legacy of meagre public revenue, defective local government, and endemic corruption in the central bureaucracy was ultimately ameliorated *by* the events of the Civil War and Interregnum. A decade of military dictatorship proved sufficient to persuade Englishmen in 1660 that the restored monarchy was, in fact, cheap at the price.

JOHN MORRILL

6. *The Stuarts*
(1603–1688)

THE Stuarts were one of England's least successful dynasties. Charles I was put on public trial for treason and was publicly beheaded; James II fled the country fearing a similar fate, and abandoned his kingdom and throne. James I and Charles II died peacefully in their beds, but James I lived to see all his hopes fade and ambitions thwarted, while Charles II, although he had the trappings of success, was a curiously unambitious man, whose desire for a quiet life was not achieved until it was too late for him to enjoy it. Towering above the Stuart age were the two decades of civil war, revolution, and republican experiment which ought to have changed fundamentally the course of English history, but which did so, if at all, very elusively. Whilst kings and generals toiled and failed, however, a fundamental change was taking place in English economy and society, largely unheeded and certainly unfashioned by the will of government. In fact, the most obvious revolution in seventeenth-century England was the consequence of a decline in the birth-rate.

Society and Economic Life

The population of England had been growing steadily from the early sixteenth century, if not earlier. It continued to grow in the first half of the seventeenth century. The total population of England in 1600 was probably fairly close to 4.1 million (and Scotland, Ireland, and Wales, much more impressionistically, 1.9 million). By the mid-century, the population of England had reached a peak of almost 5.3 million, and the total for Britain had risen from roughly 6.0 to roughly 7.7 million. Thereafter, the number stabilized, or may even have sagged to 4.9 million in England, 7.3 million in Britain. The reasons for the rise in population, basically a steady progression with occasional setbacks resulting from epidemics before 1650, and the subse-

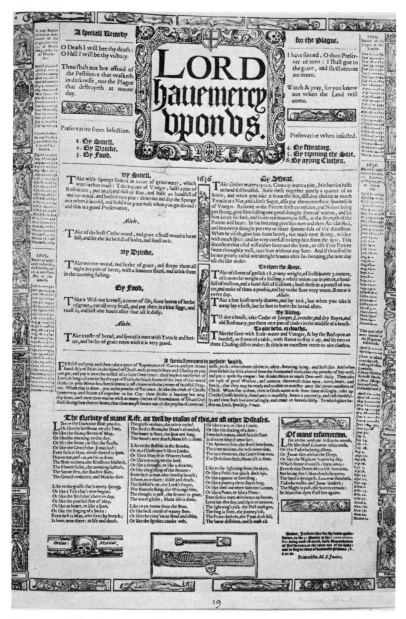

'*A memory of the plague year*'. This gives the numbers of deaths (from all causes and from plague) in London for several years between 1603 and 1636. In the centre are a number of inefficacious cures.

quent relapse, are very puzzling. The best recent research has placed most emphasis on the family-planning habits of the population. Once the plague had lost its virulence, a country like England, in which land was plentiful and extremes of weather never such as to wipe out entire harvests, was likely to see population growth. Each marriage was likely to produce more than enough children who would survive to adulthood to maintain the population. The rate of population growth was in fact kept rather low by the English custom of late marriage. In all social groups, marriage was usually deferred until both partners were in their mid-twenties and the wife had only twelve to fifteen childbearing years before her. The reason for this pattern of late marriage seems to be the firm convention that the couple save up enough money to launch themselves as an independent household before they wed. For the better off, this frequently meant university, legal training, an apprenticeship of seven years or more; for the less well off a long term of domestic service, living in with all found but little in the way of cash wages.

This pattern continued into the late seventeenth century with even later marriages; perhaps the real earnings of the young had fallen so that sufficient savings took longer to generate. At any rate the average age of first marriage seems to have risen by a further two years to over twenty-six, with a consequent effect on fertility. More dramatic still is the evidence of a will to restrict family size. Steps were clearly taken in families with three or more children to prevent or inhibit further conceptions. For example, mothers would breast-feed third or subsequent children for many more months than they would their first or second child, with the (effective) intention of lowering fertility. Crude contraceptive devices and sexual prudence were also clearly widespread. Some studies of gentry families even suggest that celibacy became much more common (the growth of the Navy may be partly responsible for this unexpected development!). In South Wales, one in three of all heads of leading gentry families remained unmarried in the late seventeenth century compared with a negligible proportion one hundred years earlier; while the average numbers of children per marriage declined from five to two and a half (which, given the high rate of child mortality, meant that a high proportion of those families died out). It is not known whether this was typical of the gentry everywhere or of other social groups. But it does graphically illustrate changing demographic patterns.

The economic, social, and political consequences were momentous. In the century before 1640, population was growing faster than food resources. One result of this was occasional and localized food shortages so severe as to occasion hunger, starvation, and death. It is possible that some Londoners died of starvation at the end of the sixteenth and at the beginning of the seventeenth centuries and quite certain that many did so in Cumbria in the early 1620s. Thereafter, famine disappears as a visible threat, in England at least. Increased agricultural production, better communication and lines of credit, and the levelling off of population solved the problem. England escaped the periodic dearths and widespread starvation that was to continue to devastate its continental neighbours for decades to come.

A more persistent effect of population growth was price inflation. Food prices rose eightfold in the period 1500–1640, wages less than threefold. For most of those who did not produce their own food, and enough of it to feed themselves and their household with a surplus to sell in the market, it was a century of financial attrition. Above all, for the growing proportion of the nation who depended upon wage-labouring, the century witnessed a major decline in living standards. In fact, a large section of the population—certainly a majority—had to buy much of their food, and these purchases took up an increasing proportion of their income. It became a central concern of government to regulate the grain trade and to provide both local machinery and an administrative code, backed up by legal sanctions, to ensure that whenever there was harvest failure, available stocks of grain and other produce were made widely available at the lowest extra cost which could be achieved.

A growing population put pressure not only on food resources but on land. With families producing on average more than one son, either family property had to be divided, reducing the endowment of each member for the next generation, or one son took over the family land or tenancy while the others had to fend for themselves. The high prices of agricultural produce made it worth while to plough, or otherwise to farm marginal lands hitherto uneconomic, but in most regions by the early seventeenth century there was little unoccupied land left to be so utilized. The way forward lay with the more productive use of existing farmed land, particularly in woodland areas or in the Fenland where existing conditions (inundations by the sea or winter rain) made for only limited usage. The problem here was that the drainage of the Fens or the clearing of woodland areas was costly, had to be undertaken by those with risk capital, and had to be at the expense of the life-style, livelihood, and modest prosperity of those who lived there. Once again, government was forced to be active in mediating (or more often vacillating) between encouraging higher productivity and guarding against the anguish and protest of those adversely affected.

A growing population also put pressure on jobs. By the early

The title-page of one of the growing number of self-confident agricultural tracts.

d 423.

THE
Engliſh Farrier,
OR,
Country-mans Treaſure.

Shewing approved Remedies to cure all Diſeaſes, hurts, maymes, maladies and griefes, in Horſes: and how to know the ſeverall Diſeaſes that breed in them, with a deſcription of every Veine, how and when to let them blood, according to the nature of their Diſeaſes.

With directions to know the ſeverall Ages of them.

Faithful'y ſet forth according to Art and approved experiment, for the benefit of Gentlemen, Farmers, Inholders, Husbandmen, and generally for all.

At London printed by *Iohn Beale*, and *Robert Bird*. 1636.

seventeenth century there was widespread underemployment in England. Agriculture remained the major source of employment, but the work in the fields was seasonal and hundreds of thousands found day labouring sufficient for part but not all of the year. Because, however, labour was plentiful and cheap, because most manufacturing relied exclusively on muscle power rather than a form of energy that would draw workers to its source, because raw materials walked about on, grew up out of, or lay dormant within the land, 'industry' in the seventeenth century took place in cottages and outbuildings of rural village communities. For some, especially in the metalworking and building trades, 'manufacturing' would be the primary source of income. For others, as in some textile trades, it could be a primary or secondary source of income. Textiles were by far the largest 'manufacture' with perhaps 200,000 workers scattered through-out England, above all in the south-west, in East Anglia, or in the Pennine region. It was a particularly volatile industry, however, with high food prices dampening the domestic market and war and foreign competition sharply reducing foreign markets in the early seventeenth century. Tens of thousands of families, however, could not balance the household budget whatever they tried. Injury, disability, or death made them particularly vulner-able to a shortfall of revenue. There was chronic 'underem-ployment': a structural problem of too many part-time workers seeking full-time work.

At Aldenham in Hertfordshire, about one in ten households needed regular support from the poor rate but a further one in four (making over one-third in all) needed occasional doles or allowances (for example of fuel or clothes) to ease them through difficult patches. For a large number of families, achieving subsistence involved scrounging or scavenging fuel or wild fruit and vegetables and seeking periodic help from local charities or the rates—what has been called the 'economy of makeshifts'. One effect of the difficulties of rural employment was to drive large numbers of men and women into the cities—above all to London—where the problems were no less but rather more volatile. There was a large amount of casual unskilled labour in the towns, but casual work could shrink rapidly in times of recession or harvest failure. High food prices meant less demand for other goods and this in turn meant less scope for non-agricultural wages. Those who most needed additional wages for food were most likely to find less work available. Once more, the government had been drawn in to organize and superintend a national scheme of poor relief, and ancillary codes of practice governing geographical mobility, house building, and the promotion of overseas trade. Thus a growing population greatly increased the duties and responsibilites of the government, arguably beyond the Crown's resources and capacity. Those who produced and sold goods, those who could benefit from the land hunger in increased rents and dues, and those who serviced an increasingly complex and uncertain market in lands and goods (notably the lawyers) wanted to enjoy the fruits of their success; others looked to the Crown to prevent or to mitigate the effects of structural change. A dynamic economy is one in which government has to arbitrate between competing and irreconcilable interests. No wonder the Crown found itself disparaged and increasingly distrusted.

By contrast, the late seventeenth century saw the easing, if not the disappearance, of these problems. The slight population decline in itself prevented the problems from getting worse. The upsurge in agricultural productivity was more important. The nature and extent of agricultural change in the seventeenth century is still much disputed. What is clear is that England ceased from about the 1670s to be a net importer of grain and became an exporter; indeed, bounties had to be introduced to ensure that surplus stocks were not hoarded. This remarkable turn-around may have been the result of a massive extension of the acreage under the plough—either by the ploughing of land not hitherto farmed or by land amelioration schemes. But it might also be the result of the introduction of new methods of farming which dramatically increased the yield per acre. By skilful alternation of crops and more extensive use of manure and fertilizers, it is possible to increase yields of grain and to sustain much greater livestock levels. Almost all the ideas which were to transform English agriculture down to the early nineteenth century were known about by 1660; indeed most of them had been tried and tested in the Netherlands. The problem is to discover how rapidly they were taken up. There was stubborn conservatism, especially among the yeomen; the good ideas lay mingled in the textbooks with some equally plausible ones which were in fact specious; the most effective methods required considerable rationalization of land use and some of them required high capital outlay. In the early part of the century, it seems likely that the most widespread innovations were not those which increased yields, but those which soaked up cheap surplus employment—especially 'industrial' cash crops that had to be turned into manufactures: dye crops, tobacco, mulberry trees (for silkworms). It was only when a falling population raised real wages and lowered grain prices that the impetus to increase productivity replaced the desire to extend the scale of operation as a primary motivation of the farmer. Changes in the way land was rented out also gave the landlord better prospects of seeing a return on the money he invested in land leased out. The new farming probably consolidated the position established earlier by the simple device of increasing the acreage under the plough. Either way, government action in the grain market and the regulation of wages became far less frequent and necessary.

In 1600, England still consisted of a series of regional economies striving after, if not always achieving, self-sufficiency. Problems of credit and of distribution hindered the easy exchange of produce between regions. Most market towns, even the large county towns, were principally places where the produce of the area was displayed and sold. By 1690 this was no longer the case. England had for long been the largest free trade area in Europe and had the Crown had its way at most points in the century, the full integration of Ireland and Scotland into a customs-free zone would have been achieved or brought nearer. That it was not owed most to the narrow self-interest of lobbyists in the House of Commons, especially in the 1600s and the 1660s. No point in England was (or is) more than seventy-five miles from the sea, and as a result of the schemes to improve river navigation, few places by 1690 were more than twenty miles from water navigable to the sea. Gradually, a single, integrated national economy was emerging. No longer did each region have to strive for self-sufficiency, producing low-quality goods in poor-grade soil or inhospitable climate. Regional specializations could emerge, taking full advantage of soil and climatic conditions, which could then be exchanged for surplus grain or dairy products from elsewhere. Hence, the spread of market-gardening in Kent.

Exactly the same could be said for manufactures. One consequence of and further stimulus to this was a retailing revolution—the coming of age of the shop. The characteristic of market towns was the market-stall or shambles, in which the stall-holders or retailers displayed their own wares which they had grown, made, or at least finished from local raw materials. By 1690, most towns, even quite small ones, had shops in the modern sense: places which did not distribute the produce of the region but which met the variegated needs of the region. The shopkeeper met those needs from far and wide. One particularly well-documented example is William Stout who, in the 1680s, rented a shop in Lancaster for £5 per annum. He visited London and Sheffield and bought goods worth over £200, paid for half in cash (a legacy from his father), half on credit. Soon he was purchasing goods from far and wide and offering the people of Lancaster and its environs a wide variety of produce: West Indian sugar, American tobacco, West Riding ironmongery, and so on. None the less, once towns became centres for the distribution of the produce of the world, people would tend to bypass the smaller towns with little choice and make for the bigger centres with maximum choice. This is why most seventeenth-century urban growth was concentrated in existing large market towns. The proportion of the population living in the twenty or so towns which already had 10,000 inhabitants rose sharply; the proportion living in the smaller market towns actually fell slightly. Some small centres of manufacturing (metalworking towns such as Birmingham and Sheffield, or cloth-finishing towns such as Manchester or Leeds, or shipbuilding towns such as Chatham) became notable urban centres. But the twenty largest towns in 1690 were almost the same as the twenty largest in 1600. All of them were on the coast or on navigable rivers.

Large towns, then, prospered because of their changing role in marketing. But many of them—and county towns especially—increasingly concentrated not only on the sale of goods; they began to concentrate on the sale of services. The pull of the shops and the burgeoning importance of county towns as local administrative centres in which hundreds gathered regularly for local courts and commissions, encouraged the service and leisure industries. Gentlemen and prosperous farmers came to town for business or for the shops, and would stop to take professional advice from lawyers, doctors, estate agents; or bring their families and stay over for a round of social exchange linked by visits to the theatre, concerts, or new recreational facilities. The age of the spa and the resort was dawning.

Paris, the largest town in France, had 350,000 inhabitants in the mid-seventeenth century. The second and third largest were Rouen and Lyons with 80,000–100,000 inhabitants. In Europe, there were only five towns with populations of more than 250,000, but over one hundred with more than 50,000 inhabitants. In England, however, London had well over half a million inhabitants by 1640 or 1660; Newcastle, Bristol, and Norwich, which rivalled one another for second place, had barely 25,000 each. London was bigger than the next fifty towns in England combined. It is hard to escape the conclusion that London was growing at the expense of the rest. Its stranglehold on overseas trade, and therefore on most of the early banking and financial activity, was slow to ease; in consequence much of the trade from most of the outports had to be directed via London. In the seventeenth century the major new 're-export' trades (the importation of colonial raw materials such as sugar and tobacco for finishing and dispatch to Europe) were concentrated there. London dominated the governmental, legal, and political world. While rural England flourished under the opportunities to feed the capital and keep its inhabitants warm, urban growth was probably slowed. By 1640, 10 per cent of all Englishmen lived in the capital, and one in six had lived part of their lives there. By 1690 the richest one hundred Londoners were among the richest men in England. No longer was wealth primarily the perquisite of the landed.

If goods moved more freely within a national economy, people may have become more rooted in their own community. Both before and after the Civil War, more than two-thirds of all Englishmen died in a parish different from the one in which they were born. But both before and after the wars, most did not move far; most stayed within their county of birth. It is possible to distinguish two patterns of migration. The first is 'betterment migration' as adolescents and young adults moved to take up apprenticeships or tenancies of farms. This migration throughout the century was essentially local except for movement from all over the country to London for apprenticeships. The second is 'subsistence migration', as those who found no work or prospect of work at home took to the road, often travelling long distances in the hope of finding employment elsewhere. Such migration was far more common in the first half of the century than in the second, partly because demographic stagnation and economic development created a better chance of jobs at home, partly because the general easing of demands on poor relief made parish authorities more sympathetic to the able-bodied unemployed, and partly because tough settlement laws inhibited and discouraged migration. An Act of Parliament in 1662 gave constables and overseers power to punish those who moved from parish to parish in search of vacant common land or wasteland on which to build cottages.

The seventeenth century is probably the first in English history in which more people emigrated than immigrated. In the course of the century, something over one-third of a million people— mainly young adult males—emigrated across the Atlantic. The largest single group made for the West Indies; a second substantial group made for Virginia and for Catholic Maryland; a very much smaller group made for Puritan New England. The pattern of emigration was a fluctuating one, but it probably reached its peak in the 1650s and 1660s. For most of those who went, the search for employment and a better life was almost certainly the principal cause of their departure. For a clear minority, however, freedom from religious persecution and the expectation that they could establish churches to worship God in their preferred fashion took precedence. An increasing number were forcibly transported as a punishment for criminal acts or (particularly in the 1650s) simply as a punishment for vagrancy. In addition to the transatlantic settlers, an unknown number crossed the English Channel and settled in Europe. The largest group were probably the sons of Catholic families making for religious houses or mercenary military activity. Younger sons of Protestant gentlemen also enlisted in the latter. Many hundreds were to return to fight the English Civil War. Thus, whereas the sixteenth century had seen England become a noted haven for religious refugees, in the seventeenth century Europe and America received religious refugees from England. The early seventeenth century probably saw less immigration from abroad than for many decades before. The only significant immigration in the seventeenth century was of Jews who flocked in after the Cromwellian regime had removed the legal bars on their residence, and of French Huguenots escaping from Louis XIV's persecution in the 1680s.

Fewer men set up home far from the place of their birth. But many more men travelled the length and breadth of England. There was a tripling or a quadrupling of the number of packmen, carriers, and others engaged in moving goods about. The tunnage of shipping engaged in coastal trading probably rose by the same amount. The roads were thronged with petty chapmen, with their news-sheets, tracts, almanacs, cautionary tales, pamphlets full of homespun wisdom; pedlars with trinkets of all sorts; and travelling entertainers. If the alehouse had always been a distraction from that other social centre of village life, the parish church, it now became much more its rival in the dissemination of news and information and in the formation of popular culture. In the early years of the century, national and local regulation of alehouses was primarily concerned with ensuring that not too much of the barley harvest was malted and brewed; by the end of the century, regulation was more concerned with the pub's potential for sedition.

In the century from 1540 to 1640 there was a redistribution of wealth away from rich and poor towards those in the middle of

A tavern brawl from the 1680s. Not all visits to the pub ended this way, even though legislators and moralists often claimed that they did so.

society. The richest men in the kingdom derived the bulk of their income from rents and services, and these were notoriously difficult to keep in line with inflation: a tradition of long leases and the custom of fixed rents and fluctuating 'entry fines'— payments made when tenancies changed hands—militated against it. Vigilant landowners could keep pace with inflation, but many were not vigilant. Equally, those whose farms or holdings did not make them self-sufficient suffered rising (and worse, fluctuating) food prices, while a surplus on the labour market and declining real wages made it very hard for the poor to make good the shortfall. The number of landless labourers and cottagers soared. Those in the middle of society, whether yeomen farmers or tradesmen, prospered. If they produced a surplus over and above their own needs they could sell dear and produce more with the help of cheap labour. They could lend their profits to their poorer neighbours (there were after all no banks, stocks and shares, building societies) and foreclose on the debts. They invested in more land, preferring to extend the scale of their operations rather than sink capital into improved productivity. Many of those who prospered from farming rose into the gentry.

Only two groups had 'social' status in seventeenth-century England—the gentry and the peerage. Everybody else had 'economic' status, and was defined by his economic function (husbandman, cobbler, merchant, attorney, etc.). The peerage and gentry were different. They had a 'quality' which set them apart. That 'quality' was 'nobility'. Peers and gentlemen were 'noble'; everybody else was 'ignoble' or 'churlish'. Such concepts were derived partly from the feudal and chivalric traditions in which land was held from the Crown in exchange for the performance of military duties. These duties had long since disappeared, but the notion that the ownership of land and 'manors' conferred status and 'honour' had been reinvigorated by the appropriation to English conditions of Aristotle's notion of the citizen. The gentleman or nobleman was a man set apart to govern. He was independent and leisured: he derived his income without having to work for it, that income made him free from want and from being beholden to or dependent upon others, and he had the time and leisure to devote himself to the arts of government. He was independent in judgement and trained to make decisions. Not all gentlemen served in the offices which required such qualities (justice of the peace, sheriff, militia captain, high constable, etc.). But all had this capacity to serve, to govern. A gentleman was expected to be hospitable, charitable, fair-minded. He was distinguished from his country neighbour, the yeoman, as much by attitude of mind and personal preference as by wealth. Minor gentry and yeomen had similar incomes. But they lived different lives: the gentleman rented out his lands, wore cloth and linen, read Latin; the yeoman was a working farmer, wore leather, read and wrote in English. By 1640, there were perhaps 120 peers and 20,000 gentry, one in twenty of all adult males. The permanence of land and the security of landed income restricted gentility to the countryside; the prosperous merchant or craftsman, though he may have had a larger income than many gentlemen, and have discharged, in the government of his borough, the same duties, was denied the status of gentleman. He had to work, and his capital and income were insecure. Younger sons of gentlemen, trained up in the law or apprenticed into trade, did not retain their status. But they were put into professions through which they or their sons could redeem it. The wealthy merchant or lawyer had some prospect of buying a manor and settling back into a gentler life-style at the end of his life.

This pattern shifted in the late seventeenth century. Conditions were now against the larger farmer: he had high taxation, higher labour costs, and lower profits, unless he invested heavily in higher productivity, which he was less able to do than the great landowners (for whom there were economies of scale). Few yeomen now aspired to the trappings of gentility, while many minor gentlemen abandoned an unequal struggle to keep up appearances. On the other hand, professional men, merchants, and town governors became bolder in asserting that they were as good as the country gentleman and were entitled to his title of respect. The definition of 'gentility' was stretched to include them without a prior purchase of land. This 'pseudo-gentility' became increasingly respectable and increasingly widely recognized, even by the heralds. It was not, however, recognized by many country gentlemen who bitterly resented this devaluation of their treasured status. They responded to the debasement of the term 'gentry' by sponsoring and promoting a new term which restored their exclusiveness and self-importance: they called themselves squires and their group the 'squirearchy'.

The century between 1540 and 1640 had seen the consolidation of those in the middle of society at the expense of those at the bottom and, to some extent, of those at the top. The century after 1640 saw some relief for the mass of poor householders, increasing difficulties for large farmers and small landowners, rich pickings for those at the top. There was emerging by 1690 (though its great age was just beginning) a group of men whose interests, wealth, and power grew out of, but which extended far beyond, their landed estates. They invested in trade, in government loans, in the mineral resources of their land, as well as in improved farming and in renting out farming land. They spent as much time in their town houses as in their country seats; they were as much at home with the wealthy élite in London as with their rural neighbours. They constituted a culturally cosmopolitan élite of transcendent wealth, incorporating many of the peerage, but not confined to them. This new phenomenon was recognized at the time and needed a label, a collective noun. It became known as the aristocracy (a term hitherto a preserve of political thinkers, like democracy, rather than of social analysis). The invention of term 'squire' and adaptation of the word 'aristocrat' in the late seventeenth century tells us a great deal about the way society was evolving. The integration of town and country, the spread of metropolitan values and fashions, the fluidity of the economy and the mobility of society are all involved in the way men categorized one another. By 1690, England already had a flexible and simple moneyed élite; access to wealth and power was not restricted by outdated notions of privilege and obsessions with purity of birth as in much of Europe.

Government and Law

Stuart governments had little understanding of these structural changes and less ability to influence them. The resources of Stuart government fell far short of those required to carry out the ambitions and expectations which most people had of their king and which kings had of themselves.

The financial and bureaucratic resources at the disposal of kings remained limited. James I inherited an income of £350,000 a year. By the later 1630s this had risen to £1,000,000 a year and by the 1680s to £2,000,000 a year. This is a notable increase. It meant that, throughout the seventeenth century, the Stuarts could finance their activities in peacetime. As the century wore on, revenues from Crown lands and Crown feudal and prerogative right fell away to be an insignificant part of royal revenues. The ordinary revenues of the Crown became predominantly those derived from taxing trade: customs duties on the movement of goods into and out of the country and excise duties, a sales tax on basic consumer goods (above all beer!). Only during the Civil Wars and Interregnum (when a majority of state revenues came from property taxes) did direct taxation play a major part in the budget. Over the period 1603–40 and 1660–89, less than 8 per cent of all royal revenues came from direct taxation—certainly less than in the fourteenth or sixteenth centuries. This, in part, reflects landowner domination of the tax-granting House of Commons; but it also reflects an administrative arthritis that hindered improvements in the efficiency and equity of tax distribution.

The buoyancy of trade, especially after 1630, was the greatest single cause of the steady growth in royal income—well ahead of inflation—that made the Stuart monarchy at almost every point the least indebted in Europe. Both James I and Charles II suffered from fiscal incontinence, buying the loyalty and favour of their servants with a rashness that often went beyond what was necessary. However, the problems of the Stuarts can fairly be laid at Elizabeth's door. All over Europe in the sixteenth and seventeenth centuries, princes used the threat of invasion by tyrannical and/or heretical foreigners to create new forms of taxation which were usually made permanent when the invasion scare had receded or was repulsed. William III was to make just such a transformation in the 1690s when England was under siege from the absolutist Louis XIV and the bigoted James II. Since the Stuarts never faced a realistic threat of invasion, they never had a good excuse to insist on unpalatable fiscal innovations. Elizabeth I had a perfect opportunity in the Armada years but she was too old, conservatively advised, too preoccupied even to attempt it. Instead she paid for the war by selling land. Although this did not make James I's and Charles I's position as difficult as was once thought, it did have one major consequence: it deprived the king of security against loans.

The Stuarts, then, whenever they put their mind to it, had an adequate income and a balanced budget. Almost alone amongst the rulers of the day they never went bankrupt, and only once, in 1670, had to defer payment of interest on loans. But they never had enough money to wage successful war. Since, throughout the century up to 1689, no one ever threatened to invade England or to declare war on her, this was not as serious as it sounds. England waged war on Spain (1624–30, 1655–60), on France (1627–30), and on the Netherlands (1651–4, 1665–7, 1672–4), but always as the aggressor. It cannot be said that these wars achieved the objectives of those who advocated them, but none was lost in the sense that concessions were made on the status quo ante. While rivalries in the colonial spheres (South Asia, Africa, North, Central, and South America) were intensifying, no territories were ceded and expansion continued steadily. There was a growing recognition of the futility of major armed interventions on the Continent which led to gradual increases in the proportion of resources devoted to the navy, while all Continental countries found that the costs of land warfare hindered the development of their navies. By 1689 the British navy was the equal of the Dutch and the French, and the wars of the next twenty-five years were to make it the dominant navy in Europe. For a country which could not afford an active foreign policy, England's standing in the world had improved remarkably during the century.

The monarchy lacked coercive power: there was no standing army or organized police force. Even the guards regiments which protected the king and performed ceremonial functions around him were a Restoration creation. In the period 1603–40 the number of fighting men upon whom the king could call in an emergency could be counted in scores rather than in thousands. After 1660 there were probably about 3,000 armed men on permanent duty in England and rather more in Ireland and Tangiers (which had come to Charles II as a rather troublesome part of the dowry of his Portuguese wife). There were then also several thousand Englishmen regimented and in permanent

Execution of the gunpowder plotters. The penalty exacted for treason—hanging, disembowling, quartering—is powerfully represented.

service with the Dutch and with the Portuguese armies who could be recalled in emergency. But there was no military presence in England, and apart from pulling up illegal tobacco crops in the west country and occasionally rounding up religious dissidents, the army was not visible until James II's reign.

It had not been so, of course, in the aftermath of the Civil War. At the height of the conflict, in 1643–4, there were probably 150,000 men in arms: one in eight of the adult male population. By the late 1640s, this had fallen to 25,000. The number rose to 45,000 in the third Civil War, waged against the youthful Charles II and the Scots (1650–1), and then fell to remain at between 10,000 and 14,000 for the rest of the decade (although between 18,000 and 40,000 more were serving at any particular moment in Scotland and Ireland). The troops in England were widely dispersed into garrisons. London had a very visible military presence, since 3,000 or so troops were kept in very public places (including St. Paul's Cathedral, the nave of which became a barracks). Everywhere troops could be found meddling in local administration and local politics (and perhaps above all in local churches, for garrisons very often protected and nurtured radical, separatist meeting-houses). The army was at once the sole guarantor of minority republican governments, and a source of grievance which hindered long-term acceptance of the Regicide and Revolution by the population at large.

Throughout the rest of the century, then, the first line of defence against invasion and insurrection was not a standing army but the militia: half-trained, modestly equipped, often chaotically organized local defence forces mustered and led by local gentry families appointed by the Crown but not subservient to the Crown. They saw active service or fired shots in anger only as part of the war effort in 1642–5.

There was no police force at all. Few crimes were 'investigated' by the authorities. Criminal trials resulted from accusations and evidence brought by victims or aggrieved parties to the attention of the justices of the peace. Arrests were made by village constables, ordinary farmers or craftsmen taking their turn for a year, or by sheriffs (gentlemen also taking their turn) who did have a small paid staff of bailiffs. Riots and more widespread disorders could only be dealt with by the militia or by a 'posse comitatus', a gathering of freeholders specially recruited for the occasion by the sheriff.

The Crown had little coercive power; it also had little bureaucratic muscle. The total number of paid public officials in the 1630s was under 2,000, half of them effectively private domestic servants of the king (cooks, stable boys, etc.). The 'civil service' which governed England, or at any rate was paid to govern England, numbered less than 1,000. Most remarkable was the smallness of the clerical staff servicing the courts of law and the Privy Council. The volume of information at the fingertips of decision-makers was clearly restricted by the lack of fact-gatherers and the lack of filing cabinets for early retrieval of the information which was available. In the course of the seventeenth century there was a modest expansion of the civil service with significant improvements in naval administration and in the finance departments (with the emergence of the Treasury as a body capable of establishing departmental budgets and fiscal priorities). Two invaluable by-products of the Civil War itself were the introduction of arabic numerals instead of Roman ones in official accounts and of the printed questionnaire. Although the Privy Council trebled in size in the period 1603–40 and doubled again under Charles II, there was a steady decrease in efficiency, and the introduction of subcommittees of the Council for foreign affairs, trade, the colonies, etc. did not improve on Elizabethan levels of efficiency.

Government in seventeenth-century England was by consent. By this we usually mean government by and through Parliament. But, more important, it meant government by and through unpaid, voluntary officials throughout England. County government was in the hands of 3,000 or so prominent gentry in the early seventeenth century, 5,000 or so in the late seventeenth century. They were chosen by the Crown, but that freedom of choice was effectively limited in each county to a choice of fifty or so of the top eighty families by wealth and reputation. In practice all but heads of gentry families who were too young, too old, too mad, or too Catholic were appointed. In the 200 or so corporate boroughs, power lay with corporations of 12–100 men. In most boroughs these men constituted a self-perpetuating oligarchy; in a large minority, election was on a wider franchise. Only in the 1680s was any serious attempt made to challenge the prescriptive rights of rural and urban élites to exercise power.

The significance of the government's dependence on the voluntary support of local élites cannot be overestimated. They controlled the assessment and collection of taxation; the maintenance, training, and deployment of the militia; the implementation of social and economic legislation; the trial of most criminals; and, increasingly, the enforcement of religious uniformity. Their autonomy and authority was actually greater in the Restoration period than in the pre-war period (the Restoration settlement was a triumph for the country gentry rather than for king or Parliament). The art of governing in the seventeenth century was the art of persuading those who ruled in town and country that there was a close coincidence of interest between themselves and the Crown. For most of the time, this coincidence of interest was recognized. Crown and gentry shared a common political vocabulary; they shared the same conception of society; they shared the same anxieties about the fragility of order and stability. This constrained them to obey the Crown even when it went against the grain. As one gentleman put it to a friend who complained about having to collect possibly illegal taxes in 1625: 'we must not give an example of disobedience to those beneath us'. Local élites were also engaged in endless local disputes, rivalries, conflicts of interest. These might involve questions of procedure or honour; they might involve the distribution of taxation or rates; or promotion to local offices; or the desirability of laying out money to improve highways or rivers. In all these cases the Crown and the Privy Council was the obvious arbitrator. All local governors needed royal support to sustain their local influence. None could expect to receive that support if they did not co-operate with the Crown most of the time. The art of government was to keep all local governors on a treadmill of endeavour. In the period 1603–40 most governors did their duty even when they were alarmed or dismayed at what was asked of them; after 1660 the terrible memories of the Civil War had the same effect. Only when Charles I in 1641 and James II in 1687 calculatingly abandoned the bargain with those groups with the bulk of the land, wealth, and power, did that coincidence of interest dissolve.

In maintaining that coincidence of outlook we should not underestimate the strength of royal control of those institutions which moulded belief and opinion. The Crown's control of schools and universities, of pulpits, of the press was never complete, and it may have declined with time. But most teachers, preachers, writers, most of the time upheld royal authority and sustained established social and religious views. This is perhaps most clearly seen in the speed with which the ideas of Archbishop Laud and his clique (which, as we shall see, sought to revolution-ize the Church of England) were disseminated at Oxford and Cambridge, through carefully planted dons, to a whole generation of undergraduates. Equally the strength of divine-right theories of monarchy was far greater in the 1680s amongst the graduate clergy than in the population at large, again as a result of the Crown's control over key appointments in the universities. At the Restoration, the earl of Clarendon told Parliament that Cromwell's failure to regulate schoolmasters and tutors was a principal reason why Anglicanism had thrived in the 1650s and emerged fully-clad with the return of the king: he pledged the government to ensure the political loyalty and religious orthodoxy of all who set up as teachers, and there is evidence that this was more effectively done in the late seventeenth century than at any other time. Even after 1689 when the rights of religious assembly were conceded to Dissenters, they were denied the right to open or run their own schools or academies.

The Early Stuarts

The Crown, therefore, had formidable, but perishable, assets. There was nothing inexorable either about the way the Tudor political system collapsed, causing civil war and revolution, or about the way monarchy and Church returned and re-established themselves. Fewer men feared or anticipated, let alone sought, civil war in the 1620s or 1630s than had done so in the 1580s and 1590s. Few men felt any confidence in the 1660s and 1670s that republicanism and religious fanaticism had dealt an irrevocable blow.

Throughout Elizabeth's reign, there was a triple threat of civil war: over the wholly uncertain succession; over the passions of rival religious parties; and over the potential interest of the Continental powers in English and Irish domestic disputes. All these extreme hazards had disappeared or receded by the 1620s and 1630s. The Stuarts were securely on the throne with undisputed heirs; the English Catholic community had settled for a deprived status but minimal persecution (they were subject to discriminatory taxes and charges and denied access to public office), while the Puritan attempt to take over the Church by developing their own organizations and structures within it had been defeated. A Puritan piety and zeal was widespread, but its principal characteristic was now to accept the essential forms and practices of the Prayer Book and the canons but to supplement and augment them by their own additional services, preachings, prayer meetings. Above all, they sought to bring a spiritualization to the household that did not challenge but supplemented parochial worship. These additional forms were the kernel and the Prayer-Book services the husk of their Christian witness, but the degree of confrontation between Puritans and the authorities decreased, and the ability of Puritans to organize an underground resistance movement to ungodly kings had vanished. Finally, the decline of internal tensions and the scale of conflicts on the Continent itself removed the incentive for other kings to interfere in England's domestic affairs. In all these ways, England was moving away from civil war in the early seventeenth century. Furthermore, there is no evidence of a general decline into lawlessness and public violence. Quite the reverse. Apart from a momentary spasm induced by the earl of Essex's attempts to overturn his loss of position at court, the period 1569–1642 is the longest period of domestic peace which England had ever enjoyed. No peer and probably no gentleman was tried for treason between 1605 and .1641. Indeed, only one peer was executed during that period (Lord Castlehavon in 1631, for almost every known sexual felony). The number of treason trials and executions in general declined decade by decade.

Early Stuart England was probably the least violent country in Europe. There were probably more dead bodies on stage during a production of *Hamlet* or *Titus Andronicus* than in any one violent clash or sequence of clashes over the first forty years of the century. Blood feuds and cycles of killings by rival groups were unheard of. England had no brigands, bandits, even groups of armed vagabonds, other than occasional gatherings of 'Moss Troopers' in the Scottish border regions. While the late sixteenth century could still see rivalries and disputes amongst county justices flare up into fisticuffs and drawn swords (as in Cheshire in the 1570s and Nottinghamshire in the 1590s), respect for the institutions of justice was sufficient to prevent a perpetuation of such violence into the seventeenth century.

Englishmen were notoriously litigious, but that represented a willingness to submit to the arbitration of the king's courts. There was still much rough justice, many packed juries, much intimidation and informal community sanctions against offenders. But it stopped short of killings. A random fanatic stabbed the duke of Buckingham to death in 1628, but few if any other officers of the Crown—lords lieutenant, deputy lieutenants, justices of the peace, or sheriffs—were slaughtered or maimed in the execution of their duty. A few bailiffs distraining the goods of those who refused to pay rates or taxes were beaten up or chased with pitchforks, but generally speaking the impression of law and order in the early decades is one of the omnicompetence of royal justice and of a spectacular momentum of obedience in the major endeavours of government. It even seems likely that riots (most usually concerned with grain shortages or the enclosure of common land depriving cottagers and artisans of rights essential to the family economy) were declining in frequency and intensity decade by decade. Certainly the degree of violence was strictly limited and few if any persons were killed during riots. The response of the authorities was also restrained: four men were executed for involvement in a riot at Maldon in 1629 just weeks after the quelling of a previous riot. Otherwise, the authorities preferred to deploy minimum force and to impose suspended sentences and to offer arbitration along with or instead of prosecutions. Riots posed no threat to the institutions of the State or to the existing social order.

The fact that few contemporaries expected a civil war may only mean that major structural problems went unrecognized. England may have been becoming ungovernable. Thus, the fact that neither crew nor passengers of an aircraft anticipate a crash does not prevent that crash. But while planes sometimes crash because of metal fatigue or mechanical failure, they also sometimes crash because of pilot error. The causes of the English Civil War are too complex to be explained in terms of such a simple metaphor, but it does seem that the English Civil War was more the consequence of pilot error than of mechanical failure. When, with the wisdom of hindsight, contemporaries looked back at the causes of the 'Great Rebellion' they very rarely went back before the accession of Charles I in 1625. They were probably right.

James I was, in many ways, a highly successful king. This was despite some grave defects of character and judgement. He was the very reverse of Queen Elizabeth. He had a highly articulate, fully-developed, and wholly consistent view of the nature of monarchy and of kingly power—and he wholly failed to live up to it. He was a major intellectual, writing theoretical works on government, engaging effectively in debate with leading Catholic polemicists on theological and political issues, as well as turning his mind and his pen to the ancient but still growing threat of witchcraft, and to the recent and menacing introduction of tobacco. He believed that kings derived their authority directly from God and were answerable to him alone for the discharge of that trust. But he also believed that he was in practice constrained by solemn oaths made at his coronation to rule according to the 'laws and customs of the realm'. However absolute kings might be in the abstract, in the actual situation in which he found himself, he accepted that he could only make law and raise taxation in Parliament, and that every one of his actions as king was subject to judicial review. His prerogative, derived though it was from God, was enforceable only under the law. James was, in this respect, as good as his word. He had several disagreements with his Parlia-

The banqueting house ceiling, showing one of the nine panels, each of which is an allegory of the beneficent reign of James I. The building was designed by Inigo Jones and the ceiling was painted by Rubens, ambassador in London for the Spanish Netherlands.

ments, or at any rate with groups of members of Parliament, but they were mostly unnecessary and mostly of temporary effect. Thus he lectured the Commons in 1621 that their privileges derived from his gift, and this led to a row about their origins. But he was only claiming a right to comment on their use of his gift; he was not claiming, and at no point in relation to any such rights and liberties did he claim, that he had the right to revoke such gifts. It was this tactlessness, this ability to make the right argument at the wrong moment that earned him Henry IV of France's *sobriquet,* 'the wisest fool in Christendom'.

His greatest failings, however, were not intellectual but moral and personal. He was an undignified figure, unkempt, uncouth, unsystematic, and fussy. He presided over a court where peculation and the enjoyment of perquisites rapidly obstructed efficient and honest government. Royal poverty made some remuneration of officials from tainted sources unavoidable. But under James (though not under his son) this got out of hand. The public image of the court was made worse by a series of scandals involving sexual offences and murder. At one point in 1619 a former Lord Chamberlain, a former Lord Treasurer, a former Secretary of State, and a former Captain of the Gentlemen Pensioners, all languished in the Tower on charges of a sexual or financial nature. In 1618, the king's latent homosexuality gave way to a passionate affair with a young courtier of minor gentry background, who rose within a few years to become duke of Buckingham, the first non-royal duke to be created for over a century. Buckingham was to take over the reins of government from the ailing James and to hold them for the young and prissy Charles I, until his assassination in 1628. Such a poor public image cost the king dear. His lack of fiscal self-restraint both heightened his financial problem and reduced the willingness of the community at large to grant him adequate supply.

James I was a visionary king, and in terms of his own hopes and ambitions he was a failure. His vision was one of unity. He hoped to extend the Union of the Crowns of England and Scotland into a fuller union of the kingdoms of Britain. He wanted full union of laws, of parliaments, of churches; he had to settle for a limited economic union, a limited recognition of joint citizenship and for a common flag. The sought-after 'union of hearts and minds' completely eluded him. James's vision was expressed in flexible, gradualist proposals. It was wrecked by the small-mindedness and negative reflexes of the parliamentary county gentry. He also sought to use the power and authority of his three crowns—England, Scotland, and Ireland—to promote the peace and unity of Christian princes, an aim which produced solid achievements in James's arbitration in the Baltic and in Germany in his early years, but which was discredited in his later years by his inability to prevent the outbreak of the Thirty Years War and the renewed conflict in the Low Countries. Finally, he sought to use his position as head of the 'Catholic and Reformed' Church of England, and as the promoter of co-operation between the Presbyterian Scots and episcopal English churches, to advance the reunion of Christian churches. His attempts to arrange an ecumenical council and the response of moderates in all churches, Catholic, orthodox, Lutheran, and Calvinist to his calls for an end to religious strife, were again wrecked by the outbreak of the Thirty Years War. But they had struck a resonant chord in many quarters.

James's reign did see, however, the growth of political stability in England, a lessening of religious passions, domestic peace, and the continuing respect of the international community. His 'plantation policy' in Ulster, involving the dispossession of

George Villiers, Duke of Buckingham, painted at about the time when his
homosexual relationship with the king began.

native Irish Catholic landowners and their replacement by thousands of families from England (many of them in and around Londonderry settled by a consortium of Londoners) and (even more) from south-west Scotland, can also be counted a rather heartless short-term success, though its consequences are all-too-grimly still with us. He left large debts, a court with an unsavoury reputation, and a commitment to fight a limited war with Spain without adequate financial means.

He had squabbled with his Parliament and had failed to secure some important measures which he had propounded to them: of these, the Act of Union with Scotland and an elaborate scheme, known as the Great Contract, for rationalizing his revenues were the only ones that mattered. But he had suffered no major defeat at their hands in the sense that Parliament failed to secure any reduction in royal power and had not enhanced its own participation in government by one jot. Parliament met when the king chose and was dismissed when its usefulness was at an end. Procedural developments were few and had no bearing on parliamentary power. Parliament had sat for less than one month in six during the reign and direct taxation counted for less than one-tenth of the total royal budget. Most members recognized that its very survival as an institution was in serious doubt. No one believed that the disappearance of Parliament gave them the right, let alone the opportunity, to resist the king. James was a Protestant king who ruled under law. He generated distaste in some, but distrust and hatred in few if any of his subjects. Charles I's succession in 1625 was the most peaceful and secure since 1509, and arguably since 1307.

Just as there is a startling contrast between Elizabeth I and James I so there is between James I and Charles I. Where James was an informal, scruffy, approachable man, Charles was glacial, prudish, withdrawn, shifty. He was a runt, a weakling brought up in the shadow of an accomplished elder brother who died of smallpox when Charles was twelve. Charles was short, a stammerer, a man of deep indecision who tried to simplify the world around him by persuading himself that where the king led by example and where order and uniformity were set forth, obedience and peace would follow. Charles I was one of those politicians so confident of the purity of his own motives and actions, so full of rectitude, that he saw no need to explain his actions or justify his conduct to his people. He was an inaccessible king except to his confidants. He was a silent king where James was voluble, a king assertive by deed not word. He was in many ways the icon that James had described in *Basilikon Doron*.

Charles I on horseback. Van Dyck invokes the king as emperor and as Knight of St. George, a potent symbol of authority and of a discipline that brought order and tranquillity. Charles surveys a gentle, tamed landscape.

Government was very differently run. Charles was a chaste king who presided over a chaste court; venality and peculation were stanched; in the years of peace after 1629 the budgets were balanced, the administration streamlined, the Privy Council reorganized. In many respects, government was made more efficient and effective. But a heavy price was paid. In part this was due to misunderstandings, to failures of communication. The years 1625–30 saw England at war with Spain (to regain the territories seized from Charles's brother-in-law the elector Palatine and generally to support the Protestant cause) and with France (to make Louis XIII honour the terms of the marriage treaty uniting his sister Henrietta Maria to Charles I). Parliament brayed for war but failed to provide the supply to make the campaigns a success. A mercenary army was sent in vain into Germany; naval expeditions were mounted against French and Spanish coastal strongholds. Nothing was achieved. The administrative and military preparations themselves, together with financial devices resorted to in order to make good the deficiencies of parliamentary supply, were seen as oppressive and burdensome by many and as of dubious legality by some.

Throughout his reign, however, Charles blithely ruled as he thought right and did little to explain himself. By 1629, king and Parliament had had a series of confrontations over the failure of his foreign policy, over the fiscal expedients needed to finance that policy, over the use of imprisonment to enforce those expedients, and over the king's sponsorship of a new minority group within the Church, whose beliefs and practices sharply diverged from the developing practice and teachings of the Anglican mainstream. In 1629, passions and frustrations reached such a peak that Charles decided that for the foreseeable future he would govern without calling Parliament. He probably believed that if the generation of hotheads and malcontents who had dominated recent sessions was allowed to die off, then the old harmony between king and Parliament could be restored. It was as simplistic as most of his assessments. But the decision was not in itself self-destructive. The three Parliaments of 1625–9 had been bitter and vindictive. But they represented a range of frustrations rather than an organized resistance. They also demonstrated the institutional impotence of Parliament. There was much outspoken criticism of royal policies, but no unity of criticism. Some MPs were anxious about the Crown's religious and foreign policies, others with the legal basis of the fiscal expedients. There was little that men such as John Pym, Sir Edward Coke, Sir Thomas Wentworth, Sir John Eliot, Dudley

Digges (to name perhaps the most vociferous royal critics in those sessions) shared in common beyond a detestation of Buckingham and the belief that the misgovernment of the present was best put right by their own entry into office. All were aspirant courtiers both because of the rewards and honours that would flow from office, and because of the principles and policies they would be able to advance. No change of political institutions and no change in the constitution was envisaged. They were not proto-revolutionaries; they lacked the unity of purpose even to stand forth as an alternative government team.

So in the 1630s the king ruled without Parliament and in the absence of any concerted action, peaceful or otherwise, to bring back Parliament. The king raised substantial revenues, adequate for peacetime purposes, and he faced obstruction, and that largely ineffective obstruction, in only one instance—the Ship Money rates used to build a fleet from 1635 onwards. Most of this obstruction was based on local disputes about the distribution of the rate, and over 90 per cent of it was collected, if rather more slowly than anticipated. Arguments about the legality of the measure were heard in open court and after the king's victory payments were resumed at a high level. By 1637 Charles was at the height of his power. He had a balanced budget, effective social and economic policies, an efficient council, and a secure title. There was a greater degree of political acquiescence than there had been for centuries.

He was, however, alienating a huge majority of his people by his religious policies, for his support for Archbishop William Laud was re-creating some of the religious passions of the 1570s and 1580s. But it was not leading to the development of an underground church or of subversive religious activity. Indeed, those who found the religious demands of Laud unacceptable now had an option not available to previous generations: they could and did emigrate to the New World. There, freed from the persecution of the Anglican authorities, they set about persecuting one another in the name of Protestant purity.

There were, however, two things about Laud which dangerously weakened loyalty to the Crown. One was that the teachings of many of those sponsored by the archbishop, and many of the practices encouraged by Laud himself and his colleagues, were reminiscent of Roman Catholic beliefs and ritual. With Laud himself maintaining that the Roman Church was a true church, though a corrupt one, it became widely believed that popery was being let in by a side door, that the Church was being betrayed and abandoned. Laud's own priorities were not, in fact,

William Laud, archbishop of Canterbury. All other sitters for van Dyck
are presented against a background that expresses their political, religious, cultural
values. Laud is presented as a simple cleric with no other pretensions.

intended to change the liturgy and observances of the Church,
but to restrict Englishmen to a thorough conformity to the letter
of the Prayer Book. The 1559 Prayer Book was not only necessary
it was sufficient. Thus the wide penumbra of Puritan practice
and observances which had grown up around the Prayer Bc
was to be curtailed or abolished. This programme incense
Puritans and worried most other men. Just as bad was I
clericism, his attempt to restore the power and authorit
bishops, of the Church courts, of the parish clergy by
lay encroachments on the wealth and jurisdiction of th

Church lands were to be restored, lay control of tithes and of clerical appointments restricted, the clergy's power to enforce the laws of God enhanced. The most notable visual effect of Laud's archiepiscopate was the removal of the communion tables from the body of the church to the east end, where they were placed on a dais and railed off. At the same time, the rich and ornamental pews set up by the status-conscious clergy were to be removed and replaced by plain, unadorned ones. In the House of God the priest stood at the altar raised above the laity who were to sit in awed humility beneath his gaze. Sinful man could not come to salvation through the word of God alone, or at all, but only through the sacraments mediated by His priesthood. Only a priesthood freed from the greed and cloying materialism of the laity could carry out the Church's mission. Such a programme committed Laud to taking on almost every vested secular interest in the State.

Despite this, in 1637 Charles stood at the height of his power. Yet five years later civil war broke out. Only a catastrophic series of blunders made this possible. The most obvious lesson the king should have learnt from the 1620s (if not the 1590s) was that the Tudor–Stuart system of government was ill-equipped to fight successful wars, with or without parliamentary help. This did not matter since no one was likely to make war on England in the foreseeable future, giving the Crown time in an increasingly favourable economic climate (the great inflation petering out and foreign trade booming). What Charles had to avoid was blundering into an unnecessary war. In 1637, however, he blundered into civil war with his Scots subjects. Governing Scotland from London had proved beyond Charles, whose desire for order and conformity led him first to challenge the autonomy of the Scots lords in matters of jurisdiction and titles to secularized Church lands, and then to attempt to introduce religious reforms into Scotland similar to those advocated by Laud in England. Protests over the latter led to a collapse of order and the king's alternating bluster and half-hearted concession led to a rapid escalation of the troubles. Within twelve months, Charles was faced by the ruin of his Scottish religious policies and an increasing challenge to his political authority there. He therefore decided to impose will by force. In 1639 and again in 1640 he planned to invade land. On both occasions the Scots mobilized more quickly, thoroughly, and in greater numbers than he did. Rather cept a deal with the Short Parliament (April–May 1640) as willing to fund a campaign against the Scots in return l but feasible concessions (certainly for less than the

Scots were demanding), Charles preferred to rely o
Catholics, Highland Catholics, and specious offers of he
Spain and the Papacy. Poor co-ordination, poor morale, a...
general lack of urgency both forced Charles to abandon the
campaign of 1639 and allowed the Scots to invade England and to
occupy Newcastle in the autumn of 1640. There they sat, refusing
to go home until the king had made a treaty with them, including
a settlement of their expenses, ratified by an English Parliament.

A unique opportunity thus arose for all those unhappy with
royal policies to put things right: a Parliament was called which
could not be dismissed at will. The ruthlessness of the way the
opportunity was taken was largely the result of that unique
circumstance. Within twelve months those institutions and
prerogatives through which Charles had sustained his non-
parliamentary government were swept away. The men who had
counselled the king in the 1630s were in prison, in exile, or in
disgrace. But the expected return to peace and co-operation did
not occur. Instead, the crisis rapidly deepened amidst ever
greater distrust and recrimination. Civil war itself broke out
within two years to the dismay and bewilderment of almost
everyone. The reasons why Charles's position collapsed so
completely, so quickly, and so surprisingly are necessarily a
matter of dispute amongst historians. But two points stand out.
One is that once the constitutional reforms which were widely
desired were achieved, Charles's palpable bad grace, his obvious
determination to reverse his concessions at the earliest opportunity, and his growing willingness to use force to that end,
drove the leaders of the Commons, and above all John Pym, to
contemplate more radical measures. In 1640 almost without
exception the members favoured a negative, restrained programme, the abolition of those powers, those prerogatives, those
courts which had sustained non-parliamentary government. No
one had intended to increase the powers of the two Houses, but
only to insist that Parliament be allowed to meet regularly to
discharge its ancient duties: to make law, to grant supply, to
draw the king's attention to the grievances of the subjects, and to
seek redress. By the autumn of 1641 a wholly new view had
emerged. It was that the king himself was so irresponsible, so
incorrigible, that Parliament, on the people's behalf, had a right
to transfer to themselves powers previously exercised by the
king. Specifically, this meant that the Houses should play a part
in the appointment and dismissal of Privy Councillors and
principal officials of State and court, and that the Privy Council's
debates and decisions should be subject to parliamentary

scrutiny. Such demands were facilitated by the fact that Charles had made very similar concessions to the Scots in his treaty with them in July 1641, and such demands were given new urgency by the outbreak of the Irish rebellion in October.

The Catholics of the north of Ireland, fearful that the English Parliament would introduce new repressive religious legislation, decided to take pre-emptive action to disarm those Ulster Protestants who would enforce any such legislation. With the legacy of hatred built into the Ulster plantations, violence inevitably got out of hand and something like 3,000 (that is, one in five) of the Protestants were slaughtered. Reports in England credibly suggested even larger numbers. Fatally for Charles I, the rebels claimed to be acting on his authority and produced a forged warrant to prove it. This reinforced rumours of Charles's scheming with Irish Catholics, of his negotiations with Catholic Spain and with the pope for men and money to invade Scotland in 1640, and it followed on from the discovery of army plots in England and Scotland earlier in the year to dissolve Parliament by force. Within weeks it was emphatically endorsed by Charles's attempt, with troops at his back, to arrest five members of the Commons during a sitting of the House. In these circumstances, to entrust Charles with recruiting and commanding the army to subjugate the Irish, an army available for service in England, was unthinkable. John Pym now led a parliamentary attack on Charles I as a deranged king, a man unfit to wield the powers of his office. In the eighteen months before the outbreak of civil war, a majority of the Commons and a minority of the House of Lords came to share that conviction. When Charles I raised his standard at Nottingham and declared war on his people, the question of his judgement, of his trustworthiness was one which divided the nation.

The first point about the outbreak of the war is, then, that Charles's actions in 1640–2 forced many men into a much more radical constitutional position than they had taken or anticipated taking. But the constitutional dynamic was a limited one. The question of trust arose in relation to an urgent non-negotiable issue: the control of the armed forces to be used against the Irish rebels. This turned attention on a further related question, the king's control of the militia and of those who ran it, the lords lieutenant and their deputies. These constitutional issues together with the accountability of the king's ministers and councillors to Parliament proved to be the *occasion* of the Civil War. But they were not the prime considerations in the mind of those who actively took sides. Certainly the question of trust drew some men to the side of the Houses; but the palpably new demands now being made by Pym and his colleagues were wholly unacceptable to many others. If the king's flirtations with Popery drove some into the arms of Pym, so Pym drove others into the arms of the king by his reckless willingness to use mass picketing by thousands of Londoners to intimidate wavering members of both Houses to approve controversial measures. But for everyone who took sides on the constitutional issue in 1642, there were ten who found it impossible to take sides, who saw right and wrong on both sides, and who continued to pray and to beg for accommodation and a peaceful settlement. In a majority of shires and boroughs, the dominant mood throughout 1642 was pacifist, neutralist, or at least localist. That is, attempts were made to neutralize whole regions, for demilitarization agreements to be reached between factions or to be imposed by 'peace' movements on both sides, or for the county establishments to impose order and discipline in the name of king or Parliament but without doing anything to further the larger, national war effort. Constitutional issues, however much they pressed them upon those at Westminster who experienced royal duplicity and the London apprentices' politics of menace, were not in themselves weighty enough to start a civil war.

By 1642, however, a second factor was crucial: religion. The religious experiments of Archbishop Laud reactivated Puritan militancy. By 1640 substantial numbers of clergy, of gentry, and especially prosperous farmers and craftsmen had decided that the system of Church government, so easily manipulated by a clique of innovators and crypto-Catholics such as they deemed the Laudians to be, had to be overthrown. The office of bishop must be abolished, the Prayer Book, which, said some, 'is noisome and doth stink in the nostrils of God', must be suppressed, the observance of 'popish' festivals such as Christmas and Easter must be stopped. A majority in Parliament initially favoured a more moderate reform—the punishment of Laud and his henchmen and legislation to reduce the autonomy and jurisdiction of the bishops. But the Scots' pressure for more change, a carefully orchestrated petitioning campaign for reform of the Church 'root and branch', and outbreaks of popular iconoclasm (the smashing of stained glass and the hacking out of communion rails was reported from many regions) led to a rapid polarization of opinion. Since many of those who campaigned against bishops also campaigned against rapacious landlords and against tithes (with implications for property rights in general), the defence of the existing Church became a defence of

Oliver Cromwell is pictured on the eve of his brutal
and victorious campaign in Ireland, 1649–50.

order and hierarchy in society and the State as well as in religion.

There was an Anglican party before there was a royalist party,
and those who rushed to join the king in 1642 were those clearly
motivated by religion. On the other side, those who mobilized

for Parliament were those dedicated to the overthrow of the existing Church and to the creation of a new evangelical church which gave greater priority to preaching God's word, greater priority to imposing moral and social discipline. It was a vision reinforced by the return of exiles from New England who told of the achievements of the godly in the Wilderness. Like the Israelites of the Old Testament led out of bondage in Egypt to the Promised Land, so God's new chosen people, the English, were to be led out of bondage into a Promised Land, a Brave New World. While the majority of Englishmen dithered and compromised, the minority who took up the armed struggle cared passionately about religion.

Those who hesitated were, then, sucked inexorably into the Civil War. Faced by escalating demands and threats from the minority who had seized the initiative, most men had to choose sides. Many, maybe most, followed the line of least resistance and did what they were told by those in a position immediately to compel obedience. Others, deciding reluctantly and miserably, examined their consciences and then moved themselves and their families to an area under the control of the side which they thought the more honourable. But fear of the king's 'popish' allies and of Parliament's religious zealots made that decision unbearable for many.

The Civil Wars

The first Civil War lasted from 1642 until 1646. It is impossible to say quite when it began: the country drifted into war. In January 1642 the king left London and began a long journey round the Midlands and the north. In April he tried to secure an arsenal of military equipment at Hull (left over from his Scottish campaign). The gates were locked against him and he retired to York. Between June and August, Charles and the two Houses issued flatly contradictory instructions to rival groups of commissioners for the drilling of the militia. This led to some skirmishing and shows of force. By the end of August both sides were recruiting in earnest and skirmishing increased. The king's raising of his standard at Nottingham on 20 August was the formal declaration of war. But the hope on all sides remained either that negotiations would succeed or else that one battle between the two armies now in the making would settle the issue. But that first battle, at Edgehill in South Warwickshire on 23 October, was drawn and settled nothing. Although the king advanced on

London and reached Brentford, he did not have the numbers or the logistical support to take on the forces blocking his path. He retreated to Oxford as the winter closed in and the roads became impassable. Only after a winter of fitful peace and futile negotiation did the real war break out. Those first armies had been cobbled together and paid on a hand-to-mouth basis. By the spring, it was clear that the nation had to be mobilized. Armies had to be raised in every region and the money and administrative apparatus to sustain those armies created. The country may have stumbled into war; but the logic of that war and its costs would turn civil disturbance into bloody revolution.

It is probable that at some moments in 1643–5 more than one in ten of all adult males was in arms. No single army exceeded 20,000 men, and the largest single battle—Marston Moor near York in June 1644, which saw the conjunction of several separate armies—involved less than 45,000 men. But there were usually 120,000 and up to 140,000 men in arms during the campaigning seasons of 1643, 1644, and 1645. Both sides organized themselves regionally into 'associations' of counties, each with an army (at least on paper) whose primary duty was to clear the association of enemies and to protect it from invasion. Both sides also had a 'marching army' with national responsibilities. In these circumstances the war was essentially one of skirmishes and sieges rather than of major battles. Some regions saw little fighting (for example, East Anglia, the south coast, mid-Wales); others were constantly marched over and occupied by rival armies (the Severn and Thames valleys were amongst the worst, but the whole of the Midlands was a constant military zone). Parliament's heartland was the area in the immediate vicinity of London. Proximity to the capital and to the peremptory demands of the Houses, and the rapid deployment of thousands of Londoners in arms (the unemployed and the religiously inclined joining up in uncertain proportions) ensured that the lukewarm and the hesitant accepted parliamentary authority. Equally, the king's initial strength lay in the areas he visited and toured: the North and East Midlands in a swathe of counties from Lancashire to Oxfordshire. The far north and the west were initially neutral or confused. Only gradually did royalists gain the upper hand in those areas.

The King had several initial advantages—the support of personally wealthy men, a naturally unified command structure emanating from the royal person, a simpler military objective (to capture London). But Parliament had greater long-term advantages: the wealth and manpower of London, crucial for the

Major battles and sieges of the English Civil Wars 1642–1651.

provision of credit; the control of the navy and of the trade routes with the result that hard-headed businessmen preferred to deal with them rather than with the king; a greater compactness of territory less vulnerable to invasion than the royalist hinterlands; and the limited but important help afforded by the invasion of 20,000 Scots in 1644 in return for a commitment by the Houses to introduce a form of Church government similar to the Scottish one.

It was always likely that the parliamentary side would wear down the royalists in a long war. So it proved. Purely military factors played little part in the outcome. Both sides deployed the same tactics and used similar weapons; both had large numbers of experienced officers who had served in the armies of the Continental powers in the Thirty Years War. In 1645 both sides 'new modelled' their military organizations to take account of the changing military balance, the king setting up separate grand commands on Bristol and Oxford, Parliament bringing together three separate armies depleted in recent months: an army too large for its existing task, the defence of East Anglia, the unsuccessful southern region army of Sir William Waller, and the 'marching army' of the commander-in-chief, the earl of Essex. This New Model Army was put under the command of an 'outsider', Sir Thomnas Fairfax, to avoid the rival claims of senior officers in the old armies, and all MPs were recalled from their commands to serve in the Houses; but otherwise commands were allocated more or less according to existing seniority. The New Model was not, by origin, designed to radicalize the parliamentary cause and it was not dominated by radical officers. Professionalization, not radicalization, was the key; the army's later reputation for religious zeal and for representing a career open to the talents was not a feature of its creation. The great string of victories beginning at Naseby in June 1645 was not the product of its zeal, but of regular pay. In the last eighteen months of the war, the unpaid royalist armies simply dissolved, while the New Model was well supplied. The Civil War was won by attrition.

The last twelve months of the war saw a growing popular revolt against the violence and destruction of war. These neutralist or 'Clubmen' risings of farmers and rural craftsmen throughout west and south-west England sought to drive one or both sides out of their area and demanded an end to the war by negotiation. Again, as the discipline of royalist armies disintegrated they were the principal sufferers. But the hostility of the populace to both sides made the fruits of victory hard to pick.

To win the war, Parliament had imposed massive taxation on the people. Direct taxation was itself set at a level of 15–20 per cent of the income of the rich and of the middling sort. Excise duties were imposed on basic commodities such as beer (the basic beverage of men, women, and children in an age just prior to the introduction of hot vegetable drinks such as tea, coffee, and chocolate) and salt (a necessary preservative in that period).

Several thousand gentry and many thousands of others whose property lay in an area controlled by their opponents had their estates confiscated and their incomes employed wholly by the State except for a meagre one-fifth allowed to those with wives and children. By the end of the war, Parliament was allowing less active royalists ('delinquents') to regain their estates on payment of a heavy fine; but the hardliners ('malignants') were allowed no redress and were later to suffer from the sale of their lands on the open market to the highest bidder. All those whose estates were not actually confiscated were required to lend money to king or Parliament; refusal to lend 'voluntarily' led to a stinging fine. In addition to those burdens, both sides resorted to free quarter, the billeting of troops on civilians with little prospect of any recompense for the board and lodging taken. Troops on the move were all too likely to help themselves and to point their muskets at anyone who protested. Looting and pillaging were rare; pilfering and trampling down crops were common. All this occurred in an economy severely disrupted by war. Trade up the Severn was seriously affected by the royalist occupation of Worcester and parliamentarian occupation of Gloucester; or up the Thames by royalist Oxford and parliamentarian Reading. Bad weather added to other problems to make the harvests of the later 1640s the worst of the century. High taxation and high food prices depressed the markets for manufactures and led to economic recession. The plight of the poor and of the not-so-poor was desperate indeed. The costs of settlement, of the disbandment of armies, and of a return to 'normality' grew.

In order to win the Civil War, Parliament had to grant extensive powers, even arbitrary powers, to its agents. The war was administered by a series of committees in London who oversaw the activities of committees in each county and regional association. Committees at each level were granted powers quite at variance with the principles of common law: powers to assess people's wealth and impose their assessments; to search premises and to distrain goods; to imprison those who obstructed them without trial, cause shown and without limitation. Those who acted in such roles were granted an indemnity against any civil or criminal action brought against them, and (after mid-1647) that indemnity was enforced by another parliamentary committee. Judgements reached in the highest courts of the land were set aside by committee decree. Only thus had the resources to win the Civil War been secured. But by 1647 and 1648 Parliament was seen as being more tyrannical in its government than the king had been in his. The cries for settlement and restoration were redoubled.

In order to win the Civil War, Parliament promised the Scots that the Elizabethan Church would be dismantled and refashioned 'according to the word of God, and the example of the best reformed churches' (a piece of casuistry, since the Scots wrongly assumed that must mean their own church). By 1646 this was accomplished, on paper at least. Episcopacy, cathedrals, Church courts, the Book of Common Prayer and the Kalendar (including the celebration of Christmas and Easter) were abolished and proscribed. In their place a 'Presbyterian' system was set up. Ministers and lay 'elders' from a group of neighbouring churches were to meet monthly to discuss matters of mutual concern. Representatives of all such meetings or 'classes' within each county were to meet regularly. The activities at parish, classical, and provincial level would be co-ordinated by a national synod and by Parliament. No one was exempt from the authority of this new national Church any more than they had been from the old Church. The new national faith would be based upon a new service book ('the Directory of Public Worship', emphasizing extempore prayer and the preaching of the Word), new catechisms, and new articles of faith. At every level, the 'godly' were to be empowered to impose moral duties, a 'reformation of manners', and strict spiritual observance through ecclesiastical and secular sanctions. But this Puritan experiment was stillborn. It gave the laity far too much control to please many strict Presbyterian ministers. It gave too little authority to the individual parishes and too much to classes, provinces, and synods to please many others. The precise doctrinal, liturgical, and disciplinary requirements were too rigid for others or just plain unacceptable in themselves. While there was 'Puritan' unity in 1642 against the existing order, the imposition of one particular alternative created a major split in the movement. Many 'Independents' refused to accept the package and began to demand liberty of conscience for themselves and a right of free religious assembly outside the national Church. Some began to refuse to pay tithes. The disintegration of Puritanism preceded any attempt to impose the Presbyterian system. At the same time, this system was bitterly opposed by the great majority of ordinary people. Over four generations they had come to love the Prayer Book and the celebration of the great Christian festivals. They resented the loss of both, and also the Puritan doctrine that forbade anyone to come to receive holy communion without first being approved by the minister and his self-righteous henchmen and given a certificate of worthiness. Throughout much of England, therefore, including East Anglia, the decrees against the Prayer Book and the celebration of Festivals were a dead letter. Ministers who tried to impose change were opposed and even thrown out, and although one in five of the clergy were ejected by parliamentary commissions for spiritual, moral, or political unfitness, a majority of their replacements sought secret episcopal ordination. The Puritan experiment was ineffective but added to popular hatred of an arbitrary Parliament.

But if the great majority, even on the winning side, became convinced that the Civil War had solved nothing and had only substituted new and harsher impositions on pocket and conscience for the old royal impositions, a minority, equally dismayed by the shabby realities of the present, persuaded themselves that a much more radical transformation of political institutions was necessary. God could not have subjected his people to such trials and sufferings without a good purpose. To admit the futility of the struggle, to bring back the king on terms he would have accepted in 1642, would be a betrayal of God and of those who had died and suffered in His cause. Once again it was the religious imperative which drove men on. Such views were to be found in London, with its concentration of gathered churches and economic distress, and in the army, with its especially strong memories of suffering and exhilaration, many soldiers aware of God's presence with them in the heat of battle. Furthermore a penniless Parliament, bleakly foreseeing the consequences of seeking to squeeze additional taxes from the people, enraged the army in the spring of 1647 by trying to disband most of them and to send the rest to reconquer Ireland without paying off the arrears of pay which had been mounting since the end of the war. In the summer of 1647 and again in the autumn of 1648 a majority in the two Houses, unable to see the way forward, resigned themselves to accepting such terms as the king would accept. His plan since his military defeat, to keep talking but to keep his options open, looked likely to be vindicated.

On both occasions, however, the army prevented Parliament from surrender. In August 1647 it marched into London, plucked out the leading 'incendiaries' from the House of Commons, and awed the rest into voting them the taxation and the other material comforts they believed due to them. In doing so, they spurned the invitation of the London-based radical group known as the Levellers to dissolve the Long Parliament, to decree that all existing government had abused its trust and was null .

and void, and to establish a new democratic constitution. The Levellers wanted all free-born Englishmen to sign a social contract, an Agreement of the People, and to enjoy full rights of participation in a decentralized, democratic state. All those who held office would do so for a very short period and were to be accountable to their constituents. Many rights, above all freedom to believe and practise whatever form of Christianity one wanted, could not be infringed by any future Parliament or government. The army, officers and men, were drawn to the Levellers' commitment to religious freedom and to their condemnation of the corruption and tyranny of the Long Parliament, and officers and 'agitators' drawn from the rank and file debated Leveller proposals, above all at the Putney debates held in and near Putney Church in November 1647. But the great majority finally decided that the army's bread-and-butter demands were not to be met by those proposals. Instead the army preferred to put pressure on the chastened Parliament to use its arbitrary powers to meet their sectional interests.

The outcome was a second Civil War, a revolt of the provinces against centralization and military rule. Moderate parliamentarians, Clubmen, whole county communities rose against the renewed oppressions, and their outrage was encouraged and focused by ex-royalists. The second Civil War was fiercest in regions little affected by the first war, insufficiently numbed by past experience—in Kent, in East Anglia, in South Wales, in the West and North Ridings. It was complicated by the king's clumsy alliance with the Scots, who were disgusted by Parliament's failure to honour its agreement to bring in a Church settlement like their own, and who were willing, despite everything, to trust in vague assurances from the duplicitous Charles. If the revolts had been co-ordinated, or at least contemporaneous, they might have succeeded. But they happened one by one, and one by one the army picked them off. With the defeat of the Scots at Preston in August, the second Civil War was over.

It had solved nothing. Still the country cried out for peace and for settlement, still the army had to be paid, still the king prevaricated and made hollow promies. As in 1647, the Houses had to face the futility of all their efforts. By early December there were only two alternatives: to capitulate to the king and to bring him back on his own terms to restore order and peace; or to remove him, and to launch on a bold adventure into unknown and uncharted constitutional seas. A clear majority of both Houses, and a massive majority of the country, wanted the former; a tiny minority, spearheaded by the leaders of the army, determined on the latter. For a second time the army purged Parliament. In the so-called Pride's Purge, over half the members of the Commons were arrested or forcibly prevented from taking their seats. Two-thirds of the remainder boycotted the violated House. In the revolutionary weeks that followed, less than one in six of all MPs participated, and many of those in attendance did so to moderate proceedings. The decision to put the king on trial was probably approved by less than one in ten of the assembly that had made war on him in 1642.

In January 1649, the king was tried for his life. His dignity and forbearance made it a massive propaganda defeat for his opponents. His public beheading at Whitehall took place before a stunned but sympathetic crowd. This most dishonourable and duplicitous of English kings grasped a martyr's crown, his reputation rescued by that dignity at the end and by the publication of his self-justification, the *Eikon Basilike*, a runaway best seller for decades to come.

Commonwealth and Protectorate

From 1649 to 1660 England was a republic. In some ways this was a revolutionary period indeed. Other kings had been brutally murdered, but none had previously been legally murdered. Monarchy was abolished, along with the House of Lords and the Anglican Church. England had four separate constitutions between 1649 and 1659, and a chaos of expedients in 1659–60. Scotland was fully integrated into Britain, and Ireland subjugated with an arrogance unprecedented even in its troubled history. It was a period of major experiment in national government. Yet a remarkable amount was left untouched. The legal system was tinkered with but was recognizably the old arcane common law system run by an exclusive legal priesthood; local government reverted to the old pattern as quarter sessions returned to constitute veritable local parliaments. Exchequer reasserted its control over government finance. Existing rights of property were protected and reinforced, and the social order defended from its radical critics. There was a loosely structured national Church. If no one was obliged to attend this national Church, they were required to pay tithes to support its clergy and to accept the secular and moral authority of parish officers in the execution of the duties laid upon them in Tudor statutes. In practice, the very freedom allowed to each parish in matters of worship, witness, and observance, permitted Anglican services and the Anglican feasts to be quietly and widely practised.

Institutionally, it was indeed a decade of uneven progress back towards a restoration of monarchy. From 1649 to 1653, England was governed by the Rump Parliament, that fragment of the Long Parliament which accepted Pride's Purge and the Regicide and which assumed unto itself all legislative and executive power. Despite the high-minded attempts of some MPs to liken themselves to the assemblies of the Roman Republic, the Rump in practice was a body that lived from hand to mouth. Too busy to take bold initiatives and to seek long-term solutions, let alone to build the new Jerusalem, the Rump parried its problems. By selling the Crown's lands, Church lands, and royalist lands, it financed the army's conquest of Ireland, which included the storming of Drogheda and Wexford and the slaughtering of the civilian population, acts unparalleled in England, but justified as revenge for the massacres of 1641, and its gentler invasion of Scotland. By the establishment of extra-parliamentary financial institutions and by the restoration of pre-war forms of local government, the Rump wooed enough men in the provinces into acquiescence to keep going and to defeat the royalists in a third Civil War. By incoherent and contradictory pronouncements on religion, it kept most men guessing about its ecclesiastical priorities, and drove none to desperate opposition. The Rump even blundered into a naval war with the Dutch and captured enough Dutch merchantmen in the ensuing months to double Britain's entrepôt trade. A demoralized royalist party licked its wounds and tried to pay off its debts; a dejected majority of the old parliamentarian party grudgingly did what they were told but little more. The Rump stumbled on.

By the spring of 1653 the army was ready for a change. With fresh testimonies of divine favour in their victories in Scotland and Ireland and over Charles II at the battle of Worcester, its leaders, above all its commander (since 1649) Oliver Cromwell, demanded the kind of godly reformation which the Rump was too preoccupied and too set in its ways to institute.

Disagreements between Rumpers and army commanders led finally to the peremptory dissolution which the latter had ducked in 1647 and 1648. Fearful that free elections would provoke a right-wing majority, Cromwell decided to call an 'assembly of saints', a constituent assembly of 140 hand-picked men drawn from amongst those who had remained loyal to the godly cause, men who shared little beyond having what Cromwell called 'the root of the matter in them', an integrity and intensity of experience of God's purpose for His people, whose task it was to institute a programme of moral regeneration and political

'The horrible tail man'. Cromwell is offered the crown, while Dutch, Irish, Scots, and royalists cut off sections of his money-filled tail. A Dutch satire.

education that he hoped would bring the people to recognize and to own the 'promises and prophecies' of God. Cromwell's vision of 140 men with a fragment to contribute to the building up of a mosaic of truth was noble but naïve. These 140 bigots of the Nominated and Barebones Parliament, leaderless and without co-ordination, bickered for five months and then, by a large majority, surrendered their power back into the Lord General's hands. Cromwell's honest attempts to persuade others to govern while he stood aside had failed. The army alone propped up the republic and could make and break governments. The army must be made responsible for governing.

From December 1653 until his death in September 1658, Oliver Cromwell ruled England as Lord Protector and Head of State. Under two paper constitutions, the *Instrument of Government* (1653–7, issued by the Army Council) and the *Humble Petition and Advice* (1657–8, drawn up by a Parliament), Cromwell as head of the executive had to rule with, and through, a Council of State. He also had to meet Parliament regularly. Cromwell saw himself in a position very similar to that of Moses leading the Israelites to the Promised Land. The English people had been in bondage in the Land of Egypt (Stuart monarchy); they had fled and crossed the Red Sea (Regicide); they were now struggling across the Desert (current misfortunes), guided by the Pillar of Fire (Divine Providence manifested in the army's great victories, renewed from 1656 on in a successful war against Spain). The people, like the Israelites, were recalcitrant and complaining. Sometimes they needed to be frog-marched towards the Promised Land, as in 1655–6 when Cromwell became dismayed by the lack of response in the people at large during an abortive royalist uprising (few royalists participated but many turned a blind eye, and few beyond the army rushed to extinguish the flames of rebellion). He then instituted a system of government placing each region under the supervision of a senior military commander. These 'Major Generals' were responsible for security but also interfered in every aspect of local government and instituted a 'reformation of manners' (a campaign of moral rearmament). At other times Cromwell tried to wheedle the nation towards the Promised Land with policies of 'healing and settling', playing down the power of the sword and attempting to broaden participation in government and to share power with local magistrates and with Parliament.

If Cromwell had settled for acquiescence and a minimum level of political acceptance, he could have established a secure and lasting regime. But he yearned for commitment and zeal, for a nation more responsive to the things of God, more willing to obey His commands. Cromwell was an orthodox Calvinist in his belief in the duty of God's elect to make all men love and honour Him, and in his belief that God's providence showed His people the way forward. He was unusual in believing that, in this fallen world, the elect were scattered amongst the churches. Toleration was a means to the end of restoring the unity of God's word and truth. This religious radicalism went along with a social conservatism. The hierarchical ordering of society was natural and good, its flaws and injustices not intrinsic but the consequence of sin. It was not society but man's behaviour within society that must be reformed.

By executing Charles, Cromwell cut himself off from justifications of political authority rooted in the past; by acknowledging that a free vote of those who held the franchise would restore the king, that is by refusing to base his authority on consent, Cromwell cut himself off from arguments of the present. His self-justification lay in the future, in the belief that he was fulfilling God's will. But because he believed that he had such a task to perform, he had a fatal disregard for civil and legal liberties. To achieve the future promised by God, Cromwell governed arbitrarily. He imprisoned men without trial. When George Cony, a merchant, refused to pay unconstitutional customs duties, Cromwell imprisoned him and his lawyer to prevent him taking his case to court. When Parliament failed to make him an adequate financial provision, he taxed by decree. When the people would not respond voluntarily to the call to moral regeneration, he created Major Generals and set them to work. Hence the supreme paradox. Cromwell the king-killer, the reluctant head of state, the visionary, was begged by his second Parliament to become King Oliver. He was offered the Crown. Ironically he was offered it to limit his power, to bind him with precedents and with the rule of law. Because such restrictions were irrelevant to the task he believed he was entrusted to perform, because God's Providence did not direct him to restore the office that He had set aside, he declined the throne.

While Cromwell lived, the army (who had the immediate military muscle) and the country gentry (who had the ultimate social authority) were kept in creative tension. Cromwell was a unique blend of country gentleman and professional soldier, of religious radical and social conservative, of political visionary and constitutional mechanic, of charismatic personal presence and insufferable self-righteousness. He was at once the only source of stability and the ultimate source of instability of the regimes he ran. If he could have settled for settlement, he could have established a prudent republic; if he had not had a fire in his belly to change the world, he would never have risen from sheep farmer to be head of state. With his death, the republic collapsed. His son lacked his qualities and succumbed to the jealousy of the senior military commanders. They in turn fell out amongst themselves and a national tax strike hastened the disintegration of the army. Eighteen months after Cromwell's death, one section of the army under General Monck decided that enough was enough. Free elections were held and Charles II was recalled.

Restoration Monarchy

Charles was restored unconditionally. His reign was declared to have begun at the moment of his father's death; those Acts of Parliament to which his father had assented were in force, all the rest were null and void (which meant, for example, that all Crown and Church land sold off by the republic was restored,

Charles II is presented with all the trappings of majesty, his seat on the throne very secure. Yet there is a relaxation and informality of posture unthinkable in his predecessors.

but also that those royalists who had paid fines or who had repurchased their estates under Commonwealth legislation went uncompensated). Parliament assured itself of no greater role in the government than it had possessed under Elizabeth and the early Stuarts (except for a toothless Act requiring a triennial session of Parliament, an Act Charles II ignored without popular protest in 1684). Since the Long Parliament and those of the Interregnum had abused their authority as freely as Charles I had done, it seemed pointless to build them up as a counterpoise to the Crown. Rather the Restoration Settlement sought to limit royal power by handing power back from the centre to the localities. Charles I had agreed to the abolition of the prerogative courts, to the restriction of the judicial power of the Privy Council (now emasculated and thus unable to enforce policy), to the abolition of prerogative taxation. The local gentry were freer than ever before to run their own shires. What is more, with remarkable nerve and courage, Charles set out to build his regime on as broad a base as possible. He refused to give special positions of favour and trust to his own and his father's friends. There was to be power-sharing at every level of government: in the council and in the distribution of office at court, in the bureaucracy, in local government. Old royalists, old parliamentarian moderates who had shunned the Interregnum regimes, Cromwellian loyalists, all found places. Indeed, the group who did least well were the royalist exiles. Charles defeated parliamentary attempts at a wide proscription and punishment of the enemies of monarchy. Only those who signed Charles I's death warrant and a handful of others were exempted from the general Act of Indemnity and Oblivion (one bitter cavalier called the Restoration an 'act of indemnity to the King's enemies and of oblivion to his friends'). It took courage to determine that it was better to upset old friends (who would not send the king on his travels again) than to upset old enemies. Plots against Charles II were few and restricted to radical religious sects. Even a government with less than 3,000 men in arms could deal with such threats.

Charles had hoped to bring a similar comprehensiveness to the ecclesiastical settlement. He sought to restore the Church of England, but with reforms that would make it acceptable to the majority of moderate Puritans. To this end, he offered bishoprics to a number of such moderates and he issued an interim settlement (the Worcester House Declaration) which weakened the power and autonomy of the bishops and made the more contentious ceremonies and phrases of the Prayer Book optional. He also wanted to grant freedom of religious assembly (if not equality of political rights) to the tiny minority of Puritans and Catholics who could not accept even a latitudinarian national Church. For eighteen months he fought for this moderate settlement only to be defeated by the determination of the rigorist Anglican majority in the Cavalier Parliament, by the lukewarmness of his advisers, and by the self-destructive behaviour of Richard Baxter and the Puritan leaders. They refused the senior positions in the Church offered them, they campaigned against toleration, and they persisted in unreasonable demands at the conference held to reform the Prayer Book. Their Scottish colleagues, more flexible and pragmatic, achieved a settlement acceptable to a majority of their brethren.

Charles finally abandoned the quest for a comprehensive Church and assented to the Act of Uniformity which restored the old Church, lock, stock, and barrel, and which imposed a number of stringent oaths and other tests on the clergy. In consequence about one in five of the clergy were ejected by the end of 1662, and many of them began to set up conventicles outside the Church. Charles then set about promoting the cause of religious toleration for all non-Anglicans. Even though his first attempt in January 1663 was a failure, he had the consolation of knowing that he had reversed traditional roles. The pre-war Puritans had looked to Parliament for protection from the king; the new non-conformists had to look to him for protection from Parliament. For fifteen years this made his position in relation to the majority of them politically safe. None the less, it was the single greatest weakness of the Restoration settlement. A comprehensive political settlement was set against a narrow, intolerant religious settlement. Few local governors were Dissenters; but many were sympathetic to them and reluctant to impose the full strictures of the vindictive laws which Parliament went on to pass against their religious assemblies.

In general, Charles's problems did not arise from the settlement but from his preferred lines of policy. In some ways, he was a lazy king. His adolescence and early manhood had been dominated by the desire to gain the throne and once he had returned from exile all his ambition was spent. He was the only one of the Stuarts not to be a visionary, not to have long-term goals. This made it easy for him to back down whenever his policies were strongly opposed. But while he lacked vision, he did not lack prejudices and preferences. He was a man with a strong rationalist streak—a worldly man with many mistresses and seventeen acknowledged bastards, a cynic with regard to human nature, an intellectual dilettante who took a lively if spasmodic interest in the affairs of the Royal Society launched at his accession. But this intellectual empiricism was joined with an emotional and spiritual mysticism which he got from his parents. He believed that he possessed semi-divine powers and

Church and court. George Fox was leader of the Quakers, the largest and most effective of the sects that emerged during the Interregnum.

attributes (no king touched so much for the king's evil, that class of unpleasant glandular and scrofulous disorders that kings were reputed to be able to cure). He was also strongly drawn to Roman Catholicism. His mother, wife, brother, and favourite sister were all Catholics and while he had a *bonhomie* which made him accessible to many, it was superficial, and he was only really close to his family. He knew that wherever Catholicism was strong, monarchy was strong. The Catholics had remained conspicuously

Barbara Villiers, countess of Castlemaine rather smugly holds up one of her four bastards by Charles II. Altogether Charles acknowledged seventeen bastards, but he rarely kept more than one mistress at once.

loyal to his father. If any theology of Grace made sense to Charles it was Catholic doctrine (of his mistresses, Charles said that he could not believe that God would damn a man for taking a little pleasure by the way). He was drawn to Catholicism and twice revealed that preference (in a secret treaty with France in 1670 and in his deathbed reception into the Catholic Church). He was much too sensible politically to declare himself except on his deathbed. But it did lead him to make clear his commitment to toleration. Both this and his obvious admiration for his cousin Louis XIV of France caused growing alarm in England.

Charles was given a generous financial settlement in 1660–1 (£1.2 million per annum), principally from indirect taxation. Bad housekeeping made this inadequate in his early years, and in general it left him with little flexibility. He had no ability to raise emergency taxation without recourse to Parliament and limited access to long-term credit. Thus although Charles had sole responsibility for foreign policy and for making war and peace, Parliament clearly would not vote the necessary revenues without a consideration of the cause for which the money was needed.

The period needed a great administrative reformer in the mould of Henry VIII's Thomas Cromwell, and it did not find one. Decision-making and policy enforcement needed restructuring and formalizing. The Council was too large and amorphous to be effective, and decisions were too often made at one *ad hoc* meeting in the king's chambers and unmade at a subsequent *ad hoc* meeting. This led to real uncertainty and eventually to panic about who was in charge. With the Council emasculated, enforcement of policy was left to individual ministers and departments without co-ordination. Patronage was chaotically handled. Equally, Parliament was inefficient and increasingly crotchety. Charles, feeling that those elected in 1661 were as loyal a group of royalists as he was likely to meet, kept the 'Cavalier' Parliament in almost annual sessions for eighteen years. In part, its inefficiency was due to a growing rivalry between the two Houses, especially over the Lords' claim to take over much of the jurisdiction of the defunct conciliar courts, and a number of sessions were wrecked by deadlock on such issues. In part, its inefficiency was due to there being no government programme for it to get its teeth into. A body of several hundred members without recognized leadership spent much time discussing what to discuss. With most senior ministers in the Lords, and a predisposition to resist management by the court, the 1660s and 1670s were years of drift. Charles ruled without serious threat to his position at home or abroad. The early euphoria gave way to a mild political depression as the final ravages of plague, the humiliating Dutch incursions up the Medway during the second Dutch war (1665–7), and the Great Fire of London (1666) sapped the self-confidence of 1660–1 that God would bless a land that had come to its senses.

There were many political embarrassments, such as the defeat of a major attempt to introduce religious toleration (1672–3), the suspension of interest payments on his loans (1672), and the political brawls in Parliament as the discredited ministers of the 'Cabal' administration blamed each other for their collective failure (1674–5). But the only challenge to his authority came in the Exclusion crisis of 1678–81. This was triggered by the revelations of Titus Oates, Israel Tonge, and other desperadoes of a popish plot to murder Charles and put his Catholic brother on the throne. This was more lucid and more plausible than many similar tales, but was just as mendacious. The mysterious death of an investigating magistrate and the discovery of conspiratorial letters in the possession of James's private secretary also heightened tension. The result was a full-scale attempt to place a parliamentary bar on the accession of James and thereby to shatter Charles's divine-right theories of government.

In fact the political leaders of the Exclusion movement were at least as concerned to use the crisis to clip Charles's wings as James's. For the first twelve months their target was not James but Charles's Cavalier–Anglican chief minister, the earl of Danby. This appears odd, but it is clear that Shaftesbury, the leader of the Opposition, saw Danby's regime as just as much a threat to liberties as James might be. Danby's principles were the very antithesis of Shaftesbury's, in that he had developed sophisticated techniques of parliamentary management, had centralized financial control, had upset the balance of interests in local government to the advantage of Cavalier–Anglicans, seemed willing to develop a standing army in peacetime, and had allied with the Dutch against the French. Shaftesbury, a turncoat in the Civil War, a member of Barebones Parliament and of Cromwell's council of state, who had served Charles as Chancellor of the Exchequer and Lord Chancellor, had a consistent record of supporting free and unfettered Parliaments, decentralization, religious toleration, a horror of standing armies, and a distaste for the Dutch. Danby's policies amounted in fact to nothing more than a programme to give Charles II a quiet life: to Shaftesbury it looked like incipient absolutism. By now there was such a conjunction in people's minds between Popery and arbitrary government, that even Danby could be portrayed as a secret agent of the papists, despite his impeccable Anglicanism. Only when Danby was imprisoned in the Tower did Shaftesbury turn to Exclusion as an end in itself and as a means to other ends. These included shattering the theoretical basis of divine right and creating the need for continued political action and cohesion (to secure Exclusion on Charles's death, for James would hardly accept it without a fight). To secure Exclusion, Shaftesbury created the first political party in English history. His 'Whigs' produced a mass of propaganda, organized petitions and demonstrations, and co-ordinated campaigns in three successive general elections (1679–81).

They failed. Charles held all the trump cards. The Whigs were fatally divided over who should take James's place as heir—Monmouth, the favoured royal bastard, or Mary, James's Protestant daughter. Almost without exception, the Whigs were committed to lawful, peaceful action only. The memories of civil war were too strong to allow violent councils to hold sway. Charles could, and did, use his power to summon and dissolve Parliament to his own advantage; he had a solid majority in the House of Lords that would vote down the Exclusion Bill time after time; a trade boom enhanced royal revenues on trade and freed Charles from financial worry; and his policy of offering concessions short of Exclusion bought off many moderates. Shaftesbury fatally assumed that Charles would weaken under pressure. He never grasped that Charles would always concede matters of policy, but never matters of principle. He would never have surrendered his divine right. His ultimate sacrifice would have been to divorce the barren queen he respected if he did not cherish, to remarry, and to solve the succession crisis via the marriage bed. It would have been the supreme demonstration of his political style.

As it was, the same iron nerve, pragmatism, and easy goodwill to all, which he had demonstrated in 1660, won him the day. A nation racked by political deadlock for three years backed off, took stock, and rallied to him. In his last years he was able to pick off those who had crossed him, reward those who had stood by him, enjoy a quiet life at last. He left a nation governed by and for those who believed in the divine right of kings, the divine right of the Church of England, and the divine right of the localities to run their own affairs. The complacency of the Tory–Anglicans knew no bounds, as they welcomed James II to the throne, the king whose rights they had protected. Such complacency was in for a rude shock.

James was in fact a bigot. His government of Scotland in the early 1680s had seen a most severe repression and extensive use of judicial torture against Protestant Dissenters ('conventiclers'). Worse still, James believed himself to be a moderate. He had no deliberate plan to set himself up as an absolutist king on the Continental model. But since a trade boom greatly enhanced royal revenues (and his first Parliament, meeting under threat of a military bid for the throne by Charles's favoured bastard, the duke of Monmouth, voted higher rates in addition), he was able to maintain an army of 20,000 men. The army's most striking characteristic was its professionalism and the apolitical views of its career commanders. James had twice urged Charles to use his tiny army to get rid of troublesome Parliaments. He would not have hesitated to use his army against a recalcitrant assembly, but he did not intend to rule without Parliament. Indeed, at the time of his fall, he was engaged in the most elaborate operation ever attempted, to 'pack' Parliament with sympathizers. Until early 1688 James's second marriage, more than a decade old, was childless. James—already fifty years old—expected to be succeeded by his Protestant daughter Mary and her Dutch husband, William of Orange. He intended to secure for all time a religious and civil equality for his co-religionists. This meant not only removing from them all the penalties and disabilities under the Penal Laws (fines for non-attendance at Anglican worship) and Test Acts (barring them from all offices and paid

A pope-burning procession on 17 November 1680 (commemorating the accession of Queen Elizabeth I)

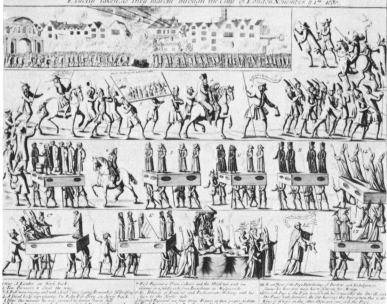

THE SOLEMN MOCK PROCESSION of the POPE, CARDINALS, IESUITS, FRYERS, NUNS
Exactly taken, as they marcht through the Citty of London Nouember 17 1680.

employments under the Crown), but also allowing the Catholic Church to be set up alongside the Anglican Church. This meant establishing a Catholic hierarchy and diocesan structure and public places of worship. It also meant allowing Catholics a share in the universities (maybe even the take-over—or 'restoration'—of some colleges to serve as Catholic seminaries). It would probably have led on to granting Catholics exemption from tithes and the authority of Anglican courts. James honestly believed that once the ban on Catholic evangelism was lifted, once the civil and religious disabilities removed, the return of hundreds of thousands to the Faith was certain. He believed that this granting of 'equal status' to Catholics was a humane and moderate programme. If, in the short term, a certain amount of positive discrimination was necessary to favour Catholics in appointments to national and local office, this too was only fair as a correcting exercise.

It need hardly be said that the Tory–Anglican political nation was outraged. Their loyalty to the Church proved greater than their loyalty to their anointed king. James soon discovered that no Tory–Anglican Parliament would repeal the anti-Catholic legislation and while a packed judiciary would uphold his suspension of that legislation, it would come back into force the moment he died and his Protestant heir took over. He therefore made a desperate bid to jettison the Tory squirearchy and to build an alternative power base in an alliance of Catholics and Protestant Dissenters. Three-quarters of all JPs were sacked, together with most lords lieutenant. The new men were of lower social origin, and James's purge constituted a greater social revolution in local government than had been attempted even in the years 1646–60. James called in the charters of most towns and reorganized their governments to give Dissenters control (this was especially vital if he was to get a sympathetic parliamentary majority). To win over the Dissenters, a Declaration of Indulgence was issued giving them full religious freedom.

The Tory–Anglicans were stung, but initially pacific. The whirlwind would blow itself out; James would die and Mary succeed him; they would take their revenge. Passive disobedience would limit James's success. Thus seven bishops petitioned him explaining why they would not obey his order to instruct their clergy to read the Declaration of Indulgence to their flocks. They also committed the Church to a future Anglican toleration of Protestant Dissenters. James had the bishops tried for seditious libel, but even his judges summed up against him and they were acquitted. However, the Tory complacency of 1687

Titus Oates did not prosper under James II.
He is shown being flogged and in the pillory. The priests in the insets
were amongst the thirty or so executed on his perjured evidence.

('we are not to be laughed out of our doctrine of Non-Resistance
and passive obedience on all occasions' wrote the marquis of
Halifax) turned to stunned horror in June 1688 with the birth of a

son and heir to James II. Now indeed the possibility of a dynasty of rabid Catholics appeared to stretch out before them.

Ironically, while many Anglican leaders came to put their religion before their political principles, many Dissenters chose to put political principles first. They had little doubt that James was using them for present purposes only. Thus leaders of both parties joined in the desperate expedient of inviting William of Orange to come to England, suitably protected with armed men, to remonstrate with James. Perhaps they really believed that this would lead to James agreeing to William's humiliating terms: the recall of the writ designed to produce a packed Parliament and new writs to return a 'free' Parliament; a declaration of war on France; and a commission to investigate the legitimacy of the infant Prince of Wales. Only a minority were willing to join William's invasion by taking up arms; but even fewer were willing to lift their little fingers to help James.

Whatever those who invited William may have expected, William himself almost certainly intended to depose James. He was taking a quite outrageous risk, justified only by the necessity of harnessing the whole of Britain's military, naval, and financial resources to the struggle against Louis XIV. But how he expected to secure the throne is less clear. In the event, he was able to get himself proclaimed joint ruler with Mary within a matter of weeks because James had what can only be called a complete mental collapse. His army and William's never met. William landed at Torbay on 5 November and moved east. James brought his army as far as Salisbury where incessant nosebleeds held him up. As his behaviour became more and more bizarre and manic, many of his professional officers and commanders deserted him. James then fled back to London and was quickly in William's hands. Even then, his position was not hopeless. A series of vague undertakings and promises would have ensured that he retained the loyalty of most peers and leading gentry. But he was beyond reason. He twice escaped (on the first occasion, to William's annoyance, being captured on the Kent coast by well-meaning fishermen and sent back). His flight to France, the public promises of Louis XIV to use French arms to restore him, and William's clear statement that he would not protect the realm unless he shared the throne with his wife, left the political nation no choice. Almost all Whigs and most Tories, rationalizing their conduct as best they could, and in a variety of ways, agreed that James had vacated his throne and that the Crown be offered jointly to William and Mary. The Glorious Revolution of 1688 was even more unanticipated and unplanned than the Great Rebel-

James II had a distinguished military and naval career blighted by his ignominious flight in 1688.

lion of 1642; its consequences probably more momentous.

Had the English Revolution had any lasting effects on the power of the Crown? The answer is that it had surprisingly little. In the 1680s the Crown was far better endowed financially, it had a growing but still inadequate civil service, and an unprecedented opportunity to create a standing army. Parliaments had shown themselves quite unable to defeat the king, in the sense of imposing on him restrictions and conditions that he disliked or taking away from him powers he had hitherto enjoyed. The royal prerogatives in the 1680s were little different from those of the 1600s. The king could veto bills he did not approve; he could dispense individuals from the operation of statutes; he could pardon whomsoever he chose. He selected his own councillors, judges, senior administrators, and he could dismiss most of them at will. He was not bound to take anyone's advice. If he had lost most of his feudal revenues and his 'discretionary' powers to raise money, he had been amply compensated by parliamentary taxes, some in perpetuity, others for life.

The only really major weakening of royal power had come in the legislation of 1641 which abolished those courts and councils which were particularly susceptible to royal control. The most important restriction was the one which took away from the Privy Council its judicial power. Its teeth removed, the Council ceased to be an executive, active body, monitoring, cajoling, and directing the work of local government, and reverted to what it had begun as: a talking shop, a place where the king sought advice. It probably never functioned as well under the Stuarts as under the Tudors; James I allowed factionalism to spill over from the Council to the floor of Parliament; Charles I did not want to hear alternative proposals from groups within the Council. He wanted puppets to confirm his own preconceptions. Charles II enjoyed policy-making in secret, summoning ministers to hasty meetings in his private quarters, so that no one knew what was going on. For different reasons, each of these monarchs encouraged the growth of secret committees of the Council comprising the holders of key offices. Here was the seed of the Cabinet councils of the eighteenth century. Other conciliar courts abolished in 1641 included Star Chamber, High Commission, Requests, and—more by chance than design—the Regional Councils of the north and in the marches of Wales. Charles II was restricted at the Restoration not by the gentry in Parliament, but by the gentry in the provinces. Almost all the methods by which Tudor and early Stuart kings could bring recalcitrant county communities to heel had been taken away. Government was more than ever by their active consent. In the 1660s all taxation except the customs, all ecclesiastical legislation (such as the Act of Uniformity, the Conventicle Acts, and the Five Mile Act), and most security matters, were entrusted to the gentry magistrates with no appeal from their decisions to the central courts.

The abolition of the monarchy and the experience of republican rule thus had a very limited direct impact. Even the memory of Charles I's public trial, conviction, and decapitation did not change the monarchy's pretensions to rule by divine right nor make them more respectful of Parliaments. After all, the political nation knew that regicide had cost them dear, that it had added to, rather than removed, their oppressions. The problems of matching resources to responsibilities had become clearer; but the problems themselves had neither increased nor diminished.

† The alternatives for England were to see either a strengthening of the central executive and administration at the expense of the independent county gentry; or else a further withering away of the centre, turning England into a series of semi-autonomous county-states, self-governing, undertaxed, stagnant. The latter was the preference of a range of 'Country parties' visible in the Parliaments of the 1620s, the neutralist groups in the Civil War, and many Whigs in the 1670s and 1680s. It was also the preference of republicans such as John Milton, who admired the Dutch republic and longed to see the same oligarchic civic humanism develop in England. Most dramatically, it was the ideal of democratic groups such as the Levellers, who wanted to make governors more accountable, government subservient to the liberties of a sovereign people, and who therefore urged devolution of power to elected local magistrates and juries. But these 'Country' ideologies were incompatible with the development of a global empire. The expansion into the West Indies and along the eastern seaboard of North America (from Carolina to the St. Lawrence); into extensive trade networks with South America, West Africa, India, and Indonesia; even the protection of the vital trades with the southern and eastern Mediterranean all required strong naval and military power. This could only be sustained by a massive increase in the ability of the State to tax and to wage war. It was the combined threat of Louis XIV and the exiled James II after 1689 to introduce Popery and arbitrary government which finally forced through the necessary constitutional and political changes, as the following chapter will show. The Stuart century was one of unresolved tensions.

Intellectual and Religious Life

For the Church of England, if not for the monarchy, the seventeenth century was an age of disillusionment. By the time of the Glorious Revolution of 1688–9 it had lost the intellectual, moral, spiritual authority it had acquired by 1603. Intellectually, Anglicanism was on the offensive at the beginning of the century. The generation living through the events of 1559 witnessed a settlement cobbled together to meet political necessities, a hybrid of Protestant doctrine and Catholic practice. The criticisms of the first generation of Puritans were the more telling because their Marian exile allowed them to speak from experience of the purity of the Continental reformed churches. The new generation of the 1590s and 1600s had known no other Church, and had come to love the rhythms of the Anglican liturgical year and the cadences of Cranmer's liturgy. The work of Jewel, Hooker, and Andrewes presented the Church of England as the best of all Churches, claiming an apostolic descent and an uninterrupted history from the Celtic Church which gave it a greater authority than the schismatic Protestant Churches, and a superiority over Rome in that it had sloughed off the corruptions and failings of the Roman Catholic Church just as it had sloughed off the usurped authority of the bishops of Rome. The Church of England had an authority as ancient and as apostolic as Rome's, and a practice more true to the injunctions of Christ. There were claims which the Puritans did not find easy to meet.

Puritans displayed an increasing willingness to work within the Church. Their response to James I's accession, the Millenary Petition, called only for modifications within the existing framework. At the Hampton Court Conference of 1604, in which James presided over a meeting of bishops and Puritans, discussion was entirely about how to make the episcopal national Church more effectively evangelical. Puritans yearned for a godly prince who, like the Emperor Constantine 1,200 years before, would bring good order to his State, and promote and protect true religion. They chafed for more to do, rather than for less. They worked within the Church and not against it. Even the 5 per cent of the nation who made up the Catholic recusants succumbed to an intellectual onslaught led by Anglican divines. The greatest single debate on any issue in the first quarter of the century was over the duties of Catholics to take the oath of allegiance and to eschew papal claims to command their political allegiance. Anglican arguments prevailed and the Catholics, while holding
+ to their faith, abandoned political resistance. The Gunpowder

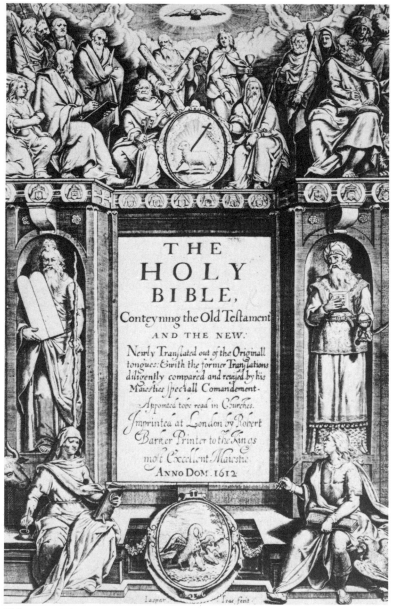

Title-page of the King James bible
(product of the Hampton Court conference of bishops and Puritans
under James I's chairmanship).

plot was the last real popish plot. As English Catholicism became controlled less by military clergy and more by a prudent peerage and gentry, its pacifism and political acquiescence grew.

Protestant unity, if not uniformity, was retained until the Long Parliament. Puritans added their own practices to those of the Church, but the number who opted out and set up conventicles or assemblies in defiance of the Church was extremely few. Some hundreds, perhaps thousands, moved to New England rather than submit to the narrow interpretation of Anglican practice required by Archbishop Laud. But there was no schism.

The Civil War and Interregnum years saw the disintegration not only of Anglicanism, but of English Puritanism. The structure of the Church of England was abolished (bishops, church courts) or proscribed (the Prayer Book, the celebration of Christmas or Easter). Cathedrals were turned into preaching centres or secularized (used as barracks, prisons, shopping arcades). In thousands of parishes the old services and celebrations were carried on despite the proscriptions. But the Church leaders lost their nerve. The bishops fled, hid, remained silent. They were not replaced as they died. By 1660 the survivors were all over seventy years of age, and Church of England bishops were an endangered species.

But those who dreamed of replacing Anglicanism by a Calvinist church like those of Massachusetts, Scotland, or Geneva were disappointed. The Presbyterian system conceived by Parliament was stillborn. The chaos of the Civil War created a bewildering variety of sects and gathered churches. The Baptists, one of the few strong underground churches before 1640, spread widely via the army. Many new groups denied Calvinist notions of an Elect predestined to salvation, and proclaimed God's Grace to be freely available. Some even proclaimed universal salvation. Such groups were most evident in London and other provincial cities. The largest of all the sects was the Quakers, whose informal missionary evangelism in the countryside gained thousands of adherents in the 1650s: denouncing the formalization of religion, and the specious authority of 'hireling priests' in their 'steeple houses', the Quakers urged men to find the divine spark within themselves, the Holy Spirit which came direct to the Christian, mediated neither by the Church nor Scripture. Their hatred of formal worship and of tithes led them into widespread campaigns of militant passive disobedience. One of their leaders, James Nayler, was tried for blasphemy by the second Protectorate Parliament in 1656. Although he escaped the sentence of death, he was subject to a variety of severe physical punishments, Parliament taking several hours to contemplate which bits of him should be sliced or cut off.

There was no recovering the old triumphalism after 1660. The Church might be outwardly restored to its ancient forms at the Restoration, but it had neither the self-assurance nor the power to reimpose a general uniformity. Anglican apologetic was defensive and edgy. With the disappearance of High Commission and the rust of disuse settled in its diocesan courts, it lacked the weapons to punish defaulters. The ignominy of its abolition left it institutionally enfeebled. In 1660 the celebration of Easter and the ubiquitous return of maypoles may have been spontaneous and have shown signs of its deep roots in popular culture. But those who chose to defy it were not going to be forced back into its assemblies. The decision in 1662 not to broaden its appeal by adapting its liturgy and by softening episcopal pretensions drove two thousand clergy out of the Church. Despite the attempts to prevent unlawful conventicles, the Baptists, Quakers, and other radicals were not to be

Ballad illustration of a maypole, showing one of the most characteristic rural customs of the century, and certainly one of the first to reappear with the king in 1660 after Interregnum proscription.

uprooted. Even more important, the tens of thousands of 'Dissenters' of 1662 who were within the moderate Puritan tradition re-examined whether their desire to be part of a national Church (though not the one on offer) outweighed their desire for a pure worship of God. In the 1580s and the 1600s they had preferred to 'tarry for the magistrate', to stay in the Church and to wait for better times. In Restoration England, they came more and more to opt for separation. In the early seventeenth century they found 'much piety in Babylon'; now they abandoned such temporizing and went into schism. The Toleration Act of 1689 was the formal recognition of the fact of religious pluralism. Unable to punish those who were not its members, and unable to compel men and women to be its members, the Church of England was a spent spiritual force.

In the early and mid-seventeenth century, most intellectuals and most governors believed that there was a divine imperative to bring godliness, good discipline, and order to the English nation. God was guiding His people towards a Promised Land of peace and justice in which men would love and worship him as it was their duty to do. The vision of a better world that could be built by man's response to the divine challenge was shared by James and Charles I, by Wentworth and Laud, by Pym and Cromwell. All political writings were suffused by the immanence of God in his Creation, by a deep sense of God's activity in human history and in His providences, His signs of Himself. Shakespeare's plays, Donne's poems, the thought of Henry Parker and the young John Milton all proclaim the same point: the plays of Marlowe are the exceptions that prove the rule.

No such hopes survived the Interregnum. The trauma of regicide left few royalists with faith in the providences of God; the much deeper sense of betrayal experienced by the radicals in 1660 largely explains their political quiescence thereafter. Psychologically, the pain of betrayal after such visible testimonies of divine favour was too great. Instead, most of the Puritans and their heirs internalized the kingdom of God. They accepted the world as the domain of sin and of imperfectibility. Within this vale of tears, each person must seek personal peace by building a temple of grace within himself or herself. This acceptance of the limits of what Church and State could achieve dominated the ideology of the late seventeenth century. It is apparent in the way Charles II's jaundiced view of the world was combined with his deep personal mysticism, in the latitudinarianism of the bishops and of the clerical establishment; in the Dissenters' abandonment of the quest for a national Church. A few men continued to seek the millennium (Sir Isaac Newton combined his successful search for physical laws with an unsuccessful search for the dating of the Second Coming from the runes in the Book of Revelation), but most settled for making the most of things as they were. John Milton heroically confronted a God who appeared to have guided his people in the 1640s and 1650s only to betray them in 1660. *Paradise Lost* looked at the Omnipotent Creator who let man fall, *Paradise Regained* looked at the temptation of Christ in the wilderness, at the false worldly ways in which Man might proclaim the gospel. Perhaps republicans had been tempted into the wrong paths. *Samson Agonistes*, most poignantly of all, studied a man given great gifts by God who failed to use them in His service. Just as Samson dallied with Delilah and was shorn of his strength, so the republicans had been distracted by the things of the flesh in the 1650s and had missed their chance to do God's will. But the more typical Puritan work of the Restoration is Bunyan's *Pilgrim's Progress* which concerns the individual's personal search for peace and salvation.

Christianity was being depoliticized and demystified. The characteristic Anglican tracts of the late seventeenth century had titles like *The Reasonableness of Christianity* and *Christianity not Mysterious*. Where God had been in the very warp and woof of nature and life, he now became the creator who set things going, and the spirit who worked within the individual and kept him obedient to moral rules. Sermons stressed the merits of neighbourliness and charity. Ministers were encouraged to preach that religious duties meant being kind to old people and animals rather than preaching about the transformation of the world. From the Dissenting side, John Locke, pleading for religious toleration, defined a church as a voluntary society of men, meeting together to worship God in such fashion as they deemed appropriate. Religion had become an unthreatening matter, almost a hobby. The authorities need not concern themselves with what consenting adults did in private meetings. The Puritans of previous generations could not have conceived anything so anaemic.

This dilution of religious energies, this breakdown of a world-view dominated by religious imperatives can be seen in literature and in science. Restoration theatre differs from Jacobean not in its vulgarity or even in its triviality so much as in its secularism. Metaphysical poetry, which rooted religious experience in the natural world, gave way to a religious poetry either more cerebral and coolly rational, or else more ethereal and other-worldly.

Secularization was also an aspect of change in the visual arts. Tudor and Stuart country houses emphasized paternalistic Christian values, being built around a great hall in which the household and a wider community gathered to do business and to eat together. There might be a 'high table', reflecting hierarchy and degree, but there was an easy informality of social relations. By the late seventeenth century, new houses had 'withdrawing' rooms and private dining-rooms, while servants and other members of the household were given separate quarters. Houses were set in spacious parks surrounded by high walls and patrolled by gamekeepers. Royal palaces showed the way in these developments.

The seventeenth century, like the sixteenth, saw little church building. Perhaps a majority of all new churches were those needed in London after the Great Fire of 1666. There was, however, a stark contrast between the intensity and devotional emphasis of early Stuart churches and chapels such as the one at Peterhouse, Cambridge, and the cool, light, rationalist air of Wren's London churches. Allegorical stained glass and dark wood panelling gave way to marble. The recumbent effigies of souls at rest gave way to an upright statuary of men and women reflecting on their moral duties.

In all the visual arts, the influence of the Counter-Reformation art of Spain, Spanish Italy, Spanish Netherlands—an ornateness

St. Paul's Cathedral under construction (c.1690).
Wren's masterpiece replaced the old cathedral destroyed in the Great Fire.

that bound together the natural and the supernatural worlds—
gave way to the influences of Louis XIV's France—self-indulgent,
revelling in its own material extravagance. In the early seventeenth century, artists, musicians, and poets joined forces to
produce the Masque, an entertainment that sought to bring
together the world of classical civilization and Christian values,
of audiences drawn into the action as performers, a merging of
fantasy and reality. The power of the illusion was so great in the
case of Inigo Jones and Ben Jonson's Masques for Charles I, that
the king came to believe that his own piety and virtue would
soon infect his subjects and that order and uniformity could be as
easily achieved in the State as on the stage. No such illusion
bedevilled the artifice of the opera, the equivalent art-form of the
late seventeenth century. While early Stuart writers wrestled
with the heroic and the tragic, late Stuart writers turned to the
domesticated homiletics of the novel and to the mock epics of
Dryden and later of Pope.

Restoration science was just as secularized. In the 1640s and
1650s, scientists had sought what they termed 'a great instauration'. Drawing on the ideas of Francis Bacon, and led by
visionary social engineers such as Samuel Hartlib and the
Bohemian exile Comenius, the scientific establishment were
lionized by the Puritan politicians and undertook to build a
Brave New World. Man would tame and gain dominion over the
natural world. Medical advances would vanquish disease, agricultural advances would conquer hunger and want. The reformation of justice and of education would bring man into peaceful
enjoyment of the new order. It was yet another facet of Protestant
eschatology, and the scientific Zion, like other Zions, evaporated
in 1660. The later seventeenth century in the Royal Society was
not an age of visions but of piecemeal enquiry and improvement.
Francis Bacon's principles of exact observation, measurement,
and of inductive reasoning, refined by the Frenchman Descartes,
allowed major advances in the classification and study of plant
and animal life. Harvey's discovery of the circulation of the
blood, just before the Civil War, led on to a series of advances in
the knowledge of anatomy and physiology in the second half of
the century. Isaac Newton's *Philosophiae Naturalis Principia
Mathematica* (1687) was the basis of understanding of the
physical laws for two hundred years, and the work of Robert
Boyle in chemistry and Robert Hooke in geology created new
disciplines on the basis of extensive experimentation and
measurement. The advance of the physical sciences hit hard at
the older mysteries. The discovery of the geometrical movement

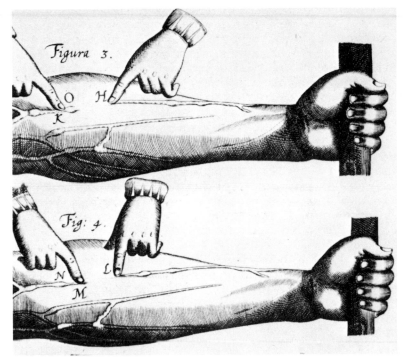

Illustration from 'De Motu Cordis' (1628), demonstrating the existence of valves in the veins. William Harvey's discovery of the circulation of the blood was one of the first great medical advances to come out of the scientific empiricism associated with Francis Bacon.

of heavenly bodies destroyed the credibility of astrology in intellectual circles. It is astonishing how quickly the discovery of natural laws bred a confidence that *everything* had a natural explanation. The realm of magic, of witches and spells, was abandoned by the educated. Within a generation of 1640 the prosecution of witches almost ceased. This was not because the people at large ceased to believe in curses and in magic, but because it was impossible to secure convictions from sceptical judges and jurors. Science and technology did not in fact advance on all fronts. The economy remained almost wholly dependent on human and animal muscle-power. No progress was made towards harnessing steam, let alone gas or electricity as energy sources. The extraction of minerals from the ground and the smelting of ore contributed another technological bottle-neck. Science was changing attitudes, not transforming the economy.

Political thought was being secularized too. Thomas Hobbes stripped sovereignty of its moral basis; in *Leviathan* (1651) the concept of legitimacy as the justification of political authority was replaced by a concentration on *de facto* power and the ability to afford protection to the subjects who lived under this power. Machiavelli remained an odious name but his ideas became more and more persuasive as a counter to the divine-right pieties of Robert Filmer and of Stuart apologists.

The English Revolution does, then, stand as a turning-point. It may have achieved little that any of the parties sought after or fought for. It may have done even less to transform political and social institutions. But it deeply affected the intellectual values, at least of the political élite. An age which derived its momentum from Christian humanism, from chivalry, from a reverential antiquarianism, gave way to an age of pragmatism and individualism. When John Locke wrote in his second *Treatise of Government* (1690) that 'all men are naturally in a state of perfect freedom to order their actions and dispose of their possessions and persons as they think fit without asking the leave or depending upon the will of any man' he was proclaiming a message not only made possible by the disillusionment with old ideals, but a message which was to make much possible in the decades to come.

145

PAUL LANGFORD

7. The Eighteenth Century
(1688–1789)

Revolution and its Repercussions

THE historical importance of the Revolution of 1688—the 'Glorious Revolution'—has inevitably fluctuated in the process of constant reinterpretation by successive generations. It has fared particularly badly at the hands of the twentieth century, and threatens to disappear altogether under the demands of modern historical scholarship. The decisive triumph of the liberal and democratic spirit, beloved of Macaulay and the Victorian Whigs, has dwindled into the conservative reaction of a selfish oligarchy. Especially when compared with modern revolutions, it seems rather to resemble a palace coup than a genuine shift of social or political power. This impression is reinforced, perhaps, by what was seen at the time as one of its most creditable features—the relative absence of physical violence. Yet this aspect can be exaggerated. In Scotland, the supporters of the deposed king had to be crushed by force of arms, a process which was completed at the battles of Killiecrankie and Dunkeld in 1689. In Ireland there was positively a blood-bath, one which still holds a prominent place in Irish myths and memories. When the siege of Londonderry was lifted, and James II decisively defeated at the battle of the Boyne, Ulster Protestants certainly considered their salvation to be glorious, but they can hardly have thought of it as bloodless.

The story might easily have been the same in England. The former royalist Nicholas L'Estrange testified that only chance, the disarray of James II's friends, and above all the king's surprising failure to raise the royal standard in his own realm, prevented a civil war as ferocious as those of the mid-century. Yet L'Estrange's very relief that his family had been saved further sacrifices in the cause of the Stuarts perhaps provides a clue to the comparative tranquillity associated with the making of the revolution in England. A perceptible sense of compromise, of the need to step back from the brink, carries over the centuries from the debates of the assembly which met in London in January 1689. The Convention, which transformed itself into Parliament by the simple expedient of passing an Act to that effect, displayed an understandable desire to legitimize what was manifestly illegitimate by following as far as possible the procedural forms employed at the Restoration in 1660. On matters of substance, the priority was plainly to find a common core of agreement rather than to test the more extreme solutions offered by either side. William of Orange was made king, with Mary as queen. Tories, led by Danby, would have preferred Mary as sole monarch, or some species of regency ruling technically in the name of James II. But the Protestant saviour would accept nothing less than the crown, and so it was. None the less, every effort was made to conceal the revolutionary nature of what was being done. Though James's supposedly illegal acts—particularly his reliance on a standing army and his recourse to the dispensing and suspending powers—were formally condemned, the Bill of Rights went out of its way to pretend that the deposed king had in effect abdicated, leaving a deserted realm no alternative but to seek the protection of the House of Orange. Implausible though this appeared, it was sufficient to secure the assent of a majority of the ruling class. There were, inevitably, exceptions. Some churchmen, led by Sancroft, the Archbishop of Canterbury, and two of the bishops who had helped bring James II down in the Seven Bishops Case, declined to take even the cautiously worded oaths designed by the Convention. Others, like the Nottingham Tories, old champions of the court in the reaction of 1681–7, wrestled with the concept of a rightful king who owed his title to a *de facto* decision of Parliament, but not to the *du jure* ordinance of heaven.

Yet the substantive acceptance of parliamentary monarchy was achieved. The profound importance of this achievement was obscured not merely by conscious attempts to avoid dogmatic prescriptions in 1689 but by the long agonies which followed. Passive obedience and non-resistance continued to be influential concepts, buttressed as they were by elaborate arguments stressing the providential nature of the Protestant Wind in 1688, and the duty of every citizen to co-operate with any form of authority rather than submit to anarchy. For a generation, these notions continued to work on men's minds, bestowing a sense of legitimacy on the rage and despair felt by many who had seen the necessity for what had happened in 1688 but found it difficult to live with all the consequences. Beyond that, they sank into the

By the grace of God. William III's successors, after Kneller. Anne is shown before her accession with her son the duke of Gloucester. In the background Britannia symbolizes the reliance placed on Princess Anne's English ancestry and patriotic standing. But Gloucester's premature death in 1700 was to bring the Hanoverian line to the throne.

Anglican orthodoxy of the eighteenth-century mind and helped secure the underlying authoritarianism which was to remain an important element of political ideology in the age of the American and French Revolutions. But, with this reservation, the major change of course carried out in 1688 can be seen to have been truly revolutionary. The Bill of Rights clearly overrode the

hereditary right which formed the basis of the restored constitution of 1660 and replaced it with the will of the nation
expressed through Parliament. First William and Mary, then
Mary's sister Anne, and finally, after the death of the latter's son
the duke of Gloucester in 1700, the Electors of Hanover
(descended from James I through the female line) all owed their
title to the determination of the propertied classes. At a time
when absolutism, both in theory and practice, seemed to be in
the ascendant in the Western world, the importance of this
transformation should not be underestimated. Eighteenth- and
nineteenth-century Whigs exaggerated the coherence and com-
pleteness of the contract theory which seemed to have triumphed
in 1689 and they underrated the tensions, contradictions, and
conflicts which it entailed. But they were fundamentally correct
in seeing it as a historic turning-point involving the decisive
rejection of an entire conception of government.

The status of the monarchy was very much the conscious
concern of the revolutionaries of 1688. It is doubtful whether
many of them foresaw the consequences of their actions in terms
of England's relations with foreign powers. In this respect,
indeed, the importance of the Revolution is undenied and
undeniable. Before 1688, the policy of successive rulers, Cromwell, Charles II, and James II, had been largely pro-French and
anti-Dutch. After 1688 France was to become a more or less
permanent enemy, and certainly a constant rival in the battle for
supremacy overseas. The scale of conflict was also novel. The
Nine Years War (1688–97) and the War of Spanish Succession
(1702–13) involved Britain in both Continental and colonial
warfare as she had not been involved since the Elizabethan
struggle with Spain, and in the interim the technological and
strategic complexity of war-making had vastly increased. The
part of Englishmen in this unexpected, if not unpredictable,
consequence of the Revolution was affected by various considerations. In terms of grand strategy, the priority was to combat
Louis XIV's expansionist policies in the Low Countries, and to
prevent the erection of a mighty new Bourbon empire comprising the Spanish as well as French monarchy. The interests of
commerce, which once had required protection against Dutch
economic enterprise, could now be said to dictate an aggressive
stance towards the more sustained challenge of French competition, and especially the assertion of Britain's right to a share in
the trade if not the territory of the Spanish empire. These
arguments were woven by the Whigs into a systematic case for an
interventionist foreign policy, expressed most clearly in the

George I appears in the regalia of the Garter.
No opportunity was lost to boost this German princeling's pretensions
to royalty; on the table rest the crown, orb, and sceptre, while the carpet is
decorated with the fleur-de-lis.

Continental campaigns of William III and Marlborough. But
such considerations would not have led many Englishmen to
approve the formidable outlay of expenditure and resources in
these years if it had not been for the dynastic issue. The Nine

Years War has appropriately been called the War of the English Succession. William would hardly have set sail for Torbay in 1688 if he had not assumed that the English alliance against France would follow logically from his own intervention in English affairs. Yet in fact diplomatic and military support from his new subjects was made much more likely by Louis XIV's imprudent championship of James II. French backing for the Jacobite camp was withdrawn when an uneasy peace was negotiated in 1697. But four years later, with the Spanish Succession at stake, and Europe on the verge of war once more, it was again Louis's support for the Stuarts, this time in the shape of James's son the Old Pretender, which convinced many reluctant Englishmen of the case for involvement in a Continental conflict.

One of the most startling aspects of the wars was the sheer success of English arms, particularly under Marlborough in the War of Spanish Succession. It was not just that the Protestant Succession was effectively secured at least for the present. More striking still was the new reputation earned by a country widely regarded as little more than a pensioner of France only a short time before. Marlborough's triumphs at Blenheim and Ramillies, not to say Rooke's at Gibraltar and Stanhope's at Minorca, established Britain as a major force in Continental politics, a substantial power in the Mediterranean, and a worthy competitor for France overseas. The latter stages of the war, in which military progress seemed to diminish in direct proportion to national expenditure, removed the loftier ambitions suggested by the dazzling victories of the Blenheim period, but when peace was made at Utrecht in 1713 sufficient was secured to retain the essential impact of the successes, and even to create the impression of what French diplomatic historians have termed the 'English hegemony' in Europe.

Hardly less important was the domestic impact of warfare. The cost of the wars amounted to almost £150 million in an age when peacetime expenditure was thought excessive at two millions per annum. This vast outlay required a corresponding rise in levels of taxation, with widespread political repercussions. But more interesting in retrospect is the fact that a large proportion of the bill, approximately one-third, was met by borrowing. Sums of this order could only be found in a buoyant and flexible money market, such as that created by the economic conditions of the late seventeenth century. Though land values were seriously affected by agrarian recession, trade had enjoyed a great upsurge in the 1680s and the investment surpluses released were to wash over the economy for a good many years. A post-revolution government, sorely in need of cash and prepared to mortgage the incomes of unborn generations of taxpayers to permit a competitive interest rate, offered promising investment possibilities. The financiers whose initiative eventually led to the foundation of the Bank of England in 1694 were not, in principle, engaging in anything new. As long as wars had been undertaken, governments had been forced to rely on loans from the business community. What was new was the political infrastructure which was necessitated by the exceptionally heavy borrowing of this period. The credit-worthiness of the new regime, based as it was on a parliamentary title, was negligible without the clear understanding that the propertied classes would ultimately be prepared to foot the bill. Without a matching recognition on the part of the regime that it must closely collaborate with those classes and their representatives, no such understanding could exist. The National Debt and all it entailed was built on this essential nexus of interest linking an illegitimate dynasty, the financial world, and the taxpaying public.

As war followed war and decade followed decade the burden of debt grew. Successive governments found it ever harder to avoid borrowing, and the main function of those taxes which were raised was often merely to pay the interest charges on the debt. With hindsight, the advantages of this system, without precise parallel in contemporary Europe, are obvious. The political security of an otherwise somewhat shaky regime was much enhanced, and national resources in wartime much boosted by this machinery for channelling private wealth into public expenditure. At the time, the disadvantages attracted more attention. The pretence that the National Debt could actually be repaid and the nation released from the threat of bankruptcy became increasingly thin. The anxieties of a society traditionally ill-disposed to taxation in general and new forms of taxation in particular made the task of the Treasury and the Committee of Ways and Means increasingly harrowing. Yet, even at the time, there were those who had a shrewd perception of one quite priceless political advantage of the new system. This arose from its impact on Parliament, and especially on the House of Commons. For everything depended on Parliament's part in this elaborate process, and Parliament was understandably jealous of its rights in matters of finance. The land tax, the basic guarantee of the taxpayer's commitment to the National Debt, was cautiously voted for a year at a time. Even the customs and excise duties, granted for much longer periods, were extended and renewed only after the most prolonged debate and haggling.

The 'budget' was nominally an achievement of the mid-century, when the term was first used during Henry Pelham's time as First Lord of the Treasury (1743–54). But its essential features can be traced back to the Revolution, and it is this aspect of 1689 which more than anything else finally secured Parliament's central place in constitutional development. At times in the seventeenth century it had been possible to see the legislature as a faintly absurd and decidedly irritating survival of England's medieval past, an irrational obstruction to efficient monarchical government which might profitably be dispensed with altogether. Now its future was secure; since 1689 Parliament has met for a substantial period every year. In this sense the Revolution gave a novel twist to an old problem: eighteenth-century politicians asked themselves not how to do away with the need for Parliament, or even how to crush it. Rather they had to consider how to manipulate it. The arts of management were to provide the key to the conduct of Georgian politics.

It was impossible in the late seventeenth century to engage in political revolution without raising the prospect or the spectre (depending on one's viewpoint) of ecclesiastical revolution. In this respect the Revolution of 1688 was perhaps important not merely for what it did but for what it failed to do. Many contemporaries hoped for a radical revision of the Church settlement of the 1660s. There was talk of a truly comprehensive national Church, and for some Dissenters, particularly the Presbyterians, the possibilities of reconcilation to the establishment seemed stronger than at any time since Hampton Court in 1604. In the event, however, their hopes were dashed. As in 1662, the Anglican squirearchy would permit no weakening of the hierarchical and episcopalian structure of the Church. It would be inappropriate to talk of a Laudian or high-church reaction at this time. But any sign of genuine *rapprochement* with the Dissenters was quickly extinguished. Instead, the latter were offered the least that could be offered against the background of recent events, a grudging toleration. The Toleration Act of 1689 in effect granted freedom of worship to Protestant nonconformists in premises licensed by Anglican bishops, provided that those concerned shared the basic doctrines laid down in the Thirty-nine Articles and sanctioned by the Act of Uniformity. This seemed a far cry from the prospect held out to Dissenters of all kinds by James II.

No doubt for this reason, it has been customary to play down the full significance of the Toleration Act. An extremely qualified liberty permitted to those whose beliefs were defined in strictly qualified terms seemed a poor reward for men who had resisted the temptations offered by the Declarations of Indulgence and had welcomed William of Orange. But such judgements depend heavily on the point of view. For Dissenters who had been vigorously persecuted as recently as the early 1680s, the Toleration Act provided an unprecedented statutory security. From the vantage point of anxious churchmen it was no less important to maintain the substance of the Restoration Settlement. The Prayer Book of 1662 was to remain the liturgical basis of Anglican worship until the twentieth century; but in 1689 it seemed to offer a precarious platform of doctrine without which established Protestantism might be lost. Paradoxically, the resulting exclusiveness of the Church had much to do˜with England's eighteenth-century reputation as a civilized society in a barbarous world. A comprehensive national Church embracing all but a small number of sectaries and papists would have been a very different matter from a restricted religious establishment, coexisting with large numbers of nonconformists. The difference was perhaps a tolerant, pluralist socity. The legal recognition of liberty of worship went far beyond what had been achieved in most of Europe, and Voltaire was to hold it up as the crucial element in the development of a free society. If so, it was to a large extent the consequence of the Revolution.

The achievements of these years had a price in the social tensions and political conflicts which marked the Augustan era. Pre-eminent among the signs of strain was indeed the plight of the religious establishment. The great cry of the period was 'The Church in Danger'. Whether it was truly in danger seems doubtful in retrospect. Toleration was obviously a fearful blow to those who dreamed of reviving a Laudian church. But the swelling tide of latitudinarian theology and sentiment made it seem innocuous enough to most. Moreover, the political monopoly enjoyed by Anglicans under the Test and Corporation Acts was left intact by the Revolution Settlement. Here, however, was the rub. For in practice there was every indication that Dissenters were able to challenge and evade this monopoly. The readiness of many nonconformists to resort to occasional conformity, annually taking the sacraments according to the Anglican rite in order to meet the requirements of the statutes, and for the rest worshipping in their own meeting houses, was a constant source of irritation to their enemies. Whether the actual practice of occasional conformity grew in this period is uncertain. But it was unquestionably more noticeable now that Dissenting chapels were publicly recognized, and now that the double standard

The church in danger. In this print of 1709, St. Paul's is assaulted by its enemies from Salter's Hall, the capital's bastion of dissent. Low-church divines lead a monstrously heretical beast; in its wake march the men of 'resistance' and republicanism, threatening the establishment in State as well as Church.

apparently observed by those who attended them was plain to all. Moreover, the general climate of the 1690s and 1700s provoked anxiety and even hysteria on the part of churchmen. Theological speculation and deistic tendencies were much discussed and much feared. John Toland's *Christianity Not Mysterious*, one of the earliest and most systematic attempts to popularize the case for 'natural' against 'revealed' religion, began a torrent of polemical debate on such matters in 1697. Nor did it help that some of the worst offenders were themselves clergy of the established Church. Samuel Clarke, the Whig sceptic whose assault on Trinitarianism brought the wrath of Convocation upon his head in 1712, and Benjamin Hoadly, who held three bishoprics in succession but denied the divine nature both of his office and of the Church itself, were only the more spectacular examples of the heretical spirit which seemed to mark the progress of the early Enlightenment in England.

The high-church reaction to these trends reached its peak under Queen Anne when the presence on the throne of a pious and theologically conservative queen provided an additional impulse. But its force derived much from other developments, many of them connected with party politics. The Tories, who frequently described themselves as 'The Church party', depended heavily for their appeal on the sense of crisis in the Church. They also drew extensively on the emotional support of the backwoods Anglican squirearchy. For the latter, the world opened up by the Revolution brought nothing but ill. The wars of the period necessitated the heaviest direct taxation since the 1650s. A land tax of four shillings in the pound came as a heavy burden on estates already afflicted by agricultural depression. Moreover, the war for which such sacrifices were required seemed designed to benefit precisely the enemies of the gentry—the merchants, manufacturers, and above all 'monied men' most active in the commercial and financial expansion of late Stuart England. Such men, it seemed, were often religious Dissenters, escaped all but indirect taxes, and invariably pursued Whig politics. The link between the old and new party systems was sometimes tenuous. The new Tories of Anne's reign were often drawn from families with a Puritan or Whiggish background; their leader, Robert Harley, was himself one such. On the other side, the Whig Junto, whose ruthless pursuit of place and power earned them an unenviable reputation for placing party before principle, seemed unlikely descendants of the Country Whigs of 1679. But there was no doubt about the intensity of party feeling in the early eighteenth century. It perhaps reached its height in 1710 when the Whigs impeached the Tory divine, Dr Sacheverell, for preaching the old doctrine of non-resistance. The popular convulsions which followed clearly revealed the potential for political instability which the Revolution had incidentally created. The Triennial Act of 1694 had principally been designed to compel the Crown to summon Parliament regularly, in which respect it proved unnecessary. But it also provided for frequent elections, and the consequence was a period of the most intense and unremitting electoral conflict, involving ten general elections in twenty years and exceeding anything which had gone before. Moreover, the effective abolition of state censorship, with the lapsing of the Licensing Act in 1695, ensured a large and growing forum for public debate. It is no coincidence that these years witnessed the decisive stage in the establishment of Grub Street, in the emergence of the periodical press, and in the growth of a genuinely popular political audience. In general, the reign of Anne has been seen by historians as the natural backdrop to the achievement of political stability. But on the evidence available to contemporaries it seemed rather to suggest that the price of limited monarchy and financial security was political chaos.

The Rise of Robinocracy

The Hanoverian Accession in 1714 brought new tensions to an already strained situation. While Anne lived, it had been possible, in terms of sentiment if not of logic, to consider her as a true Stuart occupying the throne in some sense in trust for her family. With the arrival of a German-speaking Elector of Hanover, strongly committed to intervention abroad and Whiggism at home, such pretences became difficult to sustain. From a dynastic standpoint everything was to play for in 1714. Many urged the Pretender to consider that London was worth the abandonment of the mass; had James III returned to the Anglican fold he would plainly have strengthened the chances of a second Stuart Restoration. Without this personal sacrifice, the Jacobite Rebellion of 1715 proved a damp squib. France, after the death of Louis XIV in the same year, was in no position to involve herself in English adventures. Even in Scotland, where the rebellion had its seat and indeed its heart, the prospects for the Stuarts were not particularly promising. The Scottish Union, concluded in 1708 in an atmosphere of considerably urgency, had taken much of the sting out of the succession problem. Many Scots mourned the loss of their national Parliament and thereby their independence. But the Union was shrewdly designed to preserve Scottish legal and ecclesiastical institutions, while simultaneously offering real commercial benefits through incorporation in England's imperial system. In these circumstances, the failure of the '15 was to all intents and purposes a foregone conclusion.

If the Old Pretender missed his chance, so in a different sense did his apparently successful rival, George I. By the latter part of Anne's reign, the unpopularity of the war, the electoral appeal of the 'Church in Danger'; and not least the queen's own irritation with the Junto Whigs, had placed the Tories firmly in the saddle. For most of them the interests of the established Church took precedence over sentimental attachment to the Stuart dynasty. A judiciously bipartisan policy on the part of the new regime, on the lines of William III's tactics in 1689, would have done much to ease the transition of 1714. Instead, George I displayed all too clearly his readiness to make the Hanoverian succession the exclusive property of the Whigs. The years 1714–21 witnessed a campaign for Whiggish dominance which comprehensively alienated the Tories, made the dangers of the Jacobite Rebellion greater than they need have been, and generally threatened to reshape the Revolution settlement. First the Septennial Act was passed, ensuring that the new Whig government would not have to face an unmanageable electorate until the greater part of its work was complete. It was rumoured that, when that time came, the Whigs would remove all statutory restraints on the duration of Parliaments, making possible the revival of 'long' or 'pensioner' Parliaments. At the same time, the means by which the Tories of Anne's reign had endeavoured to shackle Dissent, the Occasional Conformity and Schism Acts, were first suspended and then in 1718 repealed altogether. A Universities Bill was designed to give the Crown complete control of Fellowships and Scholarships in Oxford and Cambridge, with a view to transforming the principal nurseries of the Church and the professions into Whig preserves. Above all the Peerage Bill of 1719 was projected to restrict the House of Lords to approximately its existing size. This would have ensured permanent Whig hegemony in the Upper House, regardless of any change of mind on the part of the monarch, and provided the Whigs with a built-in check on legislation affecting their interests. With this programme, there went a steady, systematic purge of Tories in the lords-lieutenancies and commissions of the peace, in the armed forces, and in the civil service at all levels.

Complete success in this great enterprise would have created a system much like that which emerged in Sweden at this time, and which condemned that country to fifty years of national impotence and aristocratic factionalism. It would have established an oligarchy as unlimited as that absolute monarchy which generations of seventeenth-century Englishmen had so dreaded. It would also have made virtually impossible one of the eighteenth century's most characteristic achievements, a stable yet flexible political structure. That it failed owed much to the divisions among the Whigs themselves. Their plans proceeded relatively smoothly while the great Whig families united to crush their opponents during the early years of George I's reign. But this union proved short-lived. The new king's foreign policy caused severe strains by its blatant use of England's naval power to secure Hanover's Baltic ambitions. There was also an increasingly bitter struggle for pre-eminence within the ministry. The eventual result, in 1717, was the Whig split, which placed Walpole and Townshend in opposition and left Stanhope and Sunderland more firmly ensconced at court then ever. Palace politics were also subject to upheaval. The king's son, the future George II, and his wife Princess Caroline, clearly indicated their intention of siding with Townshend and thereby began a long tradition of political intrigue by Hanoverian heirs to the throne. In this situation there was little hope of completing the grandiose plans of Stanhope for the promised land of Whiggism. In the House of Commons Walpole himself played a leading part in defeating the Peerage Bill and forcing the abandonment of the Universities Bill. Any hope the ministry had of saving something from the wreckage of their plans was lost soon after in the South Sea Bubble.

In retrospect, there is a certain inevitability about the South Sea Bubble and the general financial crash which went with it. It seems to bring to a fitting conclusion the intense and inflated commercialism which had accompanied the rise of the 'monied interest' in the preceding years. Yet initially there was much to be said for the scheme which caused this convulsion. The financial interests represented in the Bank of England had enjoyed a more than favourable return on their investments during the wars, and there was obviously room for greater competition between the nation's creditors. The Tory ministers of Queen Anne's reign had indeed encouraged the formation of the South Sea Company in 1711 with a view to providing an effective alternative to the Whig Bank. Moreover, there was little doubt that the funds existed, not merely in the City, but among smaller savers generally, for a more extended and more equitable investment in the public debt. The South Sea Company's scheme of 1719 seemed well calculated to redistribute the National Debt while offering better terms to the national Exchequer. The difficulties began not with the essential logic of the scheme but with the many and varied interests involved in it. For the Directors of the Company, and especially the inner group which initiated the project, there was the need to make a substantial profit not merely for themselves but for the many courtiers, ministers, and MPs whose support was politically essential to secure acceptance of their proposals. That support was bought at a high price in terms of stock supplied on favourable terms, or even stock granted by way of open bribery. In short, many of those involved in the management of the South Sea Scheme had a strong interest in quick profits, which could only be achieved by boosting the Company's potential far beyond competing investment possibilities. Such an exercise depended heavily on the attractions of the Company's trade in the south seas. The Anglo-Spanish treaty of 1713 had given the Company a monopoly of the Spanish slave-trade and a valuable share in the Spanish American market for European goods. In theory, this offered the most promising prospects. In practice, the difficulties of managing this far-flung trade from London were to prove immense, and they were not rendered less by the often bitter conflicts between the British

The Bubble. Hogarth's 'Emblematical Print on the South Sea Scheme' displays the speculative mania of 1720. To the *left* the devil surveys his handiwork; in the *foreground* his victims religion, honesty, and honour are cynically sacrificed. The use of 'emblem' in this way was a commonplace of early eighteenth century satire.

and Spanish governments. The trade could not have proved profitable in the short run, and even with time it could hardly fulfil the wild expectations raised in 1719. But realities were quickly forgotten in the mania for speculation which prevailed in the early months of 1720. Provided the stock was rising, new speculators were constantly encouraged to invest, permitting those who had already purchased to unload their holdings at a handsome profit. The constant inflow of funds justified new issues of stock and increasingly vociferous assertions of the durability of the investment, not to say still more generous pay-offs to the politicians. In this situation, created by a corrupt regime, a naïve investing public, and a well-established National Debt, the inevitable happened. The bubble grew steadily, encouraging still more fraudulent bubbles in ever more implausible projects as it grew. When confidence eventually failed and the bubble burst the consequences were catastrophic, particularly for those who had sold substantial assets in land or other forms of property to buy at absurdly inflated prices. Little could be done for these sufferers, by no means drawn only from the wealthiest classes. Parliament rushed through a statute severely restricting joint-stock companies for the future, but this was shutting the stable door after the horse had bolted. More dramatic action was needed to minimize the damage to the regime. The king and the Prince of Wales were publicly reconciled. The opposition Whigs were welcomed back into office, Townshend to set about cultivating the goodwill of the king's mistress the duchess of Kendal, Walpole to push through the Commons a solution for the Bubble crisis which would at least protect the National Debt and save the face of the court. In this task, which earned him an enduring reputation for 'screening' corruption and fraud in high places, Walpole was in one sense aided by the very gravity of the situation. Many of those implicated in the murky transactions of 1720 were Tories who had no more enthusiasm than their Whig counterparts for public exposure. Moreover the Bubble was part of an international crisis with matching disasters in Paris and Amsterdam; it was not implausible to lay some of the blame on impersonal financial forces unconnected with individuals in the City or at court. In any event the king's ministers were, with the exception of two or three suitable scapegoats, permitted to get away with their crimes. For Walpole all this represented a great political triumph, fittingly capped by the fortuitous elimination of his rivals. Within two years, both Stanhope and Sunderland had died, leaving the way open for a new era of Walpolian supremacy, or as his opponents were to term it 'Robinocracy'.

Contemporaries, of course, could not be expected to foresee the relative stability which lay ahead. The 1720s were troubled years, not least in the most basic terms of human health and survival. The decade began, not merely with the Bubble, but with fears of a visitation from the plague which was currently devastating the south of France and which could readily be transmitted to London by way of Marseilles and the shipping lanes. In the event, the panic proved unjustified; the strains of the disease which had periodically ravished so much of Europe since the first onset of the Black Death nearly four hundred years earlier were approaching dormancy if not extinction. But this was not obvious at the time and in any case there were less exotic, home-grown maladies which continued to exert a tenacious hold on the vital statistics of demography. The later 1720s were particularly harrowing in this respect. The first three years of George II's reign, which began in 1727, were afflicted by successive waves of smallpox and influenza-like infections, imprecisely and variously described by contemporaries as agues and fevers. The demographic consequences were clearly serious. Much of the slow and slender gain in population which had occurred since the 1670s seems to have been wiped out in what was evidently the worst mortality crisis since the 1580s. By 1731 the total population stood at about 5,200,000, a figure probably lower than that for Cromwell's England in the mid-1650s.

The sense of sickness which pervaded the period was more than physiological. The greed, fraudulence, and hysteria which had characterized the South Sea Bubble were denounced both in the press and from the pulpit as the ruling vices of the years which followed. Luxury and lavish living were seen as the causes, moral decay and dissolution as the consequences. There seemed to be striking evidence of this in the great scandals which disfigured public life at this time. A whole series of parliamentary investigations uncovered extensive corruption in high places. The trustees of the Derwentwater estates were found to have connived at the sale of forfeited Jacobite property to some of their own number at artificially low prices. The directors and officials of the Charitable Corporation, whose duty it was to provide employment and assistance for the poor, were convicted of jobbery, misappropriation, and even outright peculation. In both cases, prominent MPs and supporters of the government were implicated. More sensational still was the impeachment of the Lord Chancellor, Lord Macclesfield, for organizing the sale of judicial offices. Even his ministerial colleagues declined to defend him when it emerged that this flourishing branch of commercial law had been financed from the proceeds of private property entrusted to the care of Chancery. That the guardians of equity should thus be caught in the act of infringing it seemed peculiarly shocking to an age which entertained a profound respect for rights of property. Moreover, public misdeeds could readily be matched by private ones. Crime, a distorting mirror of society, but a mirror none the less, seemed to become ever more organized, more commercial, and more cynical. Jonathan Wild, the master thief-taker, was a fitting representative of his time. Most of his profits were gained by restoring to their owners the goods stolen by his own minions. His success depended heavily on the corrupt collaboration of JPs and their officers in the metropolis. His was only one growth sector in the flourishing economy of crime. Poachers in the royal forests were often well-organized, systematic suppliers to the London market. The smugglers of the south and east coasts pursued market principles and economies of scale, again with the frequent co-operation of officials and the public at large. The authorities made somewhat

The politics of Robinocracy. Political cartoons of the Walpole era were crude but effective. (*Above*): Walpole (with wand) and Queen Caroline are shown using a magical potion to control the irascible George II, in the guise of satyr. (*Right*): The Broad Bottom or coalition ministry which succeeded Walpole shows what it thinks of pledges to reduce taxation and crush corruption. The prints incidentally reveal the limited development of personal caricature at this time; neither Walpole in the print above nor Sir John Hynde Cotton, the Tory leader in the centre of the print on the right, display anything like a physical resemblance to their subjects.

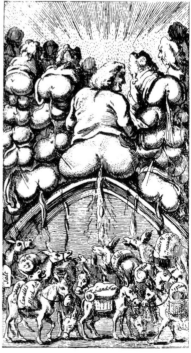

desperate attempts to combat these threats. Wild was brought to justice on a technicality. His execution in 1725 was to ensure his place in popular mythology. The poachers of Windsor Forest and elsewhere were the subject of new legislation, the draconian Black Act of 1723. They have had to wait until the twentieth century to achieve the status of folk-heroes, in their case bestowed by historians intent on treating them as authentic representatives of a popular culture. The smugglers seemed to flourish almost in proportion to the government's efforts to suppress them; at their most active in the 1730s they were capable of mounting pitched battles with George II's dragoons in their heroic service to a consumer society.

For this was what was emerging in early Hanoverian England. In this respect the South Sea Bubble is best seen not as the grand finale of post-Revolution England, but rather as a spectacular curtain-raiser to the prosperity, vulgarity, and commercialism of the mid-eighteenth century. The theatrical metaphor is peculiarly appropriate, for the period has a special significance in the history of the performing arts. The 1720s and 1730s witnessed a considerable expansion in the London theatre and an increasingly political role for it. Until the court took action to obtain extensive powers of censorship in 1737 it was the forum, along with the press generally, for a mounting campaign of criticism of the kind of society which seemed to have emerged during and after the Bubble. Nothing expressed such criticism more effectively than John Gay's *Beggar's Opera*, the great success of 1728. Whether the opera was actually intended as a political satire is uncertain, but it is significant of the contemporary climate of opinion that it was instantly accepted as such. Gay's message fitted well into the prevailing concern with illusion and unreality. It clearly depicted the court of George II as a kind of thieves' kitchen; the morality of the ruling class was put on a par with that of the London underworld. It was a point which Fielding was to reinforce by means of his unflattering comparison of Jonathan Wild with Sir Robert Walpole. It also had closely matching themes in Pope's *Dunciad*, Swift's *Gulliver's Travels*, and Bolingbroke's *Craftsman*, all products of a remarkable decade of polemical satire. Many of its elements were familiar ones: the retreat into classicism, the appeal to country values, the attraction of the rural idyll, above all the incessant criticism of the supposedly synthetic, moneyed world of early eighteenth-century commercialism. In these respects the literary and journalistic invective of the Walpole era can be seen, indeed, as the final, most violent surge of a tide which had been flowing for many years. But in inspiration for the future, or constructive analysis of alternative possibilities, it was manifestly deficient.

When Gay's audience glimpsed in Macheath the very essence of Walpolian politics, they seized upon one of the most significant aspects of the period—the close connection, seen if not established, between the political character of the Hanoverian regime and the supposed ills of contemporary society. With a few exceptions (notably the cartoonist William Hogarth, who reserved most of his energies for satirizing manners and morals), the intellectual and artistic élite of London was remarkably unanimous in its view that Walpole was the arch-villain of the piece. His characteristic image was that of a *parvenu* Norfolk placeman, enriched by a career of systematic corruption (he had been prosecuted by the Tories for official peculation in 1712) and elevated to supreme power for his utter lack of principle and total submission to the views of the court. Before 1727, his brother-in-law, Lord Townshend, had shared both his power and his unpopularity. But the death of George I and the accession of a new king placed him clearly in the full glare of public attention. By his adroit management of George II and more especially Queen Caroline, Walpole elbowed out all rivals for power, including, in 1730, Townshend himself. As a result he soon achieved a lonely eminence such as none had enjoyed, perhaps, since Danby in the 1670s. His hegemony inevitably drew the full fire of Grub Street on his personal position. He was the Great Man, the English Colossus, the Man Mountain. He also appeared as the perfect representative of the politics of illusion—the Norfolk trickster, the Savoy Rareeshowman, Palinurus the magician, Merlin the wizard, the Screenmaster-General and so on. Both his mastery of the irascible and unpredictable George II and his control of a previously unmanageable Parliament were portrayed in countless broadsides and prints as the arts of a veritable political conjuror.

At the time and ever since, the true basis of Walpole's success has been traced to his skilful use of influence and even bribery. The stability which seems to mark the period and to separate it from the political chaos of earlier years can be viewed, on this reading, as the natural culmination of forces working in favour of the executive. The expansion of government as a result of the wars, especially the vast machinery created to operate the new financial system, plainly generated a considerable quantity of new patronage. Moreover, the overwhelming necessity for post-revolution governments to obtain a working majority in the Commons provided a strong incentive to use this patronage for the purposes of parliamentary management. Hence the emergence of a much larger, much more disciplined Court and Treasury party, capable of bridging the ancient gap between Crown and Commons and inaugurating a new era of harmony between executive and legislature. It is an attractive theory, but not all the premisses are secure and not all the conclusions inescapable. Walpole's principles of management were far from novel. At least since the reign of Charles II, they had been employed by successive ministers to maintain a substantial court party in the House of Commons. Placemanship and careerism, not to say widespread evidence of corruption, had marked the reign of Anne as much as that of her successors. In some respects, indeed, the peaceful years of Walpole's ministry reduced the amount of patronage available. It is true enough that both Walpole himself and his effective successor Henry Pelham were adroit managers, and that both welded the court party into an exceptionally efficient instrument of control. But it needed more than patronage to create the classical parliamentary system of Georgian England.

This is not to deny Walpole's own inimitable talents. As a courtier he was without compare. His manipulation of the queen and (partly through her) of the king was a consummate mixture of flattery, cajolery, and bullying, brilliantly described in the memoirs of Lord Hervey, whose intimacy with Queen Caroline gave him ample opportunity to witness it. But winning courtiers were nothing new. What was more striking was the unusual combination of gifts which permitted him to handle MPs with equal skill. His decision to remain in the House of Commons as first minister was quite critical in this respect. Where previous ministers had traditionally departed to the Lords Walpole made a point of remaining in the chamber which ultimately controlled the purse-strings of government. As a debater he was somewhat crude (not necessarily a disadvantage), skilled, and extremely effective. As a conciliator, his capacity for ascertaining and implementing the views of the typical country gentleman was outstanding. But most important of all were his policies, which differed profoundly from the partisan programme of his old Whig colleagues. His desire to avoid exacerbating ancient animosities was particularly marked in his treatment of the Church. With the assistance of Indemnity Acts the Dissenters were left to enjoy their freedom of worship and even some measure of local power. But there was no serious attempt to break the Anglican monopoly in principle, and the repeal of the Test and Corporation Acts had to wait another hundred years.

Nor was there any serious talk of wholesale changes elsewhere, in the corporations, the universities, or indeed in Parliament itself. The new Whig policy of peace with France became under Walpole a policy of peace with everyone, carrying with it the priceless advantage of low taxation. In theory the Whig supremacy continued unabated. In practice Walpole subtly transformed the basis of the Hanoverian regime. The politics of coercion gave way to those of consensus; the objective of an exclusive oligarchy was replaced by the uninspiring but solid appeal of a ruling coalition open to anyone prepared to pay lip-service to undefined 'Revolution principles'.

Even without Walpole the Hanoverian regime would eventually have had an important impact on the pattern of politics. For simply in terms of corruption it was not the novelty of Walpole's management which counted, but rather the extent to which patronage was channelled in one direction. Before 1714, uncertain or inconsistent policies on the part of the court had made the calculations of placemen and patrons exceedingly difficult. From the boroughmonger at the apex of the electoral pyramid to the humble exciseman or common councillor at its base, it was far from clear where the means to profit and power lay. Much of the instability of party politics under Queen Anne arose from the resulting oscillations. After 1715 this problem was resolved for more than a generation by one simple and central fact of public life. Both George I and George II objected to the inclusion of Tories in their ministries, and with the exception of the short-lived Broad Bottom Administration in 1743, a product of the instability which followed Walpole's fall, the Tory party remained in the wilderness for more than forty years. Paradoxically, this proscription made ministerial stability more secure. Court Tories were more determinedly courtiers than they were Tories, and the prospect of permanent exclusion from place and profit was more than many could bear. Moreover, Walpole's form of Whiggism was exceptionally undemanding and there were many whose families had previously sided with the Tories who found little difficulty in subscribing to the new Whig principles. This particularly was the case with those who from interest or instinct gravitated naturally towards the politics of courts. By the 1730s the close boroughs of Cornwall, divided between Whigs and Tories at the beginning of the century, were dependable Whig preserves. In the Lords only a handful of Tory peers continued loyal to their friends in the Commons, though in 1712 Harley had achieved a Tory majority there. The change was not sudden or spectacular but it was steady and sustained, and some of the most important political names of the eighteenth century were part of it, including both the Pitt and the Fox families.

The stability of the political scene under Walpole and Pelham was unquestionably a major achievement of the Hanoverian system; but it is important not to exaggerate its extent. Politics in George II's reign did not descend into the torpor with which they are often associated. For the price of Hanoverian identification with Whiggism, albeit a somewhat watery Whiggism, was the permanent alienation of the die-hard 'country' Tory families. These families, though they rarely produced politicians of the first rank, maintained a certain resilience in opposition and provided an important focus for other potentially hostile elements. They made life difficult and unpleasant for those of their comrades who did defect; for example, when one of their aristocratic leaders, Earl Gower, joined Henry Pelham, the result at the general election of 1747 was rioting of almost unparalleled ferocity in Gower's home county of Staffordshire. In the counties, indeed, the Tories had their heartland. Among the forty-shilling freeholders of the county electorates, particularly in the Midlands, the west country, and Wales, they received consistent and even increasing support. Elsewhere they were influential if not dominating. The Toryism of the Church was bound to be diluted by the persistent drip of Whig jobbery, but one of the great seminaries of the Church, the university of Oxford, remained loyal to the Anglican gentry, and there was sufficient ecclesiastical patronage in the hands of the Tory families to maintain a powerful interest. In substantial cities there were also promising reservoirs of potential opposition to the regime. In London, Bristol, Norwich, and Newcastle, for instance, there was a long tradition of popular participation in politics, and much combustible material for Tory incendiaries. The Walpole system was too widely based to be considered a narrow oligarchy, but while a significant portion of the landed and clerical classes and a large body of middle- and lower-class opinion in the towns opposed it, the stability of the age could be more apparent than real.

Naturally enough, the conditions for genuine crisis were created only when the regime itself was divided. By the early 1730s Walpole was faced by a dangerous alliance of rivals at court. Their opportunity came with his celebrated attempt to extend the excise system, a project which was financially sound but which awakened the deepest and most violent antipathy among those numerous Englishmen who detested new taxes and feared the expansion of the government's bureaucracy. Only Walpole's readiness to withdraw his scheme in 1733 and the solid support of George II against his court rivals saved his administration; even so, the general election of 1734 produced a widespread reaction against him and a severely reduced majority in the House of Commons. An even more serious situation arose four years later. The powerful out-of-doors agitation which demanded an aggressive stance towards the Spanish Empire in 1738 and 1739 was all the more dangerous because it had support from Frederick Prince of Wales. The consequent alliance of alienated Tories, discontented Whigs, hostile business men, popular politicians, and the heir to the throne was dangerous indeed and eventually it was not only to force Walpole into a war which he profoundly disliked, but even to bring him down. The problem of the reversionary interest was particularly alarming; it was, until Frederick's death in 1751, to pose Pelham the same problems which it posed Walpole.

Even without these internal strains, the Whig supremacy faced considerable opposition. The Jacobite threat was probably exaggerated; it may be doubted whether many of those who toasted 'the king over the water' would actually have risked either their property or their lives for the House of Stuart. None the less, the more committed among them had some encouragement. The War of Austrian Succession (1740–8) found Britain involved, not merely against Spain overseas, but against a powerful Bourbon coalition on the Continent. In that war George II seemed primarily concerned to protect his beloved electorate; the consequent clash with domestic interests, and above all the unpopularity of investing British money and British blood in Germany and the Netherlands, gave patriot politicians ample ammunition for attacks on the regime. Walpole had predicted long before that warfare would mean a struggle for the English succession on English soil, and so it proved. When the Jacobite invasion came in 1745, it revealed the full extent of the danger to the Hanoverian dynasty. By European standards, the British standing army was tiny; even the small and ill-assorted force which the Young Pretender brought right into the heart of the English Midlands in December 1745 plainly stretched the defenders to the limit. An effective militia, without Tory support, had long since been abandoned; many of the country gentry offered at best sullen neutrality. The ferocious terror which was deployed against the Scottish Highlanders after the Jacobite army had been pushed back and finally crushed at Culloden was a measure of the alarm and even panic which had gripped the authorities in London. In these respects, as in others, the crisis of 1745 provides a useful corrective to excessively bland portrayals of the essential complacency of the Whig system. The customary picture of political apathy and aristocratic elegance can be a misleading one. It hardly fits the ragged but bloody progress of the rebels in 1745, nor do the relatively sedate years of the early 1750s altogether bear it out.

Pelham, for example, whose adroit management had steered his country safely if somewhat ignominiously out of the war and whose financial acumen did much to put the National Debt on a more secure basis thereafter, proved capable of misjudging the political climate. His Jew Bill of 1753, designed to soften the civil disabilities of the Jewish community in Britain, provoked a torrent of high-church hostility and intolerance and compelled him to repeal the offending measure before he could be punished for it in the general election of 1754. Again, the Jacobite alarms and excursions were far from over. As late as 1753 London was regaled with the spectacle of a Jacobite rebel being publicly hanged; in some respects, no doubt, politics in the eighteenth century was more polite, but it was not invariably so.

Industry and Idleness

The death throes of Jacobitism coincided chronologically with the passing away of pre-industrial society, for conventional accounts of the immense economic growth and change described as the Industrial Revolution locate its birth firmly in the mid-eighteenth century. Yet the period which in retrospect seems to have provided the platform for industrial take-off was widely regarded at the time as one of worrying recession, and continues to present problems of evaluation. In the 1730s and 1740s agricultural prices were exceptionally low; some important manufacturing regions, particularly the old textile centres, suffered serious unemployment and unrest. But there were also more promising developments. Low food prices permitted higher spending on consumer goods and thereby encouraged the newer industries, particularly in the Midlands. If agriculture was frequently depressed by these prices it was also stimulated by them, in East Anglia for example, to increase production. The improved techniques of mixed farming often associated with the age of 'Turnip' Townshend do not belong exclusively to this period, but their importance was certainly more widely appreciated. In other sectors there was very marked advance. For instance, the 1730s witnessed one of the most striking developments in the history of transport—the construction of a nation-

Middle-class morality. The concluding prints in one of Hogarth's
most famous series, 'Industry and Idlesness'. (*Above*): The climax
of the industrious apprentice's career; the puritan virtues
of thrift, hard work, and honest dealing are rewarded with the
Lord Mayoralty of London. (*Below*): His imprudent cousin, feckless,
idle, and immoral, is conducted to his execution; a Methodist,
reading from a volume hearing the name 'Westley' exhorts him to repent.

wide turnpike system. Before 1730, only a handful of turnpike trusts had been established. Most main roads, including the Great North Road beyond Northamptonshire and almost the whole of the Great West Road, depended for their maintenance on those unfortunate parishes which happened to lie in the immediate vicinity. The roads of early Georgian England, subjected to the immense strain of rapidly-growing passenger traffic and ever more burdensome freight services between major centres of consumption, were rightly considered a national disgrace. Turnpike trusts were a neat, if not always popular, solution, which permitted the injection of substantial sums of locally raised capital into repair and maintenance, on the security of a carefully graduated system of tolls. The heyday of the trusts lay in the four middle decades of the century. They testified strongly to the vitality of the provinces, with a large proportion of the new roads in the north and in the West Midlands; by 1770, when the canals were beginning to offer stiff competition for freight, they offered a genuinely national network of relatively efficient transport. The effect on journey times was dramatic. Major provincial centres such as York, Manchester, and Exeter were well over three days' travel from London in the 1720s; by 1780 they could be reached in not much more than twenty-four hours. Significantly these reductions, which applied to almost all important routes, seem to have stretched contemporary transport technology to the limit; they were subject to little further improvement until about 1820, when Macadam and Telford were to achieve further striking savings.

The development of the turnpikes would not have been possible without a great expansion of inland consumption, trade, and capital. But the internal growth implied in these years was more than matched by expansion overseas. Again contemporary appearances could be misleading. Patriot politicians continued to hold before the public an essentially old-fashioned view of empire. Colonies still tended to be seen primarily as valuable sources of raw materials, as dumping grounds for surplus population, or as means of adding to the nation's stock of bullion. The jewels in the imperial crown were the West Indies, with their sugar plantations; the Anglo-Spanish War of 1739, like its predecessors, was seen as a means of breaking into the eldorado of South America, with enticing prospects of gold, silver, and tropical products. Yet in retrospect it is clear that Britain's overseas trade was being recast in the direction of a quite new kind of empire. The dynamic export markets lay

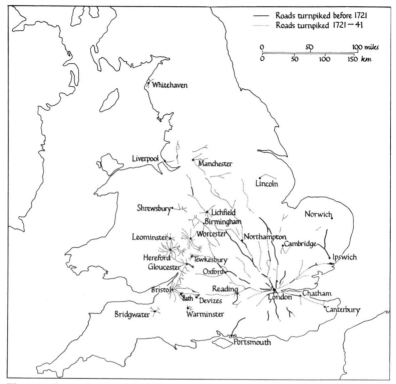

Roads turnpiked before 1721
Roads turnpiked 1721—41

The turnpike road network in 1741

increasingly outside Europe, notably in North America. Textiles, the traditional staple, benefited by this reduction, but the growth was still more marked in the newer manufacturing sectors associated particularly with the metal industries, in the production of household commodities, tools, weapons, and all kinds of utensils—in short in the vastly expanding demand for 'Birmingham goods'.

Mercantilist theories were capable of adaptation to accommodate the new trends but it took a time for the process to register clearly with contemporaries. By the 1750s, the full importance of the thirteen American colonies was beginning to be appreciated, and the eyes of businessmen and administrators alike were beginning to turn towards competition with France for dominance of the North Atlantic world. The changing emphasis also had important implications in domestic terms. The growth of

The turnpike road network in 1770

Georgian London was rapid, and its place as the greatest and most dynamic city in the Western world was already secure. But the fact was that in strictly comparative terms London was less important. A large share of the new trade in the Americas went to new or growing ports in the west, notably Liverpool, Bristol, Glasgow, and for a short but spectacular burst of commercial activity, Whitehaven. The industrial hinterland of these ports, the Severn Valley and West Midlands, the Yorkshire and Lancashire regions, and the west of Scotland, were decisively shifting the industrial base of the country away from the south, east, and west, towards the north and Midlands.

This shift is clearly seen in the demographic trends of the period. After the disasters of the 1720s, population had started growing again, albeit on a very gently rising plateau in the 1730s. The abortive Census proposed in 1750, had it been conducted, would probably have identified a total of about 5.8 million, half a million more than twenty years previously. By 1770 it stood at about 6.4 million, and by 1790 it was approaching 8 million. By nineteenth-century standards this was not a very impressive rate of growth. None the less it represented the crucial turning-point in modern demographic history. Much the same could be said of industrial and urban growth generally. There was no shortage of important innovations and new enterprises in the late seventeenth and early eighteenth centuries. But between the age of Abraham Darby and the age of Josiah Wedgwood there lay a world of difference. In this respect, the mid-century was again a watershed. The familiar giants of the early industrial revolution, Boulton and Watt, Garbett, Arkwright, Wedgwood himself, made their mark on the national consciousness in the 1760s and 1770s, and it was at the time of the Seven Years War, in the early 1760s, that the full excitement of what was occurring for instance at Birmingham and Manchester began to register. Urban improvement itself reflected the economic growth and the widespread interest in it. Contemporaries who could remember the reign of Queen Anne and who were to live on into the last quarter of the eighteenth century cited the 1760s and 1770s as a time of extraordinary change and improvement in the material life of the cities, and also to some extent of the smaller towns. The emphasis was always on space, hygiene, and order. The expanding towns of Manchester and Glasgow were much admired by visitors for their spacious squares, and neat rows of houses and warehouses. By comparison, the cluttered townscape of the older centres, with its narrow streets and timber and thatch housing, seemed outdated and even barbarous. No town with civic self-respect neglected the chance to obtain parliamentary authority for an improvement commission, equipped with extensive powers of rebuilding. Many of the better-preserved Georgian towns of today owe their character to this period of urban redevelopment. Perhaps the most spectacular example of imaginative town-planning occurred north of the border; Edinburgh's New Town continues to testify to the vigour of the City fathers in this respect. The capital of South Britain was not far behind. In a symbolic as well as practical act of modernization, the City of London's medieval gates were demolished in 1761. One of them, Ludgate, had been confidently restored and embellished, with further centuries of service in mind, less than thirty years previously. In nearby Westminster the biggest single project of urban redevelopment was begun at almost the same time in 1762. The Westminster Paving Commissioners and their collaborators in individual parishes were to transform the face of a vast area of the metropolis. Sewers and water-mains were extensively laid or redesigned. Streets and pedestrian walks were cobbled and paved, many for the first time. Squares were cleared, restored, and adorned with a variety of statuary and flora. Houses were systematically numbered; the old signs, colourful, but cumbersome and even dangerous to passers-by, were cleared away. By the 1780s the physical appearance of the capital, with the exception of its slums, was a source of pride to its inhabitants, and of wonder to its visitors, particularly foreigners.

Change was not restricted to cities and towns. Village architecture changed more gradually in most cases, but on the land itself new patterns were emerging. The most celebrated symptoms of the agricultural revolution, the parliamentary enclosure acts, were heavily concentrated in the second half of the eighteenth century. Their economic impact can be exaggerated, for they were statistically less significant than the relatively silent non-parliamentary enclosure which had been proceeding for decades and even centuries; moreover they were principally a feature of the regional belt running south and west from Yorkshire to Gloucestershire. But as pointers to the profitability of agriculture on marginal or convertible land, they are powerful evidence, and in their impact on the landscape they deeply impressed contemporaries. By the time of Adam Smith's *Wealth of Nations*, published in 1776, they suggested a confidence amounting almost to complacency about the continuance of economic growth. Curiously Smith himself did not altogether share this confidence. But Smith was an academic, his work was essentially one of theory rather than practical observation, and much of it had been conceived before the more spectacular developments of the 1760s and 1770s. His countryman John Campbell, whose *Political Survey* (1774) was an unashamed panegyric of Britain's economic progress, is in this respect a surer guide.

The gathering pace of material growth had an inevitable impact on the character of English society. To some extent the results were in line with the trends suggested by commercial diversification and the general advance of capitalism in preceding periods. In terms of social structure, therefore, the principal effect was, so to speak, to stretch the social hierarchy. Because wealth was distributed so unevenly, and because the levels and nature of taxation did so little to redistribute that wealth, real living standards rose much more dramatically in the middle and at the top of the social scale than at the bottom. In principle, this was by no means new. For example, the development of agriculture in the course of the sixteenth and seventeenth centuries had already noticeably altered the structure of the typical rural community. Enclosure, engrossing, improvement in general were gradually turning village society, characterized by the small property-owner, the freeholder or yeoman beloved of enthusiasts for Old England, into something quite new. Substantial capitalist farmers, frequently tenants of gentry landlords rather than landowners themselves, were coming to dominate an agrarian world in which all below them were increasingly reduced to landless labourers. The process has sometimes been exaggerated, for its actual incidence depended heavily on local conditions. But it certainly speeded up during the eighteenth century, and, most importantly, had a close counterpart in the development of industrial and urban society.

In this sense at least eighteenth-century England was growing into a more polarized society. Worse, the damaging consequen-

Wedgwood immortalized. Josiah Wedgwood's business skill, industrial techniques, and flair for marketing made him the prince of porcelain makers, and a fitting representative of provincial, bourgeois England in the 1770s and 1780s; here he is modelled (1782) by William Hackwood for one of his own medallions.

ces of polarization were far more apparent. Increased mobility, not to say the large contemporary improvement in literacy and communications generally, made worrying comparisons of rich and poor ever more obvious. The extravagant life-style of a ruling élite which seemed to live in a blaze of conspicuous consumption, and also the more modest but cumulatively more influential rise in middle-class standards of living, made the inequalities of a highly commercial, cash-based economy glaringly plain. The *malaise*, if it was a *malaise*, was at its most conspicuous in the capital. Conditions in London, with its relative shortage of well-established social restraints and conventions, its constant tendency to throw the wretchedly poor into close, but profitless, contact with the comfortably bourgeois and even the immensely rich, inevitably gave rise to moral outrage and social criticism of the kind which lives on in Fielding and Hogarth.

How much of the concern reflected an actual worsening of living conditions, it is difficult to judge. Before 1750, very low food prices, combined with the wage stability of a relatively static population, probably increased the real earnings of the poor. The fearful problems arising from the Londoner's thirst for gin—and the less damaging but at the time equally criticized liking of the poorer sort for tea—suggest that at least there was no shortage of disposable income at this time. After the mid-century, however, conditions seem to have deteriorated for many. A return to the older cycle of indifferent and even deficient harvests, together with the episodic slumps and unemployment characteristic of industrial economies, made life at the bottom of the heap a hazardous and harrowing business. Moreover, rapid population growth together with mechanical innovation helped to keep wages relatively low, and ensured that the advantages of industrial expansion were not necessarily shared with the humbler members of an emerging proletariat.

The eighteenth century was more sensitive to social problems than it has sometimes seemed, though it had no easy or comprehensive answers. The poor themselves fought back, mainly with traditional weapons in defence of an embattled economic order. Against dearth and high prices, they appealed to ancient laws restricting middlemen and monopolies. Against wage-cutting and the introduction of machinery, they organized combinations to defeat their masters, and clubs to provide an element of social insurance. In extremity, they rebelled and rioted with regularity and enthusiasm. This was a losing battle, although they were not without their victories. The landed gentry had some sympathy with popular resentment of the activities of moneyed and mercantile entrepreneurs. But the growth of a specialized market for the products of an improving agriculture was as essential to the landlord as to the provisions merchant. Similarly with the antiquated machinery of industrial relations: attempts to enforce the old apprenticeship laws were ineffective against the joint efforts of capitalist manufacturers and unskilled labourers to cheat them. A corporation which succeeded in operating such restrictive practices merely ensured that it did not share in new investment and industry. Associations received even shorter shrift. The friendly clubs, intended purely to provide pensions and sickness benefits, were encouraged by the upper orders. But combinations (or trade unions), even when directed against the more manifest injustices of eighteenth-century employers, such as the use of truck in the west-country clothing industry, were frequently repressed. Where they sometimes succeeded, as in the London tailoring trade, or in the royal dockyards, it was a tribute to the determination of well-established industrial groups. In most of the new industries the manufacturer swept all before him.

The most extreme manifestation of lower-class discontent was in some respects the most tolerated, no doubt because it was seen by paternalistic rulers as a necessary if regrettable safety valve. The measures used to suppress riots were rarely excessive, and punishment was used in an exemplary way on a small number of those involved. Even then, it was often surprisingly light if the provocation seemed extreme and there were no serious implications. Election riots, indeed, were regarded for most of the period as largely unavoidable; in a tumultuous town such as Coventry, with a large electorate and active involvement by those who were not even electors, they were a predictable feature of every election. The recurrent food riots associated with periods of dearth like the mid-1750s and the mid-1760s were also treated as a more or less necessary, if unwelcome, aspect of country life. Within certain limits, there was a wide tolerance in such matters. For instance, the fury of the Spitalfields silk weavers in London in 1765 (when it was believed that the duke of Bedford had worsened their plight by his support for the importation of French silks) brought about something like a full-scale siege of Bedford House. The riots were serious enough to warrant the use of troops, yet even polite London society saw nothing incongruous in treating them as an interesting diversion, worthy of personal inspection from the sidelines. Persistence, of course, was liable to lead to sterner consequences. Thus, the initial riots against turnpikes in the 1730s were treated with relative good humour, and even a hint of encouragement from some among the propertied classes who resented tolls as much as their lowlier compatriots. But exemplary sentences inevitably followed. Moreover, from the 1760s there were hints of a changing attitude towards popular disturbances. John Wilkes's protracted and controversial campaign in defence of electoral rights and the freedom of the press produced violent demonstrations on the streets. The consequent clashes with authority in the name of 'Wilkes and Liberty' had too many political implications to be viewed with complacency. The anti-papist Gordon riots of 1780, which for the first time produced a real state of terror in London, marked a further important stage in this process. It needed only the French Revolution in the following decade to complete the destruction of the old tolerance and to install the popular riot among the bugbears of the propertied mind.

There were no permanent solutions to the problems engendered by the quantitative growth and qualitative impoverishment of the lowest sort. Poor relief in the eighteenth century continued to be operated on the basis of the Elizabethan Poor Law and the 1662 Act of Settlements. At their worst, these would have put the life of a poor labourer and his family on a par with or perhaps below that of an American slave or a Russian serf. Poor relief might involve the barest minimum of subsistence dependent on ungenerous neighbours, or sojourn in a poor house with consequent exposure to a ruthless master who drew his income from the systematic exploitation of those in his charge. The laws of settlement provided for compulsory residence in the parish of birth for those not occupying a house worth at least £10 per annum, a not insubstantial sum. In practice, these draconian regulations were less forbidding. Poor relief was a major item in the expenditure of most parishes and by the late eighteenth century was already growing at an alarming rate. It frequently extended to regular outdoor relief and to some extent took account of the rising cost and the rising standard of living. The settlement laws were enforced only to a limited extent. Unhappily their chief victims were women, children, and the old, precisely those who were likely to be a burden on the parish to which they fled. But, even so, restrictions on movement by the second half of the century in reality were slight. The immense labour requirements of industry could hardly have been met if there had been any serious attempt to implement them.

Propertied people felt strongly about the poor in this as in other ages. But they felt still more strongly about crime. For a commercialized society provided ever more temptations, and ever more provocation by way of encouragement to lawlessness. The flashier forms of criminality, such as highway robbery, or the most sociologically interesting, such as offences against the game laws, have traditionally attracted most attention. But the vast majority of crime was one form or another of petty theft, an offence against propertied values which seemed to present a constantly growing threat, particularly in the urban areas. Against this tide of illegality, exaggerated no doubt, but real enough for all that, property in this period had few defences. Urban crime cried out for effective police forces offering a high chance of detection and conviction (if it did not cry out for kinder cures!). But a police force would have presented many dangers, not least its potential use in terms of political patronage. Moreover the continuing threat represented by any organized force at the command of government was taken very seriously. Few would have seen the point in keeping a standing army to the minimum while permitting a more novel and no less sinister force to spring up in its stead. In consequence, with few and partial exceptions, for example the efforts of the Fielding brothers in London, the period witnessed no significant improvement in this area. Rather, the authorities were driven back on sheer deterrence, the threat of transportation or death even for relatively insignificant offences. This was the period of the proliferation of capital sentences for minor crimes, against which early nineteenth-century reformers were to fulminate. It was in fact the only logical means to stem the flow of crimes against property. Even so it proved self-defeating. For juries would not convict and judges would not condemn in any but the clearest cases. The statistics of conviction are small compared with the actual numbers of offences. Even when the death sentence had been pronounced there was a strong chance of a reprieve at the request of the judge, or at the behest of a highly-placed patron. In this way, the processes of justice inevitably sank into the general welter of inconsistent policy and political manipulation which marked the period.

If the poor looked to the State in vain, they looked to the Church with but faint hope. The Church of the eighteenth century has a poor reputation for what would today be called social policy. Entrenched as it was in the patronage structure of the Georgian world, it could hardly be expected to offer a systematic challenge to prevailing attitudes. But it does not altogether deserve its reputation. The sheer volume of eighteenth-century charity is sometimes forgotten. No doubt this is largely because it was overwhelmingly voluntary, and

The shadow of the gallows. Lord Ferrers, a peer of the realm convicted of murder, suffers the fate of common criminals: public execution at Tyburn and anatomical dissection in the cause of medical science and deterrent example.

informal. Without the official or state papers which accompany the exercise of charity in a later or even an earlier age it can easily vanish from sight. Yet in terms of the endowment and maintenance of a host of institutions for education, health, and recreation the record is a striking one. It was marked by a frequently patronizing attitude, and motivated in part by an anxiety to keep at bay the social and political threat of the dispossessed. But this is not uncharacteristic of other periods, and the sheer quantity remains surprising. Subscription and association—the central features of this process—built schools, endowed hospitals, established poor houses, supervised benefit societies. In this the Church, or rather the churches, were heavily involved. Not the least active was a class reviled by later reformers, the dignitaries of the Anglican Establishment—its bishops, archdeacons, deans, and canons.

There was, however, a paradox about the Church's position in the eighteenth century. The influence of 'natural' religion in the early part of the century had produced a growing emphasis on works rather than faith. Christians were those who behaved like Christians, and charity was the most obvious expression of religious devotion. But rational religion, however benevolent, did not offer much spiritual consolation to those who lacked the education or the intellect to be rational. The spiritual energy of all the main churches manifestly wilted under the impact of latitudinarian tendencies. Mainstream Dissent, tortured by the theological tensions which arose from the deist challenge to the doctrine of the Trinity, visibly declined as a force in popular life and retreated for the moment at least to its traditional support among the urban middle class. The Church in the rural areas continued its somewhat erratic work, dependent as ever on the residence and personal commitment of a portion of its clergy. In the towns it was all too prone to withdraw, or to appeal, like Dissenters, to the polite middle-class congregations who could afford to supplement the poor town livings and to beautify or rebuild churches.

It was left to that rebellious daughter of the Church, the Methodist movement, to offer the poor recompense in the next world for their sufferings in this. The many facets and connections of Wesleyan Methodism make it difficult to generalize about its importance. John Wesley himself was an Oxford don of high-church views and unenlightened politics. Yet to many his influence seemed to express something of the Puritan spirit of seventeenth-century religion. His own spiritual journey was tempestuous and marked by the highest degree of what could easily be seen as recklessness and self-will. But the organization and discipline which he bestowed on his followers verged on despotism. In theological terms, Wesley was an Arminian; but Calvinism exercised a far-reaching effect on the Methodist movement. Indeed Wesley was preceded in the field by Calvinists such as Griffith Jones and Howell Harris in Wales, and George Whitefield in England. To their enemies, all such men seemed dangerous, even seditious characters. Field-preaching could be seen as an open attack on the parish clergy's monopoly of the pulpit; from the vantage point of lay authority, Wesley's readiness to preach his saving message to all ranks and degrees made squires and shires shake. Yet his political views were positively authoritarian, and he offered no challenge to social order. Through his attitudes and those of his followers ran only one concern: the total availability of the evangelist's salvation to all, above all to the poor, to the outcast communities of mining and manufacturing England, neglected by more fashionable divines. It is possible to exaggerate his achievement, for at his death there can hardly have been more than about seventy to eighty thousand committed Methodists. Yet the alarm and controversy to which his turbulent life and travels gave rise suggests the extent of his impact on Georgian society. Methodists were accused of an infinity of sins, some of them mutually incompatible. Their preachers were both papists and Puritans, Jacobites and republicans; they ravished wives or influenced them to give up all fleshly pleasures; they coveted other men's goods or denied them the use of worldly possessions. The sheer multiplicity of the charges against Methodism makes it obvious that Wesley touched a tender spot on the contemporary conscience and exposed an embarrassing deficiency in its pattern of beliefs.

The Making of Middle England

The impression confirmed by the early history of the Methodist movement is very much one of considerable social strains and problems. But it is possible to over-colour the general picture. For one thing it was widely believed at the time that English society avoided the worst of extremes. Foreigners were struck by the flexibility and cohesion of the English social fabric, not by its tensions and rigidities. A succession of French visitors, from Voltaire to the Abbé Grosley, testified in print to the lack of 'caste' in this country, and especially to the ease with which

Ladies at leisure. Satirists of the late eighteenth century were struck by the affluence and potential independence of women. John Collet's popular studies (*above and facing*) stress the unladylike nature of some ladies' activities.

individuals could move up and down the social ladder. In particular the absence of aristocratic privileges and advantages compared with the Continent earned their applause. Peers might be tried by the House of Lords, but when they went to the gallows they suffered publicly like common criminals. When Lord Ferrers was executed for murdering his servant in 1760 his fate was widely construed as clear evidence that in crime and in death alike the law of England made no distinctions. In a matter of less moment but perhaps no less significance, Grosley was astonished to discover that the tolls on the new turnpikes were paid regardless of rank and without remission for noblemen.

Moreover the degradation and dearth which threatened the lives of the urban poor seemed preferable by far to the conditions of French or German peasants. The English labourer (though it must be admitted that commentators usually meant the London labourer) seemed well paid, well fed and extraordinarily independent and articulate. Most important of all perhaps was the emphasis laid by foreigners on the flexible definition of the English gentleman. Anyone, it appeared, who chose to dress like a gentleman was treated like one. Middle-class, even lower-class Londoners aped the fashions, manners, and opinions of polite society. This, it seems clear, was the authentic mark of a society in which all social values, distinctions, and customs gave way before the sovereign power of cash. England was the outstanding example in eighteenth-century Europe of a plutocratic society.

The 'bon ton'. This cartoon of 1777 mocks the enthusiasm
of middle-class women for French fashions.

The nature of this plutocracy provides a crucial clue to the
social stability of the period. On the face of it there was little
evidence that the basic structure of property-ownership was
changing dramatically. There was no striking surge of bourgeois
capital into land, no great expropriation of the landed aristocracy
or gentry. The steady assimilation of small professional and
business families altered the precise make-up of the landed class
without significantly affecting its overall character. Higher up
the scale, the eighteenth century witnessed some strengthening
and consolidation of the great landowners. But land was only
one form of property and not necessarily the most important.
Even at the beginning of the century the primacy of land was
diminishing. Estimates of national income at the time of the
Glorious Revolution suggest that agriculture contributed nearly
a half of the total. But the proportion was changing; by 1780 it
was probably down to a third. In fact, the land itself was merely

part of the general commercialization of the English economy; in its exploitation and its improvement, it was increasingly treated exactly like an investment in stock, in trade, and in manufacturing. It was noticeable that, whereas temporary agrarian depressions had little significance for trade, the converse did not hold; commercial recessions had extremely grave implications for land prices. In the American War, when overseas trade suffered a disastrous slump, the effect was instantly seen on property values, with serious political consequences. If the landed classes had owned the greater part of non-landed property, the situation would have been very different. But they plainly did not, whatever their importance in certain sectors such as mining rights and government stocks. Movable goods in the form of industrial capital, personal wealth, and trading balances were overwhelmingly owned by the broad mass of the middle class. On them, primarily, depended the viability and growth of the national economy; and on them too depended the social flexibility and stability which were so much admired by foreigners.

The middle class or 'middling sort' was not, of course, a socially self-conscious or particularly coherent grouping. It remained diverse in point of both wealth and activity. A considerable distance stretched between the city bosses with great mercantile fortunes who ruled the capital, and the small tradesmen or craftsmen who represented the backbone of commercial England—the new 'nation of shopkeepers', a phrase often attributed to Napoleon at the end of the century but in fact used by Adam Smith considerably earlier. Nor was there necessarily much resemblance between the middling countryman, a substantial tenant farmer soon to be dignified perhaps by the title of gentleman farmer, and his urban counterparts, the business man, doctor, and lawyer, who throve on early industrial society. None the less, such men had much in common. Frequently self-made and always dependent on aggressive use of their talents, they were genuine 'capitalists' in terms of the investment of their labour and their profits in entrepreneurial activity, whether commercial or professional. Together they owned, controlled, or operated the most dynamic portions of the economy. Politically, their supremacy was rarely challenged in towns of any size, and even in many rural parishes they more nearly represented the ruling class than the lofty oligarchs and lordly magnates who seemed so important at Whitehall and Westminster.

Everywhere the dominant tone of this class, with its pragmatic attitudes and its frankly commercial logic, was discernible. Not

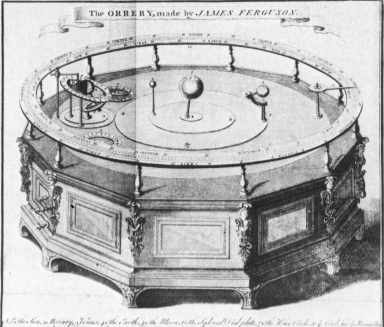

Science for the layman. (Above): A contemporary print displays
the orrery used by the scientific lecturer and writer James Ferguson
to demonstrate the movements of the planets. Ferguson's lectures
fascinated middle-class audiences in the 1750s, in the provinces
and metropolis alike. The painting of 'The Orrery'
(*facing*) is by Joseph Wright of Derby, an enthusiastic interpreter of
scientific subjects and one of the Lichfield circle of amateur scientists.

least was its influence apparent in education, a matter in which
the eighteenth century has acquired a wretched reputation.
Inspection of the great institutions of the Tudor and Stuart
academic world, the grammar schools and the universities, is not
reassuring in this respect. Grammar schools which continued
vigorously to fulfil their function of offering a scholarly education
to relatively humble children were few indeed. Most endowments proved inadequate to sustain the expenses or escape the
cupidity of those who controlled them. The clergy who taught in
them frequently did their best but rarely surmounted the
discouraging effects of low salaries and poor support. The
universities in England gave an impression of complacency and
sloth, particularly by comparison with their Scottish counter-

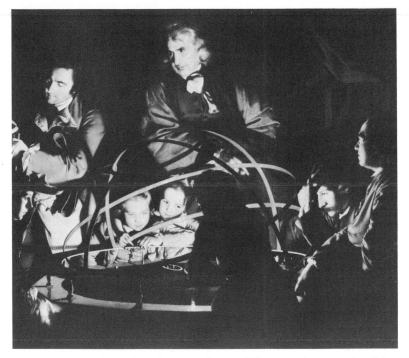

parts. North of the border, academic life was characterized by religious strife and even bigotry. But it also displayed signs of immense vigour on which the Scottish Enlightenment prospered. The Scottish contribution to the European achievement of the age in fields as diverse as moral philosophy, political economy, and medical science was substantial. The English universities fell far short by this yardstick. Their function was partly to train their clergy, partly to offer a broad education to the genteel and the wealthy. This they performed with more zest than they are generally allowed. The disciplined and innovative instruction offered at a new foundation like Hertford in Oxford, or the genuine progress of mathematical scholarship at Cambridge by no means confirm the impression given by Rowlandson prints or anti-clerical propaganda. Even so, they plainly did not meet the demands of the middle class.

But the fact was that they were not expected to. In default of the grammar schools and the universities, the characteristically middle-class devices of subscription and fees were bringing into existence a great mass of practical, progressive education designed to fit the sons of the middling sort to staff the professions and the world of business. These schools were often short-lived, and when they passed they left so little behind them that it was easy for censorious Victorians to assume that they had never existed. Even the greatest of the eighteenth-century schools, including dissenting academies like those at Northampton and Warrington, among the best of their kind, withered before very long. But in the meantime they offered exactly the basic, unpretentious education on which the business classes depended.

The result was emphatically a middle-class culture, with an unmistakably pragmatic tone. If there was an English Enlightenment it was perhaps in this sense, an enlightenment of the practical mind. The fascination of the mid-eighteenth century was neither with theological polemics nor with philosophical speculation, but rather with applied technology. The Society of Arts, founded in 1758, was an appropriate expression of this

The seaside. Rates for the social round at Margate, with a boarding-house menu, taken from *A Description of the Isle of Thanet, and Particularly of the Town of Margate,* 1763.

(68)

SUBSCRIPTIONS *and* RULES *for* Mitchener's Assembly-Room. *Margate* 1763.

	s.	d.
Subscriptions to the Room for the season to each Gentleman or Lady,	5	0
Dancing Assembly on *Monday* night, (Tea inclusive,) each Subscriber, Gentleman or Lady,	2	6
Each Non-subscriber,	5	0

CARD-ASSEMBLY, on *Thursday* night.

	s.	d.
Whist, &c. each table	6	0
Lottery-table	12	0
Each Non-subscriber for admission, (Tea inclusive,)	1	0

BREAKFASTING.

	s.	d.
To Subscribers	0	8
To Non-subscribers	1	0

TEA *in the* AFTERNOON.

	s.	d.
To Subscribers	0	6
To Non-subscribers	1	0

COFFEE-ROOM.

	s.	d.
Subscriptions for the Coffee-Room, to each Gentleman for news-papers, extra post, pens, and paper.	2	6

At

(69)

At the New-Inn, Margate, *a house I have long used, the prices of provisions, &c. are as follow :*

	s.	d.
Each person		
Bread, cheese, or butter	0	1
Welsh rabbit	0	2
Beef stakes, veal cutlets, mutton or pork chops	0	9
Veal or beef collops	1	0
Tripe boiled or fryed	0	9
Ditto in fricasée	1	0
Eggs and bacon	0	9
Cold meat	0	8
Servant breakfast, dinner, or supper	0	6
Breakfast, tea, coffee, &c.	0	8
Pigeon roasted or boiled	0	8
Ditto boiled with bacon and greens	1	0
Ditto stewed	1	0
Chicken or fowl roasted or boiled	2	0
Ditto broiled with mushroom sauce	2	6
Ditto white or brown fricasée	2	6
Ditto roasted with egg sauce	2	6
Ditto boiled with bacon and greens	3	0
Duck roasted	2	0
Ditto with onion sauce	2	6
Capon roasted or boiled	3	0
Turkey roasted with sauces, &c.	5	0
Ditto boiled with oyster or lemon sauce	5	0
Goose roasted with sauces, &c.	5	0
Wild duck and dressing	2	6
Teal and dressing	1	6
Woodcock and dressing	2	6
Eels and dressing, by the pound	1	6
Trout and dressing by the pound	2	0
Cray		

spirit. Perhaps its most controversial project during its early years was a scheme to bring fish from the coast to London by road, thereby breaking the monopoly of the Thames fish dealers, and dramatically lowering the price of a valuable and (it was stressed) a nutritious commodity. It was faintly bizarre, no doubt, but its object was pre-eminently practical. The Society of Arts was a great national concern, but it was only the most famous of many formal and informal, enduring and ephemeral, clubs and associations which fed on the interest in scientific or pseudo-scientific knowledge. Such interest was at least as enthusiastic in the provinces as in the metropolis. Again, the Lichfield circle associated with Erasmus Darwin and the Lunar Society were only the most celebrated of many amateur groups with very earnest attitudes. The stream of literature which they helped to generate also provides a rough index to the growth of popular interest in matters scientific. Even the monthly magazines, designed primarily with a view to entertainment, featured the myriad inventions and speculations of an age deeply committed to the exploration of the physical world.

Middle-class work and study required middle-class play and diversions. The eighteenth century will for ever be associated with the amusements of a fashionable oligarchical society, represented most notably in the prime of the first of the great spa towns. Yet Bath would have been a shadow of its Georgian self without its middle-class clientele. The enterprise of the Woods as developers and of 'Beau' Nash as the first master of ceremonies was dependent not merely on the names of the great but also on the money of the middling. For every nobleman reported as taking the waters or attending the Assembly, there had to be a host of those paying for a share in the genteel atmosphere which was created. In this respect, as in so many others, it was the constant fidelity of the middling sort to the fashions and habits of their social superiors which sustained the commercial viability of leisure and luxury while maintaining the impression of a dominant and patronizing aristocratic élite. Bath, in any case, was hardly unique. The spas were after all a regional as well as a national phenomenon, offering in the provinces a number of fair imitations of their more celebrated model. When Daniel Defoe toured England in the early 1720s he discovered many spa towns. Tunbridge, he noted with surprise, was a town in which 'company and diversion is the main business of the place'. But Tunbridge had several competitors around the capital: Epsom, Dulwich, and Sydenham Wells all provided attractive resorts for Londoners seeking country air and mineral salts. In the Peak

District, already a favourite area for the ancestor of the modern tourist, he found the demands of visitors outstripping the available accommodation at Buxton and Matlock. Buxton, especially, was to grow rapidly in the mid-eighteenth century, though by the 1780s its own rivalry with Tunbridge for second place to Bath was under pressure from a newcomer, Cheltenham.

Spa water, of course, was in limited supply, but there was no shortage of another valuable commodity, sea water. In this as in the case of the spas, the appropriate combination of health and recreation was provided by the co-operation of the medical profession, which hastened to testify to the inestimable benefits of salt water and sea air. Brighton was not developed to any extent until the 1790s. But the development of seaside resorts had begun long before. Dr Russell's *A Dissertation on the Use of Sea Water in the Diseases of the Glands*, published in 1749, was an important influence in this process. Weymouth, which made much of the high proportion of minerals in the waters of the English Channel, was already a flourishing resort by 1780. Margate and Ramsgate with easy access from London had established themselves even earlier, and offered more sophisticated and varied arrangements. Scarborough on the Yorkshire coast was equally advanced. The medical element in these developments was certainly important. But it is difficult not to see the essential impetus as deriving from more mundane social needs. Between fashionable society with its ritual divisions of the year and its court-orientated timetables, and the despised fairs and holidays of the lower sort, there was a considerable gap, a gap which the new resorts filled with immense success and profit. They were essentially middle-class, urban living transported temporarily to new surroundings, the bourgeois equivalent of the aristocrat's retreat to country-house life. Their underlying basis was the generally felt need for distinctively middle-class recreations. The use of fees or subscriptions ensured respectable company and a decently moneyed atmosphere. Particularly for women, in some ways the most obvious beneficiaries of the new affluence, such a flexible, yet protected environment was crucial. Long before the emergence of the resorts, its character had been fully displayed in what Defoe called the 'new fashion'd way of conversing by assemblies'. Assemblies, providing dancing, cards, tea-drinking, and general social mixing, were commonplace by the middle of the century. Even in many market towns they provided an invaluable focus for activities as businesslike as the marriage market, and as casual as country gossip. In the largest cities, spectacular displays

The seaside. An unusual early sketch of the attractions of Blackpool.

of civic pride could be involved; at Norwich the theatre and the assembly hall erected in the 1750s featured striking designs by the local architect, Thomas Ivory. They went up at much the same time as a magnificent new dissenting church, a not inappropriate demonstration of the social link between religion and recreation. Many of those who paid for their admission to the almost daily 'routs' in the Assembly also made their way on Sunday to the chapel.

To force all the cultural developments of a complex age into a single pattern might seem incautious. Yet there is little doubt that the dominating tone of the mid-Georgian arts closely corresponded to the needs of a large, wealthy, and pretentious middle class. There was no simple retreat from austere aristocratic classicism to bourgeois romanticism. Rather the classical tradition continued to be interpreted as it had been for generations since the Renaissance. But about the ubiquitous Adam fireplaces and Wedgwood pottery there was a distinctly new and even anti-aristocratic spirit. The triumphs of the Augustan arts had been the triumphs of an élite, intended primarily for the consumption of an élite. Order, structure, and form were the hallmarks of early eighteenth-century art and a sophisticated sense of their classical significance the key to interpreting them. The Horatian satires of a Pope, the Palladian designs of a Burlington, and the still essentially formal landscape gardening beloved of classicists such as William Kent, belonged to the same world. But twenty years later few pragmatic products of a middle-class education would have appreciated the linguistic nuances of a satire and fewer still would have understood or identified with the Venetian Renaissance. By contrast the cultural achievements of the mid-century required neither sophistication nor subtlety. The picturesque gardening publicized by William Shenstone, and still more the vogue for 'natural' landscaping exploited by 'Capability' Brown, represented a major break with the early eighteenth-century passion for classical imitation and allusion. This was also markedly true of the new literary developments. The specifically bourgeois nature of the novel, whether in its picaresque or puritanical form, needs little emphasis. Sometimes, as in Richardson's jaundiced portrayal of rakish aristocrats in *Pamela* and *Clarissa* it was almost painfully prominent. At other times, as in the adventure stories of Smollett and Fielding, it took the form of a moralistic interest in the social life of the lower and middling sort. In any event these trends came together and produced their most characteristic expression in the triumph of sentiment in the 1760s. Laurence Sterne's *Tristram Shandy*, for example, invaded the palace as well as the parlour, and appealed to the plutocrat as well

Professional art. Johann Zoffany's portrayal of William Hunter at the Royal Academy, *c.*1772. The serious purpose of the newly-founded Academy is clearly suggested in this representation of a lecture by one of London's most celebrated physicians. In the front row Sir Joshua Reynolds can be seen with his ear trumpet.

as the tradesman. But the widespread enthusiasm for the sentimental movement should not be allowed to obscure its significance as a vehicle of middle-class values and attitudes. Sentiment consummated in fantasy what the wealth of commercial England was bringing nearer in reality, the acquisition of gentility by a consumer society. Sentiment made 'natural' taste, the taste of the virtuous man, regardless of upbringing or breeding, the true criterion of gentility; it also boosted the domestic morality of the middle class with its stress on family life and its devotion to Calvinistic conceptions of virtue, against heroic but hierarchical notions of personal honour. After George II's death in 1760, the new king and queen were to prove altogether appropriate emblems of such ideals, giving to court society an air which can seem almost Victorian. In this, they faithfully reflected the mores of many of their subjects. Earlier middle classes had merely aped their social betters. Now there was, in theory at least, no need for aping them. Manners in this Brave New World needed no acquiring and a Man of Feeling, like the hero of Mackenzie's influential work of that name, was effectively classless.

If a middle-class culture was sentimental it was also marked by a certain insularity, tempered only by the anxiety of artists themselves to demonstrate their openness to external influences. But activities of intellectual trend-setters in this respect could be somewhat misleading. Sir Joshua Reynolds, the recognized maestro of English art in the new reign, consciously appealed to Continental models, and saw himself transmitting to a vulgar but expectant public superior traditions of European art. Yet in a way he embodied many of the new trends at home. For Reynolds, like his colleagues Hayman and Gainsborough, depended as much on a newly moneyed public as on more aristocratic patrons. In a way too, his influence neatly reflected both the national vitality and organized professionalism characteristic of the period. The emergence of the Royal Academy in 1768 saw at one level a representative association comparable to the professional bodies which were beginning to appear on behalf of doctors and lawyers. At another level it brought to a peak a vigorous native art such as Hogarth had heralded but never seen. Not that foreign influences were unimportant in this or in other fields of cultural endeavour. Angelica Kauffmann was the most sought-after decorator of fashionable London, Johann Zoffany one of its most successful protraitists. But neither played the part that foreigners had earlier in the century. There was no Verrio dominating the art of grand decoration, no Handel towering over

English musicians, no Rysbrack or Roubiliac leading the way in monumental sculpture. Instead, there were the Adams to embellish the Englishman's house, a Burney or Boyce to educate his ear, a Wilson to commemorate his passing.

The new cultural confidence was nowhere more marked than among the painters themselves. What had been most striking about Hogarth's self-conscious attempts to create a truly native tradition had been his isolation in this grand enterprise. What was striking about his successors of the English school was the ease with which they felt free to appropriate Continental techniques without a sense of inferiority or dependence. In this respect Joseph Wright of Derby, not the most praised but perhaps the most innovative of mid century artists, was also thoroughly representative. Appropriately he was a friend of Erasmus Darwin, grandfather of Charles and himself a distinguished physician, scientist, and even poet. Wright was at his best with his semi-educational studies of scientific experiments and discoveries. But he was also the skilled manipulator of light in ways which would not have shamed Caravaggio. Like everyone, Wright went to Italy, but after his major masterpieces not before; when he returned he seemed to many to have lost rather than gained inspiration.

The Politics of Protest

The social changes which made their mark on mid-Georgian England were profound, extensive, and of the utmost consequence for the future. But their immediate impact on the political structure, at a time when the power of prescription and force of custom were overriding, is difficult to assess. Superficially there were few changes in the character of politics around the middle of the century. The administrations of North (1770–82) and the younger Pitt (1783–1801) were to provoke comparisons in point of both technique and policy with those of Walpole and Pelham. Of great constitutional changes there were few indeed; the torrent of agitation and reform which threatened the *ancien régime* in the nineteenth century seems in retrospect an unconscionable time arriving. Yet appearances in this respect were deeply deceptive. The language, the objectives, even the mechanics of politics were all influenced by awareness of a large political nation which lay beyond the immediate world of Whitehall and Westminster. If nothing else the extent and bitterness of the polemical warfare which occurred in news-papers, prints, and pamphlets in the 1750s and 1760s would be adequate testimony to the vitality of public debate and the concern of politicians to engage in it. In this debate, one of the latter seemed to occupy a special place. The elder Pitt's reputation is such that, even after two centuries, it is difficult to give him the critical treatment which such an influential figure requires. Before 1754 Pitt's career had been far from an unqualified success. The younger son in a spendthrift and eccentric family, Pitt had joined and eventually married into one of the great Whig houses, that of Temple of Stowe. As a young man he made his political name as a patriot orator of fearsome rhetoric and imprudent vehemence. His anti-Hanoverian outbursts during the War of the Austrian Succession acquired widespread publicity and earned him useful popularity, but they rendered him almost permanently *persona non grata* with the king. When, in 1746, the Pelhams were able to offer him office it was on terms which provided profit without prospects. As Paymaster-General, Pitt was excluded from the making of high policy and effectively muzzled in parliamentary debate. It seemed yet another example of a patriot's progress, sacrificing principle to promotion. But Pitt's fortunes were dramatically changed by the events of the mid-1750s. The sudden death of Henry Pelham in 1754 seemed even at the time a watershed, indicated not least by the king's own observation on its significance: 'Now I shall have no more peace.' Pelham's successor was his brother, Newcastle, a shrewd, experienced minister, and by no means the ridiculous mediocrity portrayed by Whig legend. But in the Lords he found it difficult to exercise the controlling influence either of his brother or of Walpole. Pitt's principal rival in the Commons, Henry Fox, lacked the political courage or weight to replace Pelham. The 'old corps' of Whigs, the dominant force in Parliament since the Hanoverian accession, was almost without leadership. Their Tory opponents, by now increasingly restive under continuing proscription and no longer disposed to think seriously of a king over the water, also sought inspiration. Could not Pitt provide what both needed?

That he was able to do so owed much to circumstance, and in particular to the international situation. The War of Austrian Succession had identified major areas of conflict for the future without beginning to settle them. The principal focus overseas was no longer the fate of the Spanish Empire, but the worldwide conflict threatening between Britain and France, in a mercantilist age the most successful mercantilist powers. In North

Heroic death. Benjamin West's interpretation (1770) of the death of Wolfe (*above*) enjoyed an immense vogue, and was consciously exploited by J. S. Copley in a matching portrayal (1780) (*facing*) of the collapse of the elder Pitt when addressing the House of Lords on the subject of the American War in 1778. Pitt did not die for another six weeks but the dramatic possibilities of his last speech and the poignant comparison with Wolfe's fall at Quebec presented too good an opportunity to miss. The comparison was also employed by the poet William Cowper in his poem of 1785, *The Task.*

America, the French sought to forge a chain from Quebec to Louisiana, cutting off the English colonies. In the West Indies there was constant bickering over disputed sugar islands, as there was in West Africa over the trade in slaves and gum. In India the factiousness and feebleness of native princes combined with the rapacity of the French and English East India Companies to create a highly volatile situation. Everything pointed to a desperate and conclusive war for empire. When it came it began disastrously both for England and for Pitt's political rivals. In 1755–6, failure to deal the French navy a decisive blow in the Atlantic, and the loss of Minorca in the Mediterranean, if anything heightened by the ruthlessness with which the hapless Admiral Byng was sacrificed, left the old Whig regime discredited if not devastated. This was the making of Pitt, and perhaps of the First British Empire.

The ensuing years have taken their place in history as a period of exceptional importance and exceptional achievement. The

successes of the Seven Years War, which decisively defeated France in North America and India, and turned back the Bourbon threat elsewhere, represented a high point of imperial achievement and made Pitt the most gloriously successful war minister in British history. Moreover, his triumph in trouncing the 'old corps' politicians seemed to suggest a new kind of politician and a new kind of politics, neatly encapsulated in Dr Johnson's contrast between Walpole as a 'minister given by the king to the people', and Pitt as a 'minister given by the people to the king'. Yet Pitt made his way to power more by shrewd political judgement and sheer luck than by public acclaim. His supposedly popular support was engineered by his friends in the City of London and by his new-found Tory associates in the provinces. His first essay in power, the Pitt–Devonshire ministry of 1756–7, was weak and shortlived; his second, the coalition of 1757, was much more successful, thanks partly to a deal with Newcastle, partly to the support of the Prince of Wales, the future George III. This combination of the reversionary interest and the 'old corps' was as cynical an exercise in political manoeuvre as anything conceived by Pitt's predecessors and opponents; it corresponded closely with what Walpole had done in 1720 when he and Prince George (the later George II) had bullied and wheedled their way back to court.

Nor did the war quite present the unblemished record which

Pitt's admirers were to make of it. The fundamental strategy which Pitt pursued was completely at variance with the patriot programme which he had previously espoused. His commitment to an expensive alliance with Prussia and his generous deployment of British resources both in money and men to maintain an army in Germany followed naturally from the diplomatic strategy of Pelham and Newcastle. Pitt's own most characteristic contribution to the war, his use of combined operations against the coast of France, designed to divert French attention from the war in Germany, was a desperate attempt to prove his patriot credentials to his friends the Tories, already increasingly dismayed by his 'Hanoverian' policies. In military terms, they were wasteful and largely ineffective. When victory eventually came, it owed much to forces over which Pitt had little control. In general, the French paid heavily for their failure to build up resources for naval and colonial warfare. In India, the advantage enjoyed by the British East India Company was marginal but it was decisive, particularly when the talents of Clive were thrown into the balance. Pitt's description of Clive as a 'heaven-born' general was a rhetorical admission that he could not claim the credit for Clive's appointment himself. Even Wolfe, whose heroic assault on Quebec captured the national imagination, was only the last of a number of commanders whose activities in North America by no means achieved uniform success. But victory solves all problems in war, at least until a peace has to be negotiated. Before the *annus mirabilis* of 1759, when the tide turned both in the West Indies and in North America, Pitt's coalition with Newcastle was precariously balanced on the brink of disintegration. Pitt's Tory supporters constantly talked of deserting a minister whose policies filled them with alarm, while his ally Newcastle repeatedly threatened to ditch a colleague who spent money like water in pursuit of costly defeats. In 1759 these difficulties dissolved.

Pitt did not fully deserve the credit for the fortunes of the Seven Years War but there were two important respects in which his historical reputation seems justified. For if Pitt's popular credentials have been exaggerated, his role in changing the character of eighteenth-century politics was none the less an important one. In the mid-1750s the mould was plainly cracking. The proscription of Toryism, and the ability of the Whig families to keep the control of patronage within a narrow circle, had a very short future. Pitt offered at least the hope of a break with the old politics, especially in the metropolis where his connections went deep into a genuinely popular electorate. Similarly, as a war leader he did provide one crucial quality which no rival possessed at this time, without which the war could not have been continued, let alone brought to a triumphant conclusion. Political courage, and with it a confidence which was difficult to distinguish from unthinking arrogance, gave other more competent and cautious men the moral base on which to fight and win a brilliant war. Pitt's faith in his own leadership provided a key component in the direction of the war at the very moment when the leaders of the old Whig gang, Newcastle and Fox, had manifestly lost their nerve. If political laurels go in the last analysis to those prepared to risk everything, then in this sense at least Pitt deserved them.

Whatever the nature of Pitt's achievement, his controversial activities in these years formed a fitting prologue to the drama which was shortly to follow. The transformed character of politics in the 1760s will be for ever associated with the new king George III and with one of his most turbulent subjects, John Wilkes. So far as the king was concerned these years were to prove traumatic in the extreme. Yet much of what George III did was the logical culmination of trends in his grandfather's reign. This was particularly true of his supposedly revolutionary determination to abolish the old party distinctions. The validity of such distinctions had already been diminished by the success of Frederick Prince of Wales and Pitt in enlisting the aid of the Tories. The difference in 1760 was one of tone rather than substance with reluctant and grudging toleration being replaced by unavowed pride in the accessibility of the new regime to the old Tories. At court, they were welcomed back with open arms and with a judicious distribution of offices, honours, and peerages. In the counties, they returned, where they had not returned during the preceding decade, to the commissions of the peace; in the midland shires the commissions once again resembled a roll call of the country gentry, many of them of old Tory and even old royalist stock. One redoubtable Tory was granted a special place in the sun. Dr Johnson, the literary giant of the age, basked in the political approval of the new regime, signalized with a pension from Lord Bute in 1762. His new acceptability was not without irony. In the 1730s Johnson had written a bitter patriot attack on the pro-Spanish policy of Walpole in relation to the Caribbean, and British claims there. Now, under the new king, he was to pen an equally powerful and more compelling piece in defence of George III's supposed appeasement of Spain over the British claim to the Falkland Islands, which he described as 'a bleak and gloomy solitude, an island thrown aside from human use, stormy in winter, and barren in summer'. This was not the end of the Falkland Islands as an issue in the history of British foreign policy. What Johnson's progress as an individual signified was still more strikingly endorsed institutionally in the history of Oxford University. For forty-six years the home and shrine of sentimental Jacobitism had suffered in the political wilderness, as successive generations of Whig churchmen monopolized the places of honour and profit. The ecclesiastical masters of early Hanoverian England had generally been trained either at Cambridge or at the tiny minority of Whig colleges at Oxford. In the new reign, there was no doubt which university made its

Royalty refulgent. (*Below*): Zoffany's painting of the royal family captures both the confident regality of the new king, George III, and the somewhat theatrical neo-classicism of the 1760s. The new king was not afraid to challenge comparison with his Stuart forebears, as the Van Dyck costumes show; the Jacobite threat was dead and the appeal of Charles I could be safely used to glorify the Hanoverian line. (*Right*) Lord Bute's role as royal favourite brought him exceptional vilification in the press. This cartoon of 1767 employs a commonplace image for eighteenth-century Prime Ministers—'The Colossus'—but also specifically attributes Bute's success to fraud (his use of royal influences) and lust (his supposed seduction of the king's mother, the Princess Dowager of Wales).

emotional home-coming. Oddly enough, Oxford had contributed more than one Prime Minister even to early Hanoverian
government. But Pelham had made little attempt to prevent his
brother's direction of ecclesiastical patronage to Cambridge, and
Pitt had at one time stooped to making capital of his own
university's Jacobite associations. Under George III, Oxford was
to have in Lord North a Prime Minister who was also its
Chancellor, and one who fittingly represented the old Tory
families of the cavalier counties.

If the return to court of the Tories was unsurprising, George
III's other new measures seem hardly less so. The reign began in

a haze of good intentions and lofty aspirations. Any notion that a new 'patriot king' might seek to strengthen the royal prerogative was quickly crushed. The Demise of the Crown Act, which stipulated that judges would not as in the past resign their offices at the death of the sovereign, removed any suspicion that kings might use their legal rights to sweep away the Whig judicial establishment. At the same time, the Civil List Act provided for a strictly controlled royal allowance of £800,000 per annum; this was the same as that granted to George II but there was the important additional provision that any surplus produced by the civil list duties was for the future directed to the Exchequer not to the Crown. With inflation, this stipulation was seriously to impede the Crown's capacity to cope with the rising tide of court expenses and ironically proved to be a most damaging concession by the king in the name of patriotic propriety. This was the true legacy of the Leicester House party under Frederick Prince of Wales—not a fanciful scheme for the creation of a new benevolent despotism, but further limitation of the Crown's prerogative.

These, however, were minor matters compared with the most important of the new regime's priorities—peace. The old ministers, Pitt and Newcastle, both resigned from office, the former in 1761 because George III and Bute declined to extend the war to Spain at his insistence, the latter specifically in protest against the peace terms the next year. But most of the arguments which they deployed carry little weight in retrospect. Peace could not be secured without restoring to the Bourbons a proportion of the gains made during the war. The return of the principal French West Indian Islands and the preservation of French fishing rights in Canadian waters were not excessive concessions, nor would Pitt and Newcastle, in the diplomatic circumstances of 1762, have been able to make less without continuing the war to the bitter end. Moreover the immense successes of recent years had been gained at a fearful financial cost, which by 1761 was provoking widespread alarm. The case against further prosecution of the war, put repeatedly in newspapers and pamphlets and led by Israel Mauduit's *Considerations on the German War*, was a strong one. War *à outrance* would end in bankruptcy; moreover its object—continued support of Frederick the Great and the acquisition of some additional colonial possessions—seemed of doubtful value. It is possible that George III and Bute, moved in part by the reflection that the war, for all its glory, was not their war, and influenced also by the need to make a quick peace, surrendered rather more than they needed to, particularly in the terms they made with Spain. But in essentials their peace was a prudent, defensible measure and was overwhelmingly approved by parliamentary and public opinion.

Why, in these circumstances, did the new reign prove so controversial? Mainly, perhaps, it was because the new men brought to their otherwise innocuous activities a degree of personal animosity towards the old regime which was bound to cause difficulties. The chosen instrument of George III's reforms was his former tutor, Lord Bute, a Scottish peer of intellectual bent whose experience and skills were slight. Most of the instruction with which he had prepared the young king for his task was more naïve than knavish. There was no great conspiracy against liberty and the constitution, nor any determination to introduce a new authoritarian system. But there was undoubtedly on the part of the new king and his minister a deep-seated resentment of the men who had monopolized power under George II and a readiness if not a determination to dispense with, even to humiliate them. For 'black hearted' Pitt, who was seen as betraying the prince's court in 1757, there was outright hatred, and it is difficult to see how Pitt and Bute could have co-operated in the new circumstances. But Pitt was a megalomaniac with whom only a saint could have co-operated for long. The great Whig families were another matter. Their rank, weight, and inherited importance would make them dangerous enemies. No doubt they treated the new king with a measure of condescension. Families such as the Cavendishes were apt to regard themselves as kingmakers, for whom the electors of Hanover were at most *primi inter pares.* Newcastle, after a lifetime in office, might be forgiven for expecting to have his advice taken seriously by a donnish, ineffectual Scottish peer who was chiefly known for the shapeliness of his legs and his patronage of botanists. There were, in short, good reasons for proceeding cautiously, and above all reasons for ensuring as smooth a transition as possible between the new and the old politics. This was by no means out of the question. The 'old corps' Whigs knew well that the substance of Bute's demands must be granted. Most of them, in the absence of a charismatic leader of their own, were content to labour on under changed management. A typical figure was Lord North, himself a cousin of the duke of Newcastle, a future Prime Minister and in the new reign a passive adherent of George III's court. Even the senior men, who saw themselves as victims of the new order, were reluctant to declare war on it. Hardwicke, the doyen of Whig

The Younger Pitt: for and against. The favourable portrayal (*above*)
is Gainsborough's, the unfavourable (*facing*) Gillray's. Comparison of the
latter with the cartoons on p.162 above demonstrates how far the art
of political caricature had advanced since the Walpole era.

lawyers and one of the pillars of the Pelhamite system, sought
only dignified provision for his friends and a continuing supply
of places at court for his family. Given this background, it was
maladroit of Bute and George III to drive out Newcastle and his
friends. When they did so, ostensibly over the peace terms in the
spring of 1762, they created one of the most enduring enmities in
modern British politics.

Perhaps the alienation of the old political establishment would have been a price worth paying if the new plans had worked out. But Bute himself, having beset his young charge with powerful enemies, chose to resign from office after only a year, with the lordly intention of directing affairs from the back-benches, or rather (as it was inevitably seen) from the backstairs. And so to the folly of antagonizing the old Whig families was added that of providing them with a legend of intrigue and influence with which to sustain and inspire their opposition. This opposition and the equivocal conduct of Bute set the pattern for twenty years or more of politics. In the short run, the 1760s featured a nightmarish cycle of ministerial instability, as George III sought a minister who was both congenial in the closet and capable of presiding in Parliament. In the process, the Whigs themselves

under Lord Rockingham, Pitt, and the duke of Grafton were tried and found wanting, until in 1770 Lord North emerged as a figure capable of wearing the mantle of Walpole and Pelham. Running through these years of tortuous, factious politics there was always the *damnosa hereditas* of Bute's inconsequential yet damaging flirtation with power, the suspicion of the Whig families, and the myth of a continuing improper secret influence. When Edmund Burke produced his comprehensive and classic analysis of the politics of the period, *Thoughts on the Cause of the Present Discontents* (1770), it was this influence which gave him the basis for a systematic onslaught on the new court and its system. The *Thoughts* were to pass into history as the authorized version of the Whig party, and for many later generations the standard account of the misdeeds of George III.

There was other inflammable material at hand in the 1760s. The war was succeeded by a serious economic slump which clearly demonstrates the uneven distribution of economic rewards in the age of enterprise. The period was marked by a series of violent industrial disputes which created widespread unrest in urban centres such as Manchester and Newcastle, and threatened to spill over into political agitation. Even in the countryside these were years of bad harvests, rising prices, and serious dearth. In this atmosphere the activities of John Wilkes found ample support. Wilkes's historical reputation as an amiable rogue has, to some extent, obscured his political shrewdness and inventiveness. Circumstances and opportunism were the making of Wilkes. The grievances which he took up would have made little impact ten years earlier. The general warrants, which permitted arbitrary arrest for political offences, and which caused so much controversy when Wilkes's journalistic activities provoked George III's ministers to deploy them, had been a familiar feature of Hanoverian government. They were used, for example, by both Pitt and Newcastle in their time. But then they had been justified by reference to the Jacobite threat, and they had been used against proscribed Tories rather than vociferous Whigs. Similarly when, in 1768, Wilkes stood for the county of Middlesex and found himself barred from his seat in the Commons there were tolerable precedents and adequate legal arguments for his exclusion. But the Middlesex election involved a popular county intimately connected with the feverish politics of the capital; the Middlesex electors could not be treated as if they were a handful of voters in a rotten borough. Three years later, when Wilkes and his friends attacked the right of the House of Commons to prevent the public reporting of its debates, they were attacking an old and jealously guarded privilege of the legislature. But the defence of that privilege proved hopelessly impracticable in the new climate. The Wilkesite radicals were typically small businessmen, craftsmen, and artisans. They represented the 'middling and inferior sort' at its most concentrated, its most articulate, and its most volatile. When they took their grievance to the country they found support not only among provincial gentlemen worried by the threat to electoral rights but also among their own counterparts in towns up and down the country. The middle class, the crucial element in their campaign, had no unified politics, and protest was not necessarily their preferred political role. But their part in the Wilkesite movement unmistakably signalized their novel importance in the politics of George III's reign. Yet this importance was only in part of their own making. The rules by which the political game had been played under the early Hanoverians no longer applied, whatever precedents they offered; for the men who had found them advantageous now found it convenient to abandon them. The old Whigs, by their readiness to use any weapon of revenge against George III, did much to legitimize the new spirit of popular opposition to the court. Without this collaboration from highly respectable elements in the ruling class, the popular convulsions associated with Wilkes would have been a matter of much less consequence.

Rebellion and Reform

The early years of the new reign have always attracted attention for their colourful politics. Yet in some ways the most striking changes of the period concerned Britain's role overseas, especially the new awareness of empire which inevitably succeeded the Seven Years War. The effective hegemony of North America was especially entrancing. Imperial civil servants and ministers enjoyed a brief period of uninhibited inventiveness in the early 1760s as they planned a new and rosy future for the transatlantic colonies. Quebec was to provide a veritable cornucopia of fish and fur. The American colonies, reinforced by settlement in Canada and the Floridas, would form a vast, loyal market for British manufactures, a continuing source of essential raw materials, and even (enticing prospect for a debt-ridden mother country) a new source of revenue for the Treasury. The West Indies, firmly entrenched in a more effectively policed mercantilist system, would maximize the benefits of a flourishing slave trade, provide a steady flow of tropical products, and form a valuable base for commercial incursions into the Spanish Empire. In the East still more speculative and still more exciting prospects appeared. After Clive's victory at Plassey in 1757 Britain had emerged as the dominant European power on the subcontinent. There was, technically, no territorial presence in the East Indies, but in reality from this time the British East India Company was inextricably involved in effective colonization. In this respect 1765, when Clive formally accepted the *diwani* (land revenues) of Bengal on behalf of the company and thereby committed it to direct political control rather than mere commercial activity, was a landmark as important as Plassey itself, though it followed logically from it. These events transformed the British perception of India. The exotic character of the new possessions and the fact that they brought to light a previously unappreciated culture made the impact of the new empire particularly powerful. This impact was early expressed by Francis Hayman's massive portrayal of Clive receiving the submission of native princes, erected at that pantheon of genteel amusements, Ranelagh, in 1765. Imports of Asian curiosities soared and for the first time something like an informed and genuine interest in Indian society began to take shape. Other aspects of the new acquisitions in the East were less refined and less affecting. In the general election of 1768, a noticeable feature of press reporting was the appearance in a number of constituencies of men who had returned from service in the East India Company and were using their allegedly ill-gotten wealth to buy their way into Parliament. The 'nabobs' had arrived. Their influence was invariably exaggerated, as were their misdeeds and villainies. Moreover, in principle they were no different from the West India planters, the 'Turkey merchants', the 'monied men', and others whose unconventional profits had incurred the enmity of older less 'diversified' families. But their appearance was inevitably a matter of intense curiosity and eventually concern. Clive himself was the embodiment of the rapacious 'nabob'; the ruthlessness and unashamedness with which he had acquired personal riches while in the service of the company seemed all too representative of an entire class of men who saw empire as the means to a fast and even felonious fortune. Nor, it seemed, were temptations restricted to India. The furious speculation in East India stock which followed the grant of the *diwani*, the consequent recurrent crises in the Company's financial affairs, and not least the government's growing interest in its activities all brought the complex and frequently corrupt character of East India politics into an unwelcome and glaring light.

America had no nabobs, but the economic and political problems caused by the preservation and extension of the American empire were greater even than the results of Eastern expansion, and their ramifications still wider. British ministers saw all too clearly the potential value of their transatlantic subjects, but they did not appreciate the extent to which the thirteen colonies had developed a highly independent attitude when it came to intervention from London. Nor did they grasp the capacity of a distant, wealthy, and resourceful population of some two and a half millions to obstruct and resist imperial power. The result was a decade of cyclical crisis in Anglo-American relations, beginning with the Stamp Act, which raised the American cry of 'no taxation without representation' in 1765, and finally culminating in rebellion and war in 1775. It is not easy to identify what, in the last analysis, was at issue from the British standpoint, even at two centuries' distance. By 1775 most of the aims of the post-war ministers had been explicitly or tacitly abandoned. Not even the most optimistic can have thought by 1775 that America was going to prove what Lord Rockingham called a 'revenue mine'. Quelling the colonies by force was bound to be as expensive as its ultimate consequences were bound to be unpredictable. European enemies would plainly see the War of Independence as an opportunity to redress that balance which had tilted so much to their disadvantage in the Seven Years War. Moreover there were those who challenged the entire basis of the war as a logical conclusion from mercantilist principles. Adam Smith's *Wealth of Nations*, published in the same year as the Declaration of Independence (and incidentally at the same time as the first volume of Edward Gibbon's pessimistic survey of the Roman Empire), systematically demolished the economic case for empire. Yet with a few exceptions, notably the radical politicians of the metropolis and some of the religious dissenters, Englishmen strongly supported the war against America. Its central principle, the defence of unlimited parliamentary sovereignty, was naturally important in this, the great age of that principle. William Blackstone's celebrated *Commentaries on the Laws of England*, published in 1765, had announced with uncompromising clarity the unbounded legal authority of the Crown-in-Parliament; the conflict with America was its clearest possible expression. Moreover, the economic arguments which seem so attractive in retrospect made little impression when they were first put. For most Englishmen the

Father and son. The contrast between George III and his son was even more striking than that between other Hanoverian fathers and sons. The king and his wife (*above*) provided for Gillray a model of sober domesticity; here they are shown on their way to their beloved Windsor, much in the manner of any other farmer and his wife returning from market. Prince George (*below, right*), on the other hand, identified himself with the morally dissolute and politically subversive; he is shown the morning after his ill-concealed and unauthorized marriage to Mrs Fitzherbert in 1785.

only viable concept of empire was the old mercantilist one. Colonies which declined to accept the full extent of parliamentary supremacy were not merely worthless, they were positively dangerous. Against this belief that an empire out of control was worse than no empire at all, more imaginative minds made little progress. Here, if ever, there was a clash of chronology and culture. Americans at heart were defending the rights of seventeenth-century Englishmen. For them, resistance to the stamp tax was on a par with Hampden's struggle against ship money; a sovereignty which overrode provincial assemblies and local rights was unthinkable. Englishmen, on the other hand, were deploying an eighteenth-century weapon, parliamentary supremacy, in what was one of the eighteenth century's most cherished doctrines, the indivisible and unlimited authority of metropolitan power in a mercantilist system. Only force would decide the outcome.

In due course, the outcome was determined in favour of the new United States. In the interim the war proved a disaster for Britain—worse by far than anything since the Second Dutch War of 1665–7. It grew from being a colonial insurgency to an all-out war against the Bourbon monarchies, and eventually involved hostilities with the Dutch and a state of 'armed neutrality' with other powers. At the peace negotiations of 1782–3 a certain amount was saved from the wreckage. Although the thirteen colonies were lost irretrievably, a brilliant naval victory at 'the Saints' by Admiral Rodney in 1782 preserved the British West Indies and above all saved George III the embarrassment of surrendering what Cromwell had gained over a century before, the much-prized jewel of Jamaica. In the Mediterranean, Spain's attempt at the reconquest of Gibraltar was foiled. In India, Warren Hastings's desperate defence of Clive's acquisitions staved off both French *revanche* and princely rebellion. Contemporaries found the independence of America a bitter pill to swallow, but most of the empire outside the thirteen colonies remained intact, and at least the utter humiliation feared in the darkest days of the war was averted.

Almost more important than the overseas consequences of the American War were the domestic implications. The economic problems caused to a nascent industrial society by a world war and the accompanying embargoes on trade were immense. In the

ensuing recession both the stock market and land values plunged to alarmingly low levels, unseen in many years. Unprecedentedly high taxes and the rapid growth of the National Debt reinforced the financial crisis and created serious economic problems. Fundamental questions were raised about government, Parliament, and the political system generally. In the ensuing chaos, relatively conservative forces, not least the country gentry, were swept into what looked like an open attack on the constitution, with the Association movement of 1779–80. The Associations had widespread support in the counties, the capital, and provincial cities, and in their demands for reform went further than all but the wilder radicals of the Wilkesite movement. Christopher Wyvill, the Yorkshire cleric and country gentleman, who came close to exercising national leadership of the movement, was hardly himself such a radical. Yet his demands for the elimination of rotten boroughs, the extension of the franchise, and the introduction of the secret ballot, had a futuristic ring about them. Moreover, there was about the Associations a hint, or in the mouths of metropolitan agitators such as John Jebb and Major Cartwright, a definite suggestion, that Parliament, if it resisted reform, should be superseded by the delegates of the counties. Contemporary fears of this new phenomenon were unnecessarily colourful. Yet in retrospect it is difficult not to be struck by the vigour and extent of the Association movement. It arguably brought reform nearer than at any time in the ensuing fifty years, and at its height in 1780 it achieved an extraordinary degree of national consensus. At this point even the House of Commons, notwithstanding the weight of vested interests in and out of government, passed a resolution declaring that the 'influence of the crown has increased, is increasing and ought to be diminished'. This was the signal for almost five years of intense political controversy and sustained ideological conflict.

Why, then, did the Association movement fail to fulfil its promise? When Lord North gave way to a brief period of Whig rule in 1782 Burke and his colleagues pushed through Parliament a handful of reforms abolishing some of the more notorious sinecure places and providing for a more intensive scrutiny of Crown finances. But parliamentary reform proved elusive. Even when the younger Pitt was granted supreme power in 1784 and reform was actually proposed from the Treasury bench with the Prime Minister's authority, there was nothing like a parliamentary majority for it. In large measure this had to do with the circumstances in which the Association movement was born.

Civilizing mission. Despite the success of the Union, Scots endured much hostility in England. This comment on the unfamiliarity of a Scotsman with the conveniences of London life was originally published at the time of the Forty-Five but reproduced on subsequent occasions.

Genuine enthusiasm for root and branch reform was limited, and generally confined to the articulate and the urban. It sometimes made a disproportionately loud noise but real support even among the urban bourgeoisie was restricted. Association sprang from a national crisis in which any systematic critique of the existing politics would prove attractive. The outcry of the reformers against the waste and inefficiency of the court system seemed particularly appropriate. The same phenomenon was to appear for the same reason thirty years later when the immense expenditure of the Napoleonic Wars and the economic crisis associated with it produced similar protests. But these conditions were short-lived and most of the interest in reform died with them. By the mid-1780s there was a growing sense of commercial revival and financial recovery, not least due to the impact of the younger Pitt's policies. Prosperity removed the stimulus to reform more effectively than any argument could.

An additional consideration was the wide and growing concern at the measures of the extremists. The lunatic fringe of the reform movement seemed to be challenging not merely the corrupt politics of the court, but the constitutional framework which supported it, and even the propertied order itself. What was to become the 'Rights of Man' school was already visible in the writings of the early reform movement. Men such as Richard Price and Joseph Priestley were, by the standards of a later age, moderate enough. But they were challenging some of the most entrenched attitudes and commonplace ideas of their day and it needed very little to force apart their fragile alliance with backwoods gentry and provincial business men. In this context the Gordon Riots proved particularly damaging. There was no direct connection between the reformers and the Gordon rioters, who held London at their mercy for nearly a week and engaged in an orgy of murder and destruction in the spring of 1780. Their cause was unashamed religious prejudice, their aim to repeal the liberal measure of relief for Roman Catholics which had been passed with the support of both government and opposition in 1778. As with the Jew Bill in 1754, it was clear that the legislature could easily get out of step with popular feeling. The leader of the anti-papists, Lord George Gordon, called his movement the Protestant Association, and it was easy enough for frightened men of property to make a connection between the rioters and the political activities of more respectable Associators. The conservative reaction so marked in England during the following years could be traced back in origin to this episode.

The early 1780s were not only turbulent in the extra-parliamentary sense; they also provided the same spectacle of political instability as the 1760s. This, too, was an element in the failure of reform. Before 1782 reformers in Parliament had congregated loosely around the two main Whig groups, Lord Rockingham's party and those who followed Lord Shelburne. The two wings of recognized Whiggism represented distinct traditions going back to Newcastle and the old Whig clans in the case of Rockingham, and to the elder Pitt in that of Shelburne.

The most promising talent in each was also a familiar name. Charles James Fox, one of Rockingham's most radical supporters and also his most popular, was the son of that Henry Fox who had been a rival to the elder Pitt, and in the new reign briefly a tool of Lord Bute. Among Shelburne's associates was the younger Pitt—in Burke's phrase, not 'a chip off the old block' but 'the block itself'. Both were authentic reformers, both seemed to offer a fresh approach to a jaded, yet optimistic age, both held out the hope of leadership against the discredited politics of the men who had mismanaged the American War. Unfortunately, if perhaps inevitably, they turned out to be rivals rather than allies, and in the complex, bitter politics which followed Lord North's resignation in 1782, their enmity proved crucially important. The initiative was taken by Fox, who sought nothing less than total control of the Cabinet, a monopoly of power which the king detested in one whom he also found personally objectionable. Fox's weapon in the battle which followed the death of Rockingham, in the summer of 1782, was an unholy alliance with his old enemy, North. It was a deeply offensive and widely despised alliance, but the prize, control of the Commons and, therefore, as Fox saw it, of the government, seemed big enough to override demands for consistency. But there were flaws in Fox's logic. His ministry, the notorious Fox–North coalition, was short-lived. It was strongly opposed by the king himself, who systematically plotted its destruction, and also by Pitt, who wanted no dependence on Fox and cordially detested North. When Fox obligingly provided an issue on which Pitt and the king might appeal to the country, in the shape of a radical restructuring of the East India Company, in effect he committed political suicide. George III instructed the House of Lords to defeat the East India Bill, Pitt was placed in power, and in the spring of 1784 a general election was called. There could be no quarrelling with the result. Fox was roundly defeated not only where the Treasury could exert its influence, but also in the larger, more open constituencies where public opinion mattered and where the popular revulsion against him was manifest. When the dust settled, Pitt was Prime Minister on an outstandingly secure tenure, and the Whigs were thoroughly 'dished'. Above all, reform, the hoped-for product of a hoped-for alliance between Fox and Pitt against the combined forces of George III and North, was dead—killed, it seemed, by the irresponsible antics of Fox, that 'darling of the people'.

Perhaps reform was dead anyway. Once he had nodded in the direction of his youthful principles by putting a motion for reform which he knew could not be successful without the backing of the Crown, Pitt as Prime Minister showed little taste for radical political activity. A reformer he proved, but not in matters affecting the constitution in Church and State. Many of the demands of the 'economical reformers' for a reduction in the corruption and waste of the court were to be carried out under Pitt. Moreover, the first, extremely hesitant steps towards free trade were taken under his guidance, notably in the commercial treaty with France in 1787. Difficult imperial questions were also treated with a mixture of caution and innovation. The Irish had already, in the crisis of the American War, demanded parliamentary independence of Westminster, and after obtaining it in 1782 achieved a measure of home rule. Pitt would have given Ireland commercial equality with the mother country had the manufacturers of the Midlands and Lancashire allowed him to do so. His failure in this respect left Anglo-Irish relations in an equivocal and uncertain state. India was put to rest at least as a major issue in British politics with an East India Act which finally gave government the ultimate say in the Company's affairs, at least when they did not exclusively concern trade. In 1791 Canada, with its incursion of loyalist settlers after the American War and its intractable 'ethnic' problem in Quebec, was given a settlement which was to endure, albeit uneasily, until 1867.

In many ways, Pitt's supremacy had a very traditional appearance. He was essentially a beneficiary of the court and of the king's support. His triumph in 1784 could be made to seem as much a triumph for the Crown as anything done by a Danby or a Sunderland. The opposition to Pitt looked traditional too. Fox depended much on the heir to the throne, the future George IV, whose antics, political, financial, and sexual, were as much the despair of the king as those of any heir to the Crown before him. But in other respects Pitt and his activities reflected the transformations of recent years. His administrative and economic reforms take their place among a great host of changes in contemporary attitudes which can easily be lost behind the political conservatism of the age. That most flourishing product of the Enlightenment mind—Utility—was already in sight. Jeremy Bentham and the philosophical radicals were yet to achieve a significant breakthrough in practical politics, but the flavour which they imparted or perhaps adopted was everywhere, as was the religious influence of Evangelicalism. The reforms which really did make an impact in this period were precisely those moral, humanitarian, pragmatic 'improvements' which delighted the Evangelical mind. John Howard's famous campaign belonged to the 1770s and 1780s. His 'voyage of discovery' or 'Circumnavigation of Charity', in Burke's words, provided a powerful stimulus to the work of prison reform, freely supported by many local magistrates. The Sunday Schools sprang from the same era of earnest endeavour, as did the widespread drive to establish friendly societies supervised by the clergy. Traditional recreations of the lower classes came increasingly under the disapproving inspection of their social superiors, particularly when, like cock-fighting and bull-baiting, they involved cruelty to animals. There was also a distinct shift in attitudes towards imperial responsibility. Burke's campaign against Warren Hastings, the saviour of British India, proved intolerably protracted and eventually unsuccessful; the impeachment had little to commend it despite Hastings' apparent guilt on some of the charges. But Hastings was the victim of changing standards of public morality. What would have been tolerated in a Clive was tolerated no longer. The treatment of subject peoples was no longer a matter of indifference at home. The interest in 'uncivilized' peoples from the Red Indians to Captain Cook's South Sea islanders, like Burke's indignation on behalf of more sophisticated but equally subjugated Asians, revealed a new sensitivity, tinged with romanticism, to the plight of the victims of empire. The most notorious target of the new sensibility was, of course, the slave trade. The campaign, led by Granville Sharp in the formative years of the 1770s, and by William Wilberforce in the 1780s, was to wait many years before success. But there were victories along the way. In the case of Sommersett, 1772, a Negro slave brought by a West Indian planter to London was freed on the grounds that no law of England authorized 'so high an act of dominion as slavery'. The publicity value of this decision was out of all proportion to its legal significance, but the interest which it aroused caught the essence of the late eighteenth-century mind, with its emphasis on human equality, religious redemption, and political conservatism. For Wilberforce and his friends were staunch defenders of the establishment in Church and State, and utterly uninterested in radical politics. In this they expressed the serious-minded, Evangelical enthusiasm of the business classes of the new industrial England. For all the supposedly unrepresentative nature of the political system it was these classes which Wilberforce's friend Pitt best represented. It was also their instinct for obstinate defence of the interests of property, combined with thrusting commercial aggressiveness and unlimited moral earnestness, which was to carry the England of the younger Pitt into the era of the French Revolution.

FURTHER READING

5. THE TUDOR AGE

GENERAL WORKS

P. Williams, *The Tudor Regime* (Oxford, 1979), the most enlightened general survey of the Tudor age.

C. S. L. Davies, *Peace, Print and Protestantism, 1450–1558* (London, 1976), a lucid introduction especially useful on social and economic history.

S. Ozment, *The Age of Reform, 1250–1550* (New Haven, 1980), a superb and thought-provoking guide to the European background.

A. G. Dickens, *The English Reformation* (London, 1964), a dispassionate and comprehensive account.

A. L. Rowse, *The England of Elizabeth* (London, 1950), which captures the spirit of the Elizabethan age.

J. Wormald, *Court, Kirk, and Community, 1470–1625* (London, 1981), the best survey of early modern Scotland.

D. M. Palliser, *The Age of Elizabeth: England under the Later Tudors, 1547–1603* (London, 1983), the best synthesis of social and economic conditions.

BIOGRAPHIES

S. B. Chrimes, *Henry VII* (London, 1972), a sound synthesis of recent research.

J. J. Scarisbrick, *Henry VIII* (London, 1968), an enthralling and original biography accepted as standard.

A. F. Pollard, *Wolsey* (London, 1929), a dated but indispensable work.

A. Fox, *Thomas More: History and Providence* (Oxford, 1982), the best biography, achieving a breakthrough in its understanding of More's mind.

D. M. Loades, *The Reign of Mary Tudor* (London, 1979), a solid but essential conspectus.

C. Read, *Mr. Secretary Cecil and Queen Elizabeth, Lord Burghley and Queen Elizabeth* (London, 1955, 1960), a two-volume study valuable on diplomacy, but which pays insufficient attention to domestic patronage and faction.

P. Johnson, *Elizabeth I: a Study in Power and Intellect* (London, 1974), a fair-minded assessment by a professional biographer, but Elizabeth's influence is over-rated.

STUDIES OF SPECIAL TOPICS

G. R. Elton, *Reform and Renewal: Thomas Cromwell and the Common Weal* (Cambridge, 1973), the most convincing portrait of Thomas Cromwell by the leading authority.

M. Bush, *The Government Policy of Protector Somerset* (London, 1975), an important anatomy of Somerset's obsessions.

J. Loach and R. Tittler (eds.), *The Mid-Tudor Polity* (London, 1980), a provocative collection of essays by revisionist historians.

P. Collinson, *The Elizabethan Puritan Movement* (London, 1967), an authoritative study by the acknowledged expert.

P. McGrath, *Papists and Puritans Under Elizabeth I* (London, 1967), which is especially sensible about Catholic history.

G. Mattingley, *The Defeat of the Spanish Armada* (London, 1959), an absorbing book by a writer who knew Spanish as well as English sources.

L. Stone, *The Crisis of the Aristocracy* (Oxford, 1965), an important if controversial study of Tudor high society.

K. Thomas, *Religion and the Decline of Magic* (London, 1971), a sparkling and original study of the mentality of Tudor Englishmen.

R. Strong, *The Elizabethan Image* (London, 1969), a useful cultural catalogue by the leading expert.

6. THE STUARTS

POLITICAL AND CONSTITUTIONAL HISTORY

B. Coward, *The Stuart Age* (London, 1980), the best introductory survey.

R. Ashton, *The English Civil War 1603–1649* (London, 1978).

C. Russell, *The Crisis of Parliaments 1509–1660* (Oxford, 1971).

J. R. Jones, *Country and Court 1658–1714* (London, 1979).

F. M. G. Higham, *Catholic and Reformed: A Study of the Church of England 1559–1662* (London, 1962), excellent study of religious thought.

J. P. Kenyon, *The Stuarts* (London, 1958).

S. J. Houston, *James I* (London, 1973).

R. Ollard, *The Image of the King: Charles I and Charles II* (London, 1979).

J. Miller, *James II: A Study in Kingship* (London, 1978).

J. S. Morrill, *The Revolt of the Provinces* (London, 1976).

A. Woolrych, *Battles of the English Civil War* (London, 1961).

G. E. Aylmer, *The Levellers in the English Revolution* (London, 1975), a brief essay and key texts.

C. Hill, *The World Turned Upside Down* (Harmondsworth, 1973), re-creates the world of the religious radicals of the 1650s.

C. H. Firth, *Oliver Cromwell and the Rule of the Puritans* (Oxford, 1900).

J. P. Kenyon, *The Popish Plot* (London, 1972).

J. R. Jones, *The Revolution of 1688 in England* (London, 1972).

G. Donaldson, *Scotland: James V to James VII* (Edinburgh, 1965).

T. W. Moody, F. X. Martin, F. J. Byrne (eds.), *A New History of Ireland*, vol. iii 1534–1691 (Oxford, 1976), a long narrative.

M. MacCurtain, *Tudor and Stuart Ireland* (Dublin, 1972) a short analysis.

SOCIAL, ECONOMIC, CULTURAL

D. C. Coleman, *The Economy of England 1450–1750* (Oxford, 1977), a brilliantly crisp synthesis.

K. Wrightson, *English Society 1580–1680* (London, 1982), re-creates the mental world of the seventeenth-century villager.

P. Laslett, *The World We Have Lost* (London, 1971).

L. Stone, *The Crisis of the Aristocracy* (abridged version, Oxford, 1967).

J. Hook, *The Baroque Age* (London, 1976).

R. Strong, *Van Dyck: Charles I on Horseback* (London, 1972).
C. Webster, *The Great Instauration* (London, 1970).
K. V. Thomas, *Religion and the Decline of Magic* (London, 1971).
M. Spufford, *Small Books and Pleasant Histories: Popular Fiction and its Readers in 17th Century England* (London, 1981).
C. Hill, *Society and Puritanism in Pre-Revolutionary England* (London, 1964).
J. Bossy, *The English Catholic Community 1570–1850* (London, 1975).
T. C. Smout, *A History of the Scottish People 1560–1830* (London, 1969).

DOCUMENTS AND CONTEMPORARY TEXTS
Samuel Pepys, *Diary*, various editions, but all previous ones superseded by that of R. C. Latham and W. Matthews, 11 vols. (London, 1970–83).
The Illustrated Pepys, ed. R. C. Latham (London, 1978), a marvellous sampler.
John Evelyn, *Diary*, various editions and extracts, principally the edition by E. S. de Beer, 6 vols. (Oxford, 1955).
J. Aubrey, *Brief Lives* (again many editions but e.g. Harmondsworth, 1962).
R. Gough, *The History of Myddle* (Harmondsworth, 1981), a splendid evocation of life in a seventeenth-century parish, written by its vicar.
J. P. Kenyon, *The Stuart Constitution* (Cambridge, 1962), for texts and stimulating commentary.
J. Thirsk and J. P. Cooper, *Seventeenth-century Economic Documents* (Oxford, 1972).

BIBLIOGRAPHY
M. F. Keeler, *Bibliography of British History: Stuart Period, 1603–1714* (Oxford, 1970), a comprehensive guide to publications up to 1960.
J. S. Morrill, *Critical Bibliographies in Modern History: Seventeenth Century Britain* (Folkestone, 1980), complements Keeler and offers comments on the works discussed.

7. THE EIGHTEENTH CENTURY

GENERAL WORKS
J. R. Jones, *Country and Court: England, 1658–1714* (London, 1978);
W. A. Speck, *Stability and Strife: England, 1714–1760* (London, 1977);
I. R. Christie, *Wars and Revolutions: Britain, 1760–1815* (London, 1972): three books in Arnold's *New History of England* which together provide a general survey of the period.
J. B. Owen, *The Eighteenth Century, 1714–1815* (London, 1974), one of the more recent and most useful of the many outline histories of the eighteenth century.

POLITICS
J. H. Plumb, *The Growth of Political Stability in England 1675–1725* (London, 1967), one of the most influential studies.
J. Cannon (ed.), *The Whig Ascendancy: Colloquies on Hanoverian England* (London, 1981), discusses the recent literature on stability and on many other themes.
H. T. Dickinson, *Politics and Literature in the Eighteenth Century* (London, 1974), includes representative selections from contemporary works.
——*Liberty and Property: Political Ideology in Eighteenth-Century Britain* (London, 1977), a useful account for those interested in the history of ideas.

J. Cannon, *Parliamentary Reform 1640–1832* (Cambridge, 1973, rev. edn. 1982), deals with a particularly important theme.

J. R. Jones, *Britain and the World 1649–1815* (London, 1980), describes international relations in a British context.

I. R. Christie and B. W. Labaree, *Empire or Independence 1760–1776* (London, 1976);

P. J. Marshall, *Problems of Empire: Britain and India 1757–1813* (London, 1968); discussions of two particularly important imperial problems, America and India, respectively.

ECONOMIC, SOCIAL, RELIGIOUS, CULTURAL

E. Pawson, *The Early Industrial Revolution: Britain in the Eighteenth Century* (London, 1979), a useful addition to the many economic history textbooks on the eighteenth century.

R. Porter, *English Society in the Eighteenth Century* (London, 1982), presents a colourful picture of social conditions, opportunities, and developments.

G. E. Mingay, *English Landed Society in the Eighteenth Century* (London, 1963), deals with the gentry.

R. W. Malcolmson, *Life and Labour in England 1700–1780* (London, 1981), deals with the lower orders.

J. Stevenson, *Popular Disturbances in England 1700–1870* (London, 1979), also useful on popular politics.

P. Corfield, *The Impact of English Towns 1700–1800* (Oxford, 1982), a survey of eighteenth-century urban growth.

D. Hay, P. Linebough, E. P. Thompson, *Albion's Fatal Tree: Crime and Society in Eighteenth Century England* (London, 1975), a pioneering study in the now flourishing history of crime.

A. Armstrong, *The Church of England, the Methodists and Society 1700–1850* (London, 1973), a brief summary of the religious history of the period.

R. Paulson, *Emblem and Expression: Meaning in English Art of the Eighteenth Century* (London, 1975), transmits something of the flavour as well as some of the most important aspects of cultural controversy.

CHRONOLOGY

1485	Death of Richard III at Bosworth; accession of Henry VII
1487	Rebellion of Lambert Simnel
1491	Birth of Prince Henry
1509	Accession of Henry VIII
1510	Execution of Empson and Dudley
1512	War with France and Scotland
1513	Battle of Flodden: English victory over Scotland
1515	Wolsey appointed Lord Chancellor
1522	War with France
1525	Peace with France
1527	Divorce crisis begins
1528	War with Spain
1529	Peace of Cambrai; fall of Wolsey: Sir Thomas More succeeds as Lord Chancellor
1532	More resigns
1533	Henry VIII marries Anne Boleyn; Act of Appeals; birth of Princess Elizabeth
1534	Act of Supremacy
1535	Execution of More and Fisher
1536	Dissolution of the Monasteries; Pilgrimage of Grace; union of England and Wales
1542	Battle of Solway Moss; English victory over invading Scottish army
1543	War with France
1547	Succession of Edward VI; ascendancy of Protector Somerset; battle of Pinkie: English victory over Scotland
1549	First Book of Common Prayer; Northumberland's coup
1553	Accession of Mary
1554	Pole returns; reunion with Rome; Wyatt's rebellion
1555	Persecution of Protestants begins
1557	War with France
1558	New Book of Rates; accession of Elizabeth I
1559	Peace of Cateau-Cambrésis; religious Settlement in England
1566	Archbishop Parker's *Advertisements* demand religious conformity
1568	Mary Stuart flees to England
1569	Northern Rebellion
1570	Papal bull declares Elizabeth excommunicated and deposed
1580	Jesuit missionaries arrive in England
1585	War with Spain
1587	Execution of Mary Stuart
1588	Defeat of the Spanish Armada
1594	Bad harvests begin
1601	Essex's rebellion

1603	Death of Elizabeth; accession of James VI of Scotland as James I; peace in Ireland; Millenary Petition of the Puritans
1604	Peace with Spain (treaty of London); Hampton Court Conference (king, bishops, Puritans)
1605	Gunpowder Plot, the last major Catholic conspiracy
1606–7	Failure of James's plans for union of kingdoms
1607	Settlement of Virginia
1609	Rebellion of the Northern Earls in Ireland; beginnings of the Planting of Ulster by Scots and English Protestants
1610	Failure of Great Contract (reform of royal finance)
1611	Publication of Authorized Version of the Bible (Anglican–Puritan co-operation)
1612	Death of Prince Henry, James's promising elder son
1613	Marriage of Princess Elizabeth to Elector Palatine, Protestant zealot, enmeshed Britain in continental politics
1617–29	Ascendancy of George Villiers, duke of Buckingham
1619–22	Inigo Jones designs the Banqueting House, the first major royal public building since the reign of Henry VIII
1620	Pilgrim Fathers inaugurate religious migration to New England
1622–3	Prince Charles and Buckingham go to Spain to woo the king's daughter and are rebuffed
1624–30	War with Spain
1625	Death of James I; accession of Charles I and marriage to Henrietta Maria, sister of Louis XIII of France
1626–9	War with France
1628	Petition of Right; publication of Harvey's work on the circulation of the blood; assassination of Buckingham
1629	Charles I dissolves Parliament, determines to govern without one
1630	Large-scale emigration to Massachusetts begins
1633	William Laud translated to be Archbishop of Canterbury
1634–40	Ship Money case
1637	Hampden's case supports Charles I's claim to collect Ship Money
1637–40	Breakdown of Charles's government of Scotland and two attempts to impose his will by force
1640	Long Parliament summoned
1641	Remodelling of government in England and Scotland; abolition of conciliar courts, abolition of prerogative taxation, triennial bill, Grand Remonstrance; rebellion of Ulster Catholics
1642	King's attempt on the Five Members; his withdrawal from London; the 19 Propositions; the resort to arms: Civil War
1643	King's armies prosper; Scots invade on side of Parliament
1644	Parliamentary armies prosper, especially in the decisive battle of the war, Marston Moor (June)
1645	'Clubmen' risings of armed neutrals threaten both sides; Royalist armies disintegrate, but parliamentary forces reorganized (New Model Army)
1646	King surrenders to the Scots; bishops and Book of Common Prayer abolished, Presbyterian Church established
1647	Army revolt; radical movements criticize parliamentary tyranny; king prevaricates
1648	Second Civil War: Scots now side with the king and are defeated; provincial risings (Kent, Colchester, S. Wales, Yorks., etc.) crushed
1649	Trial and execution of Charles I: England a Republic

1649–53	Government by sovereign single-chamber assembly, the 'Rump' Parliament thoroughly purged of royalists and moderates
1649–50	Oliver Cromwell conquers Ireland (Drogheda massacre)
1650–2	Oliver Cromwell conquers Scotland (battles of Dunbar and Worcester)
1651	Thomas Hobbes's *Leviathan* published
1652–4	First Dutch War
1653	Cromwell dissolves Rump, creates the Nominated or Barebones Assembly; it surrenders power back to him, and he becomes Lord Protector under a paper constitution (*The Instrument of Government*)
1655–60	War with Spain
1655	Royalist insurrection (Penruddock's rising) is a complete failure
1657	*Instrument of Government* replaced by a parliamentary paper constitution, the *Humble Petition and Advice*; Cromwell rejects title of King and remains Lord Protector, but nominates his own House of Lords
1658	Cromwell dies and is succeeded by his son Richard
1659	Richard overthrown by the army; Rump restored but displeases many in the army
1660	Charles II restored
1662	Church of England restored; Royal Society receives its Charter
1663	Failure of first royal attempt to grant religious toleration
1665–7	Second Dutch War
1665	Great Plague (final major outbreak)
1666	Great Fire of London
1667	Milton's *Paradise Lost* published
1672–3	Failure of second royal attempt to grant religious toleration
1672–4	Third Dutch War
1674	Grain bounties introduced (England self-sufficient in food); Bunyan's *Pilgrim's Progress*, part I, published
1678	Titus Oates and the Popish Plot
1679–81	The Exclusion Crisis; emergence of Whig and Tory parties
1683	The Rye House Plot; Whigs proscribed
1685	Charles II dies; accession of James II; rebellion by Charles II's protestant bastard, the duke of Monmouth, fails
1687	James II's Declaration of Indulgence; Tories proscribed; Newton's *Principia Mathematica* published
1688	James II's son born
1688	William of Orange invades: James II takes flight, accession of William III (of Orange) and Mary
1689	Bill of Rights settles succession to the throne and declares illegal various grievances; Toleration Act grants rights to Trinitarian Protestant dissenters
1690	Battle of the Boyne: William III defeats Irish and French army
1694	Bank of England founded; death of Queen Mary; Triennial Act sets the maximum duration of a parliament at three years
1695	Lapse of Licensing Act
1697	Peace treaty of Ryswick between allied powers of the League of Augsburg and France; Civil List Act votes funds for the maintenance of the royal household
1701	War of Spanish Succession begins; Act of Settlement settles the royal succession on the descendants of Sophia of Hanover
1702	Death of William III; accession of Anne

1704	Battle of Blenheim: British, Dutch, German and Austrian troops defeat French and Bavarian forces; British capture of Gibraltar from Spain
1707	Union of England and Scotland
1710	Impeachment of Dr Sacheverell; Harley ministry
1713	Peace treaty of Utrecht concludes the War of Spanish Succession
1714	Death of Anne; accession of George I
1715	Jacobite rebellion aimed at overthrowing the Hanoverian succession fails
1716	Septennial Act sets the maximum duration of a parliament at seven years
1717	Whig split; suspension of convocation
1720	South Sea Bubble: many investors ruined after speculation in the stock of the South Sea Company
1721	Walpole ministry
1722	Atterbury Plot, the most notable Jacobite plot
1726	Jonathan Swift's *Gulliver's Travels* published
1727	Death of George I; accession of George II
1729	Alexander Pope's *Dunciad* published
1730	Walpole/Townshend split
1733	Excise crisis: Walpole has to abandon his plans to reorganize the customs and excise
1737	Death of Queen Caroline
1738	Wesley's 'conversion': the start of Methodism
1739	War of Jenkins' Ear: Anglo-Spanish naval war
1740	War of the Austrian Succession
1741	Samuel Richardson's *Pamela* published
1742	Fall of Walpole
1744	Ministry of Pelham
1745	Jacobite Rebellion led by 'Bonnie Prince Charlie'
1746	Battle of Culloden: the duke of Cumberland routs the Jacobite army
1748	Peace of Aix-la-Chapelle concludes War of the Austrian Succession
1752	Adoption of Gregorian Calendar
1753	Jewish Naturalization Bill
1754	Newcastle ministry
1756	Seven Years War: Britain allied with Frederick the Great of Prussia against France, Austria, and Russia
1757	Pitt–Newcastle ministry; battle of Plassey: British victory over Bengal
1759	Capture of Quebec: British victory over the French
1760	Death of George II; accession of George III
1761	Laurence Sterne's *Tristram Shandy* published
1762	Bute's ministry
1763	Peace of Paris concludes Seven Years War; Grenville ministry; Wilkes and General Warrants
1765	Rockingham ministry; American Stamp Act attempts to make the defence of the American colonies self-financing: repealed 1766
1766	Chatham ministry
1768	Grafton ministry; Middlesex election crisis
1769	James Watt's steam engine patented
1770	Lord North's ministry; Edmund Burke's *Thoughts on the Present Discontents* published; Falkland Islands crisis

1773	Boston Tea Party: American colonists protest against the East India Company's monopoly of tea exports to America
1774	Coercive Acts passed in retaliation for Boston Tea Party
1776	Declaration of American Independence; Edward Gibbon's *Decline and Fall* and Adam Smith's *Wealth of Nations* published
1779	Wyvill's Association movement
1780	Gordon Riots develop from a procession to petition parliament against the Catholic Relief Act
1781	Surrender at Yorktown: American victory over British troops
1782	Second Rockingham ministry
1783	Shelburne ministry; Peace of Versailles recognizes independence of American colonies; Fox–North coalition; Younger Pitt's ministry
1784	East India Act
1785	Pitt's motion for parliamentary reform defeated
1786	Eden commercial treaty with France

THE TUDORS 1485–1603

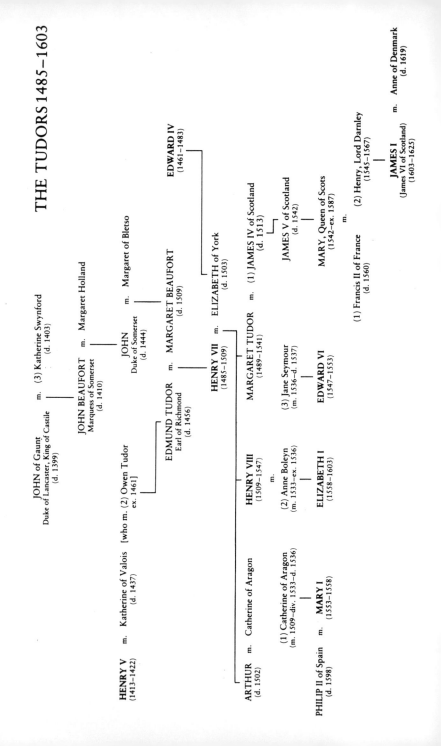

STUARTS AND HANOVERIANS 1603–1837

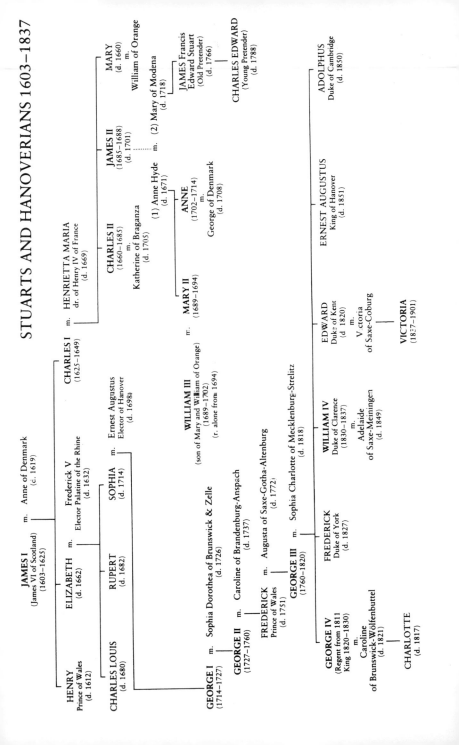

ACKNOWLEDGEMENTS

THE illustrations on pages 120 and 202 are reproduced by gracious permission of Her Majesty the Queen.

Photographs and illustrations were supplied by, or reproduced by kind permission of, the following: BBC Hulton Picture Library 82; Bodleian Library, Oxford 188, 190; British Library 55, 136, 143, 203; British Museum 25, 28, 50, 53, 61, 87, 117, 128, 141, 154, 159, 162, 181 (top), 207, 212, 213, 215; Courtauld Institute of Art, London 19 (Thyssen Collection), 40 (Petworth Collection), 170, 184, 185; Derby City Museum and Art Gallery 189, Mary Evans Picture Library 148; Ipswich Museums and Art Galleries 32; The Iveagh Bequest 206; A. F. Kersting 63; Mansell Collection 45, 72, 130, 193; National Gallery, London 98; National Gallery of Canada, Ottawa 198; National Portrait Gallery, London 11, 65, 96, 101, 106, 124, 132, 147; Public Record Office 13; Royal College of Physicians 194; Tate Gallery 198; Wedgwood 176.

Maps: Those of pp. 172 and 173 are based on two in *Transport and Economy: The Turnpike Roads of Eighteenth-Century Britain* by Eric Pawson, by kind permission of Academic Press Inc. (London) Ltd.

INDEX

Persons are indexed under the name or title used in the text, with cross references where necessary to alternative names. Page numbers in *italics* refer to illustrations or maps.

Tories, 127, 154–5, 157–60, 166–8,
  197–209 *passim*
Nottingham Tories, 146
Tory–Anglicans, 127, 129, 155, 167
towns and town life, 78–80; *see also*
  markets; seaside resorts; spas
Townshend, Charles (1674–1738), 157,
  160, 164
trade, 78–80, 171; *see also* free trade;
  markets; retail trade
trade unions, 178
Treasons Act (1534), 29
Triennial Act (1694), 155
turnpike roads, 169–71, *172–3*, 179,
  184–5
Tyburn execution, *181*
Tyndale, William (d. 1536), 22

Ulster, 95, 104, 145; *see also* Ireland
Uniformity, Acts of (1549, 1552, 1559,
  1662), 43, 49, 122, 134
universities, 129, 157, 188
Utopia, 24, 25, 26
Utrecht, peace of (1713), 150

Van Dyck, Sir Anthony (1599–1641),
  98, 101
Vere, Sir Francis (1560–1609), 54
Vergil, Polydore (1470?–1555?), 17, 36
Villiers, Barbara, countess of
  Castlemaine, duchess of Cleveland
  (1641–1709), *124*
Villiers, George, *see* Buckingham,
  duke of
Voltaire, François Marie Arouet de
  (1694–1778), 153, 183

wages and prices, 3–8, 9, 73–4, 76–8,
  177–8
Wales, 2
  religion, 182
  Union with England, 35–6
Waller, Sir William (1597–1668), 110
Walpole, Sir Robert (1676–1745), 157,
  160, *162*, 163–8, 199
Walsingham, Sir Francis (1530?–1590),
  52
Warbeck, Perkin (1474–99), 12, 38
Warrington (Lancs.), dissenting
  academy, 190
'Wars of the Roses', 10–12
Warwick, earl of, *see* Northumberland

Watt, James (1736–1819), 174
Wedgwood, Josiah (1730–95), 174, *176*,
  193
Wentworth, Thomas, 1st earl of
  Strafford (1593–1641), 99, 139
Wesley, John (1703–91), 182–3
West Africa, 134, 198
West Indies, 134, 171, 198, 204, 209,
  213
Westminster, 174
Westmorland, Charles Neville, 6th
  earl of (1543–1601), 51
Wexford, 116
Weymouth, 192
Whigs, 127, 131, 148, 156–60, 165–9,
  197–209 *passim*, 216–17
Whitefield, George (1714–70), 183
Whitehaven (Cumbria), 173
Whitgift, John, Archbishop of
  Canterbury (1530?–1604), 59
Wilberforce, William (1759–1833), 219
Wild, Jonathan (1682?–1725), 162, 164
Wilkes, John (1727–97), 179, 201, 208–9
William III of Orange (1650–1702), 86,
  128, 131, 146, 149, 150
William 'the Silent', prince of Orange
  (1555–84), 51, 52
Wilson, Richard (1714–82), 196
witchcraft, 143
Wolfe, James (1727–59), *198*, 200
Wolsey, Thomas, Cardinal and
  Archbishop of York (1475?–1530),
  15, 20–1, 26, 28, 34, 64–5
women in society, *184–5, 186*
Wood, John, Sen. (1705?–1754) and
  Jun. (d. 1782), 191
Worcester, 111
  battle of, 116
Worcester House Declaration, 121
Wren, Sir Christopher (1632–1723),
  141, *141*
Wright, Joseph (1734–97), *188–9*, 196
Wyatt, Sir Thomas (1503?–1542), 66
Wyatt, Sir Thomas (1521?–1554), 47
Wyvill, Christopher (1740–1822), 214

yeomen, 84
York, 9, 38, 107, 108, 171

Zoffany, Johann (1733–1810), *194*, 195,
  202